Counting Out the Scholars

William Bruneau and Donald C. Savage

Counting Out the Scholars

HOW PERFORMANCE INDICATORS UNDERMINE UNIVERSITIES AND COLLEGES

A CAUT Series Title

James Lorimer & Company Ltd., Publishers

Toronto, 2002

James Lorimer & Company Ltd. acknowledges the support of the Ontario Arts Council. We acknowledge the financial support of the Government of Canada through the Book Publishing Industry Development Program (BPIDP) for our publishing activities. We acknowledge the support of the Canada Council for the Arts for our publishing program.

Cover illustration: Brian Gable

National Library of Canada Cataloguing in Publication Data

Bruneau, William A., 1944–
    Counting out the scholars : the case against performance indicators in higher education

"A CAUT series title."
Co-published by the Canadian Association of University Teachers.
Includes bibliographical references and index.
ISBN 1-55028-711-7

1. Universities and colleges—Canada—Evaluation. 2. Education, Higher—Canada —Evaluation. 3. Educational indicators—Canada. 4. Industry and education—Canada. I. Savage, Donald C., 1933– II. Canadian Association of University Teachers III. Title.

LB2331.65.C3B78 2002   379.1′58′0971   C00-933237-5

A CAUT Series Title
James Lorimer & Company Ltd., Publishers
35 Britain Street
Toronto, ON M5A 1R7
www.lorimer.ca

Printed and bound in Canada.

Contents

Acknowledgement

We have been encouraged and sustained in this work by friends throughout the Canadian and international academic communities.

Colleagues in Europe, the United Kingdom, the United States, New Zealand, Australia, and every Canadian province and region have offered assistance.

It would be difficult, and possibly invidious, to try to name them all. Let this general note of thanks be our best expression of gratitude.

Foreword

"Now, what I want is, Facts. Teach these boys and girls nothing but Facts. Facts alone are wanted in life. Plant nothing else, and root out everything else. You can only form the minds of reasoning animals upon Facts.... [T]he schoolmaster [and the other grown persons present] swept with their eyes the inclined plane of little vessels then and there arranged in order, ready to have imperial gallons of facts poured into them until they were full to the brim."
—Charles Dickens, *Hard Times* (1854)

THIS BOOK IS NOT, to put it mildly, a manual on how to make performance indicators (PIs) work better, nor a technical discussion of their mathematical strengths and weaknesses. We deny outright neo-conservative claims that PIs are a means of assuring accountability. We contend they in fact weaken and even deny true public accountability in universities and colleges. Arguing that PIs undermine the guiding principles of our public education system, we suggest ways citizens might act to reverse these negative developments.

Robert Birnbaum recently defined performance indicators as "ratios of operational statistics... major tools for management control and decision making."[1] These ideas from the business community have become immensely popular in the last decade among politicians and their bureaucrats, business people, journalists, and business officers of universities and colleges. The phrase covers a multitude of practices, mostly to do with tying costs to the production of a particular good. It is the job of effective managers to establish those data and use them to drive costs down, as in costs-per-square-foot of manufacturing space. Ratios can be used to measure the costs of machinery, staff, or whatever one wants, and to tie them to the bottom line.

Enthusiasts, particularly in the English-speaking world, seek to apply this business model to all operations of the university. In New Zealand the government toyed with the idea of costs-per-square-foot as a reasonable

---

[1] Robert Birnbaum, *Management Fads in Higher Education: Where They Come From, What They Do, Why They Fail* (San Francisco: Jossey-Bass, 2001), 81. Prof. Birnbaum here summarizes the views of R. Elkin and M. Molitor, *Management Indicators in Non-profit Corporations* (Baltimore: University of Maryland School of Social Work and Community Planning, 1984).

indicator, ignoring any distinctions between Victorian and Edwardian splendours and modern concrete boxes. Others suggest treating the graduate with a degree as a "product." One can establish cost ratios for the amount of staff, library, and computer costs it takes to produce such a graduate—then drive down the costs. One can produce comparative figures for a given geographical area along with averages—which, of course, mean that half of the institutions involved will always fail and thus must strive even harder to cut costs. On this view universities do not differ from salmon canneries or bicycle factories.

Professor Birnbaum cautions that performance indicators by themselves cannot produce excellence, and thus are not much use to those who want to make our universities better educational institutions. Nor can they decide primary questions: If a university is not performing well according to the indicators (whatever they may be), should government close it down or spend more money to improve it? This conundrum is aggravated by the difficulty that universities do not start on a level playing field— particularly in the southern United States and South Africa, where former white universities have a significant head start, given their major capital legacies, over former black schools. Performance indicators cannot decide whether one should fund the poverty-stricken or the rich. That is always of necessity a political decision.

A popular variant is to give numerical awards to various PIs, add them up for the entire institution, then use the result to indicate (supposed) comparative quality. Indicators in this class include the percentage of students who complete their degrees in a fixed time, dollars-per-faculty member raised from the private sector, and percentage of graduates employed. The "league tables" created by this approach are fundamentally misleading. Not only do the individual indicators ignore key aspects of higher education, they very frequently carry perverse effects that nullify any supposed gain in quality. Items measured are sometimes not within the control of the university, but rather the effects of economic conditions and of government funding policy in education. Such PIs might well be better applied to governments than to universities....

These approaches to quantity and control were billed as a new wave that would render old-fashioned statistics obsolete, dealing with outputs rather than inputs. A university might boast fine buildings, a celebrated staff, and an excellent library, but these did not guarantee students would actually learn—as witness the infamous gentleman's C in the Ivy League. The past decade has shown how hard it is to measure what the university actually does. How does one measure the intangibles of education—critical thinking, creativity, tolerance, wisdom? Nevertheless, measurement is what the universities are forced to do. Many governments have decreed that what is not measurable is not valuable. We discuss the consequences in subsequent chapters.

Performance indicators have a long history. But it is no accident that PIs became the vogue in the Thatcher/Reagan era and beyond—one part of the movement to transform universities into business corporations complete with CEOs and the top-down structures favoured by the business community.[2] Collegial governance, academic freedom, and the like thus became simply impediments to trade. The market should govern universities, and business managers run them. Performance indicators were to be a key tool in ensuring better markets, whether for governments as purchasers of higher education or for students as career customers. All this was to liberate universities from the dead hand of government. In the end the result has been the exact opposite—the imposition of costly and highly centralized bureaucracies onto the university system, and the triumph of a right-wing *nomenklatura*. As we note in our chapter on the United Kingdom, even Margaret Thatcher has been taken aback by this unintended result.

In the English-speaking world the rise of performance indicators went hand in hand with relentless cutting of university budgets as part of the general movement to dismantle the state and to cut taxes. Performance indicators neatly transformed blame for the consequences of these cuts from the governments which inflicted them to the universities and their faculty. With this has come a series of sometimes vituperous attacks on the university community by neo-conservative critics who insisted the university was to blame for its own difficulties, not the relentless budgetary attacks of Thatcherite governments.[3]

In fact, despite perpetual financial crises, universities have indeed transformed themselves in the past forty years in teaching and research. They are also much more open institutions than ever before. Social groups and classes once systematically excluded from public higher education now enjoy much greater access. University mandates are understood to encourage an education in the arts of critical thinking as they apply to life in a democratic society, and to creative work in one's chosen profession.[4]

There is also a new objective: a practical requirement that post-secondary institutions encourage problem solving skills in business and politics, and even a certain pragmatism in the character of the people who come to universities and colleges to learn and to do research. Students are now expected to be made "life-ready" for the market-place and the agora. The job of post-secondary education is different and more complicated than at any time in the past two centuries. Those who criticize universities

---

[2] An energetic discussion of this point, from a Canadian perspective, may be found in Janice Newson and Howard Buchbinder, *The University Means Business: Universities, Corporations and Academic Work* (Toronto: Garamond Press, 1988).

[3] David J. Bercuson, Robert Bothwell, J.L. Granatstein, *The Great Brain Robbery: Canada's Universities on the Road to Ruin*, McClelland and Stewart, 1984; Peter C. Emberley, *Zero Tolerance: Hot Button Politics in Canada's Universities* (Toronto: Penguin Books: 1996).

[4] Paul Axelrod, 'Challenges to Liberal Education in an Age of Uncertainty', *Historical Studies in Education/Revue d'histoire de l'éducation*, 10, 1/2 (Spring/Fall 1998): 1–19.

as glacial and immobile should revisit the universities of the nineteen fifties and compare them with the institutions of 2001.[5] Much remains to be done, but the gains of the past half-century should not be ignored.

Performance indicators could, of course, produce the exact opposite conclusion to that of the cost-cutters. They might be used to show that universities need more faculty, better equipment, and improved student aid. There is, after all, a rather grand tradition of employing statistics in the service of social reform and democratic government. Numerical characterizations of higher education do have a place in public debate on the goals of the public education system—when properly combined with historically-grounded and socially-minded descriptions. We can imagine a world where good universities and colleges are portrayed *in part* by indicators of various kinds. But we insist that PIs in their modern form are not such indicators, nor would they be recognized by progressive reformers of the past century. PIs have become much more narrow in intent, and much more controlling in effect. They threaten to force public higher education backward to an authoritarian past.

We counter with suggestions on how to rebuild public higher education and make it truly accountable in the public interest. There is no point in dreaming of a past when universities were isolated from the community and could more or less run their own affairs without having to explain much to outsiders. Mass higher education, and the money it requires, necessitate better and more public forms of accountability. We think this can be done without continuing the catastrophic policies of the past decade. Nor can university faculty avoid reasonable forms of academic scrutiny such as external departmental reviews. The days when professionals could wrap themselves in an incomprehensible mystique to avoid such unpleasantness have also passed.

■

We have arranged this book to move from a history of PIs to a close study of their logic. Three cautionary studies of countries where PIs have been tried and found wanting—the United Kingdom, New Zealand, and the United States—lead to a consideration of the problem as manifested in Canada and, finally, to a call for new forms of accountability and a return to fundamentals of educational quality. We cannot promise that any

---

[5]See esp. Mark Kingwell, *The World We Want: Virtue, Vice and the Good Citizen* (Toronto: Viking 2000); Eamon Callan, *Creating Citizens: Political Education and Liberal Democracy* (Oxford: Oxford University Press, 1997) and also the remarkable study of first principles in higher education policy and provision by the Scot, George Davie, *The Democratic Intellect: Scotland and Her Universities in the Nineteenth Century*, 2nd ed. (Edinburgh: Edinburgh University Press, 1997).

particular section will make for pleasant reading, but together they constitute a gripping modern educational horror story.

We have put emphasis on post-secondary education in the English-speaking world, particularly universities in our four selected jurisdictions. This calls for justification, given the unfortunate impact of PIs in Mexico,[6] Central and South America, and numerous regions of Africa and Asia. We would be remiss not to add to the list the members of the European Community, all of whom (even nations with well-developed conceptions of quality and accountability) have shown interest in PIs and, therefore, in privatization, intense centralized control, and continuous budget-cutting.

Because the examples of the United Kingdom and the United States have had influence far beyond their national borders, and for at least a century, they struck us as the natural starting place for our argument. The British exported their university structures throughout the old British Empire, and the United States in the 20th century became the dominant scientific power. We consider in detail New Zealand and Canada as cases of societies whose social-democratic ethos have been much modified in the past twenty years by American views of university management. Canada itself is a long-standing example of the marriage of British and American ideas about the structure of public and private post-secondary education. We made these choices knowing that New Right ideology is essentially an Anglo-American construct which continues to have enormous impact across the world. We hope others will take up the work of writing the history and politics of PIs and similar devices in regions and nations we have been unable to discuss at length.

In our final chapter, we make practical recommendations for ways in which academics and other members of the public may deal with PIs. We found few examples of sustained policy on or against PIs in the course of our research. One significant exception to the rule is the full-scale Policy on Performance Indicators developed in the mid-1990s by the Canadian Association of University Teachers.[7]

We wanted in our final chapter to show alternatives to PIs, demonstrate how readily one could construct them, and urge how important it is to move quickly toward them. There are many roads to accountability, quality, effectiveness, and responsible public finance in higher education, and PIs are an unhappy one among those many.

Our final chapter has a secondary purpose, that of defining "by application" what PIs are. Our work of definition begins in the opening

---

[6]See, for instance, the imaginative and helpful discussion in Miguel A. Izquierdo S., *Sobrevivir a los estímulos: académicos, estrategia y conflictos* (México, D.F.: Universidad Pedagógica Nacional, 2000). Professor Izquierdo's work concerns the effects of merit pay, bibliometric and other output measures, all applied to Mexican higher education in the name of "quality."

[7]*http://www.caut.ca/english/bulletin/97_nov/pi4.htm.*

pages and carries on, through historical and contemporary example, to the end. We sought long and hard for a reliable and widely-agreed definition of PIs, but as Martin Cave *et al.* said as recently as 1997:

> Despite the growing attention paid to PIs for higher education, there is no single authoritative definition or interpretation of their nature... [a] survey carried out in the mid-1980s under the Organisation for Economic Cooperation and Development (OECD)'s Institutional Management in Higher Education (IMHE) Programme defined an indicator as "a numerical value used to measure something which is difficult to quantify."[8]

For reasons we happily lay out below, the authors have become extremely fond of this last definition.

---

[8]Martin Cave *et al.*, *The Use of Performance Indicators in Higher Education: The Challenge of the Quality Movement,* 3rd ed. (London: Jessica Kingsley Publishers, 1997), esp. 21.

Part I:
Control by Number—
Theory and Practice

1

The Surprisingly Colourful History of Performance Indicators

"The ideas of economists and political philosophers, both when they are right and when they are wrong, are more powerful than is commonly understood. Indeed the world is ruled by little else. Practical men, who believe themselves to be quite exempt from any intellectual influences, are usually the slaves of some defunct economist."
—J.M. Keynes, *General Theory*, quoted in

A.M. Schlesinger, Jr., *A Life in the Twentieth Century: Innocent Beginnings, 1917–1950* (Boston: Houghton Mifflin, 2001), 361.

"C'est un homme expéditif, qui aime à dépêcher ses malades; et quand on a à mourir, cela se fait avec lui le plus vite du monde."
—Molière, *Monsieur de Pourceaugnac*, I, vii.

THE LONG VIEW

Performance indicators are merely the latest visible signs of a perpetual struggle over control of social services: military organization, medical care and community health, education, communications, social welfare, transportation, police and corrections, or pension administration. This is an old fight, in which it is not always easy to recognize who is battling whom, or why. Governments since antiquity have demanded quick results, while debating precisely how to hold their military and civil servants accountable. The conundrum has always been how to measure success beyond the question of who won a particular battle. Better triremes or better leadership? Virtue or technology?

In the modern era, John Locke and some of his contemporaries took the view that the making of wealth was the rightful work of some people, but not all. One task of the state was to ensure exact knowledge of how many would be found in each class of persons, and to make policies and create civil services to ensure the rational functioning of the whole system as he saw it. Locke conducted detailed research on the poor-house system (1697), the monetary system (1674, 1695), and labour supply (1693), all in aid of "performance indicators" that would show whether state services such as poor-houses were a necessary and efficient device for the production of wealth.[1] Efficiency thus became the touchstone, as modern practitioners would agree. But as Locke's analysis implies, efficiency is shorthand for larger political and social policy objectives. Efficiency is not an end in itself—one must ask, efficiency in aid of what goals? A central goal must be power, since without it political, social, or economic policies are unlikely to be realized.[2]

Although the application of PIs to higher learning is a phenomenon of the nineteenth and twentieth centuries, there are reverberations from an earlier period. Governments have long sought control of universities for political reasons. Renaissance monarchs in England, Spain, and Bavaria created university visitors to ensure that these institutions were kept in line with officially-approved doctrine of the moment.[3] There is certainly an echo of this approach in the current Research Assessment Exercise in the United Kingdom and its imitators elsewhere.

---

[1]Cf C.B. McPherson, "The Social Bearing of Locke's Political Theory," *Western Political Quarterly*, 7, 1 (1954 March): 1–22; see also P.H. Kelly, ed., *Locke on Money* (Oxford: Clarendon Press, 1990–1, 2 volumes), esp. II, 489–94.

[2]Cf Janice Gross Stein, *The Cult of Efficiency* (Toronto: Anansi, 2001).

[3]W. Gordon Zeeveld, *Foundations of Tudor Policy* (Cambridge: Harvard University Press, 1948) on the connection between state policy, internal and external, and the universities. On church, state and university, see J.K. McConica, *English Humanists and Reformation Policies under Henry VII and Edward VI* (Oxford: Clarendon Press, 1965).

The early modern period in Europe saw vigorous arguments about who should pay for the exploration of the world, who would reward scientific explorers, and how the findings of such explorations could best be converted into political and economic capital.[4] The reasons people explored the world were extremely various, as are the reasons for doing science in its broadest definition, and those reasons often had little to do with politics and economics. This fact has never stopped legislators, investors, and commentators from seeking to reduce the tasks of exploration and science to mere political-economic calculation. If this reductionist thinking sounds like the reasoning of Prime Minister Thatcher in 1979, that is not surprising. The ideas that everything can be reduced to a matter of money and property, and the business of the state is to ensure everything is reduced in that way, are not new.[5]

Although the main development of PIs for post-secondary education occurred in the last hundred years, "[T]here is," Conrad Russell wrote in 1977, "nothing new about politicians aching to stick their noses into the management of education, nor about their belief that because they have received education, they know all about it."[6] What was new were the ways industrializing societies put old words indicator, efficiency, effectiveness, accountability together in new combinations, and under new ideologies. Similarly, it was a new thing when the educational establishment, composed of university teachers, students, and some administrators, was defined as an enemy entity standing in the way of the new dispensation. Thus the power of teachers and students must be destroyed ruthlessly and efficiently. What made such a *démarche* necessary? Politicians in the late 20th century promised at one and the same time to increase the quality of higher education and to denude the state of the finances necessary to maintain, much less increase, such excellence. Only black magic could possibly resolve this contradiction, and what better sorcery than PIs?[7]

It was hardly novel, on the other hand, that administrative power should be used to defend and to promote the ideology of the moment: that the operation of the market solves all problems, and applies as much to universities as to any commercial undertaking. PIs demonstrate how

---

[4]J.H. Parry, *The Establishment of the European Hegemony, 1415–1715: Trade and Exploration in the Age of the Renaissance*, 3rd ed. (New York: Harper Row, 1966); Dava Sobel, *Longitude: The True Story of a Lone Genius Who Solved the Greatest Scientific Problem of His Time* (New York: Penguin, 1996).

[5]Niall Ferguson, *The Cash Nexus: Money and Power in the Modern World, 1700–2000* (New York: Basic Books, 2001).

[6]Conrad Russell, "Leave it to the Teachers," *London Review of Books,* 19, 6 (1997 March 20).

[7]Or honesty. "Being cost-effective does not necessarily mean giving a better, but rather a more efficient service," to quote the Rt. Hon. John Moore, MP, UK Secretary of State for Social Security, 1989 May, in Conrad Russell, *Academic Freedom* (London: Routledge, 1993), in particular ch. 4, pp. 83 ff.

business practices have come to fascinate and to captivate civil servants, journalists and business-boosters alike, leading them to assert that those practices should and could replace the messy practices of democratic organizations, and the still more complicated ways-of-life one finds operating in free universities in free countries.

We do not claim to derive "lessons" from the past, but we assert that the rise of modern PIs to centre stage is better understood in an historical perspective than without its help. PIs, benchmarks, and quality measures are beneficiaries of several streams of social and political practice. When proponents of PIs make their confusingly diverse arguments, they nearly always draw on some permutation or combination of those ancient streams. Only rarely do they acknowledge their debt to the past. They are wise to keep us in the dark, for the roots of PIs are deep in the night soil of world history.

∎

Performance indicators owe much to the mid-19th-century appearance of mass elementary education in Europe and North America. There was broad consensus that any solution in North America and in Europe for problems ranging from vagrancy, indigence, and crime to the supply of modestly literate, numerate, and quiescent workers, rested partly in the universal provision of elementary education.[8] But it was commonplace to ask questions about who should have authority over it, who should pay for it, and who should be responsible for its success or failure (however one might measure them): the church? the guilds, professions, or unions? businesspeople? the family? And how, in the end, would one know if one's time, money, and energy had been well spent?

It took the Great War to publicize and to popularize the movement for broadly accessible (and finally, compulsory) secondary education, which raised the same questions.[9]

From about 1850 and on both continents, the provision of post-secondary education began to raise questions of quite another sort. The creation of so-called Red Brick universities in Britain was part of the United Kingdom's modernization of post-secondary education, as was the passage in the United States of the Morrill Act for Land-Grant Universities. It was by no means a matter of carefully-conceived state policy that these universities were founded and supported. Many of them just "happened," founded by civic and private initiative. But it was not long before they played a part in public and social policy.

---

[8]Alison Prentice, *The School Promoters: Education and Social Class in Mid-19th Century Upper Canada* (Toronto: McClelland Stewart, 1975).

[9]R. Gidney and W.P. J. Millar, *Inventing Secondary Education: The Rise of the High Schools in Nineteenth Century Ontario* (Montréal and Kingston: McGill-Queen's University Press, 1990).

Whether one wanted to ensure the nation could compete with the Prussians (as Leeds, Manchester, and London would do), or assist in the domestication of an entire continent (as the Land Grant universities would do), or prepare the members of ever-lengthening lists of professions for their life work,[10] by the 1890s colleges and universities came on both sides of the Atlantic attracted public-policy attention just as elementary and secondary schools had done.[11]

The trouble was that the abstract and indirect purposes of universities did not lend themselves to statistical celebration or to statistically-based control. Schooling could be connected through the numbers to reduced vagrancy, reductions in the numbers of child labourers, and rising productivity, even if it remained far from clear just how schooling caused these happy outcomes. It was far harder to demonstrate cause-effect linkages between higher education and improved industrial production, or success in imperial administration, let alone to prove them statistically. Yet members of the public, journalists, high civil servants, legislators, and businessmen alike were now keen for statistics on universities.

Until 1910, the statistical pickings were slim, certainly by comparison to the exhaustive enumerations published annually of prisons, schools, armies, and post offices. The new universities in Europe and the United Kingdom, like those of the latter 19th century in North America, maintained a close and vital connection with local industries while aiming to meet the social requirements of their regions and countries. All this they did without statistical aid. But with time, these newcomer universities took up sustained programmes of research and advanced professional education, all the while broadening their programmes of liberal education to match their older sister universities. They simply announced they were doing these things, produced skeletal reports to prove it, and hoped for the best when their supporting government authorities determined annual grants.[12]

Thus until about 1910, statistical evidence of progress in most states, provinces, and counties served to depict the increasing number and size of higher education institutions, and thereby the provision of professional and liberal education to more and more people.

---

[10]On higher education and professionalization, see Gidney and Millar, *Professional Gentlemen: The Professions in Nineteenth-Century Ontario* (Toronto: University of Toronto Press, 1994).

[11]United States Office of Education, *Survey of Land-Grant Colleges and Univesities* (Washington, DC: U.S. Office of Education, 1930), esp. vol. 1, pt. I. See also Richard Wayne Lyke's *Higher Education and the United States Office of Education 1867–1953* (Washington, DC: U.S. Office of Education, 1930), Chs. 1 2.

[12]Roger Geiger, *To Advance Knowledge: The Growth of American Research Universities, 1900–1940* (New York: Oxford University Press, 1986), esp. pp. 3–56; also, A.H. Halsey, "Oxford and the British Universities," in Brian Harrison, ed., *The History of the University of Oxford, VIII: The Twentieth Century* (Oxford: Clarendon Press, 1994), 577–606.

Statistics were a way of noting, encouraging, and celebrating increasing public and private commitment to higher education, including higher technical and professional education. But meanwhile, the numbers began to be interpreted by legislators and businessmen as evidence that science had been tamed, domesticated, and harnessed to a new economic order. Soon these numbers *had* to be produced, because custom or law demanded it.

From this moment, in 1910 *annus magni momenti*, the old and relatively non-invasive world of the 19th century began to pass away. Now indicators and descriptors passed through at least four more phases in fairly quick succession. In each, from about 1910 to the end of the 20th century, indicators acquired more, and more controlling, uses. The relatively benign indicators of 1900 evolved into the worrisome and destructive numbers of 2000. How did this happen, and why?

We've shown precedent for tying post-secondary education to industrial and political purposes. But the 20th century brought with it new schemas of industrial practice, new psychologies, and a revised set of neo-conservative ideologies. Together these permitted rapid development of PIs as we have come to know them in the 2000s.

PIs IN FIVE PHASES

PIs made their appearance in five phases, relying on five different justifications, between the 1850s and the present. For convenience, we use the examples of Canada, the United Kingdom, and the United States to illustrate each phase. Notice that the policies and practices that appear in each phase were not displaced by those of the next phase; instead, directions in funding, teaching, and research were added, or accreted, to the ones before. This, too, helps to explain PIs' remarkable staying power.

Phase I : Nineteenth Century Origins

This phase includes great campaigns from 1850 to World War I for compulsory public education and a growing movement on behalf of post-secondary educational provision. Everywhere, these campaigns led to statistical and anecdotal reports on the "progress" of education.[13] The reports were read from the start not just by legislators but in board rooms and

---

[13] One of the single most useful discussions of statistics in the early 19th century, warts and all, and particularly with respect to private and public provision of health and education services, is Michael J. Cullen, *The Statistical Movement in Early Victorian Britain: The Foundations of Empirical Social Research* (New York: Harvest Press/ Barnes and Noble, 1975). Our treatment of PIs owes much to Professor Cullen's careful disinterment of the Janus-like history of social statistics. On one hand, moderate progressives used them to press for change; others (one thinks of Babbage) saw statistics as neutral and interesting in the way geological or geographical facts were "interesting," but no more.

newspaper editorial offices.[14] Indeed, the opening of the campaign for tax-supported education was as much the doing of businessmen as educators and intellectuals-at-large.[15] Efficiency and minimum costs were the watchwords of the period. Education inspectors and ministerial accountants had the task of ensuring locally that money was not wasted and teaching was "excellent." But—and this is a big "but"—public and private expenditure on education was constantly increasing in real terms. The purpose of detailed statistical reporting was not so much to compel change in educational practice, as to show that social and economic conditions required new, substantial funding. Further, the rationale for detailed accounting and statistics had little to do with markets, competition, or time-and-motion efficiencies, all of which were to be featured in Phases II and after.[16]

By the end of the long 19th century, a new category of user was reading the statistics and the anecdotal reports: social reformers. They were convinced social problems demanded educational solutions rather than more policing or market-oriented reform. Meanwhile, annual public funding of public universities had acquired significant momentum. University funding was not tied to the schemes of social reformers in quite the same way as was public schooling; post-secondary education was still open to no more than 3% or 4% of the secondary school-leaving cohort in any one year, and its social impact and uses still an open question.[17] Early 20th-century legislators were persuaded that if their countries, provinces, or states were to have first-rate professions and professionals

---

[14]Note that several Canadian provinces' Annual Reports of Education departments once included the names of every single teacher, enrollments of boys and girls in every single classroom, list of what subjects were taught to whom, and so on. This form of disclosure persisted until the early 1950s. Meanwhile, although universities got only a couple of pages in government sessional papers, their accounts attracted increasingly detailed scrutiny in Treasury Boards across Canada, and Regents' committees in the United States. Only in the United Kingdom were some universities spared the demands of nosy chartered accountants, and those the ancient ones, Oxford and Cambridge. On the other hand, they were the subject of five major Royal Commissions of Inquiry in the 19th century alone, and several more in the 20th. See below, as an instance, the discussion of statistics in the Dearing Report, United Kingdom, our Chapter 3.

[15]Cf. Christopher Kent, *Brains and Numbers: Elitism, Comtism, and Democracy in Mid-Victorian England* (Toronto: University of Toronto Press, 1978), esp. the "Epilogue," pp. 155 ff.

[16]We do not suggest, even remotely, that markets, competition, and efficiency studies were the inventions of the 19th century, but rather that they featured in the development of PIs in ways particular to that narrow history.

[17]For estimates of one university's impact on its social context, see Cathy James, "Practical Diversions and Educational Amusements: Evangelia House and the Advent of Canada's Settlement Movement, 1902–09," *Historical Studies in Education/Revue d'histoire de l'éducation*, 10, 1&2 (Spring/printemps & Fall/automne 1998): 48–66; and R. Gidney and W.P.J. Millar, "Quantity and Quality: The Problem of Admissions in Medicine at the University of Toronto, 1910–51," *Historical Studies in Education/Revue d'histoire de l'éducation* 9, 2 (Fall/automne 1997): 165–89.

not just in theology, but in law, medicine, dentistry, education, social work, and nursing, then universities must become larger, more numerous, and more diverse.

Phase I of higher education closed on a pattern of moderately detailed public reporting.[18] Reports served the purposes of those who imagined the solution of great economic and social problems to be just within reach. It is more than a little ironic that they served equally well the purposes of bureaucrats, bankers, politicians, and businessmen. But nobody in the professoriate much cared. The indicators could be understood as supporting them, and encouraging continued public-private subvention of higher education. Universities and colleges remained small, taking in only in a tiny proportion of the post-secondary age cohort. Even if they attracted negative attention, did it matter much?

It did matter. This first development phase of PIs saw reinforcement of public faith in numbers. Thus it became certain that the forms and forces of production, and techniques of managing them, would soon be applied to the university.

Phase I might be described as an intensification of a 19th-century-long movement to connect higher education to various markets. Sheldon Rothblatt describes the English and the American markets for higher learning, showing how many of them could operate at one and the same time. There was a sellers' market among physicists who had studied in Germany, but a buyers' market for art historians. There was a market among industrial, banking, and certain other professional interests that would take up the graduates of newer universities and colleges, but not those of conservative, classics-oriented older ones. There was a public market for lectures and innovation and reports of discovery, a particularly convenient source of money and of popularity for hard-pressed professors and university administrators.

> From the perspective of quality, or lasting contributions to science or to science as a collective activity, the development of a market for intellectual products had mixed results. Considerable diversification of mental and artistic endeavour occurred, but there was also work that was unimaginative, shoddy, cynical and silly.... Competition led to conduct

---

[18]For statistical reporting and in its purposes, see for Canada: *Historical Compedium of Education Statistics from Confederation to 1975/Recueil de statistiques chronologiques de l'éducation de la naissance de la Conféderation à 1975* (Ottawa: Statistics Canada. Education, Science and Culture Division, Projections Section, 1978), and F.H. Leacy, M.C. Urquhart, and K.A.H. Buckley, eds., *Historical Statistics of Canada*, 2nd ed. (Ottawa: Statistics Canada, 1983), sec. W; for Europe, B.R. Mitchell, ed., *International Historical Statistics: Europe, 1750–1993*, 4th ed. (London: Macmillan, 1998), sec. "Education," but also Fritz Ringer's invaluable *Education and Society in Modern Europe* (Bloomington, Indiana: Indiana University Press, 1979), complete with comparisons to the United States.

that was morally suspicious, actions that were regarded as reprehensible, sometimes because they were unprecedented.[19]

These markets were increasingly well organized, and more willingly accepted by university and college teachers and administrators, after the turn of the 20th century than before. But in fact they had already operated one way or another for centuries.

The new danger, almost unnoticed in 1910, was that a means might be found to compel a tight and automatic relationship between education and markets. It is this feature the use of force, compulsion the illiberal and destructive use of market indicators that would flower, in four more phases, in the century to come.

Phase II: The Cult of Efficiency & Taylorism

Annual reports of universities and education ministries in the 1910s and 1920s show a sharp change in outlook and even appearance. The reason is the arrival of what Raymond Callahan memorably calls the "cult of efficiency." He argues that its heyday began as early as 1910 in the worlds of public and higher education alike.[20]

Certainly the look of publications about post-secondary education supports Callahan. At the University of Michigan, budgets for gardening, maintenance, lighting, and heating become a regular feature of reports on the academic progress of that large state institution. Even at Harvard and Princeton, the cost of secretarial help became a subject of interest as the idea of efficiency in all aspects of institutional life took hold. Previously reports about universities or colleges concentrated on innovations in residence life, or rising numbers of freshmen and women, or the installation of new fields and departments, or the high international reputation of a library or a laboratory, or the books and articles and journals of the professoriate, or the fine social services provided by these institutions. Now the tone became mechanical: what President Webster of Clark University (to whom we'll return in a moment) called the "engineering aspect of my life as a leader of thinking men."

There had been studies of industrial practice and time-work discipline in the production of textiles, carriages and automobiles from the 1860s. There had been persistent signs that both government and the private sector had grown fond of statistics. But the arrival of the efficiency expert

---

[19]Sheldon Rothblatt, *The Modern University and Its Discontents: The Fate of Newman's Legacies in Britain and America* (Cambridge: University Press, 1997), 423; but see also pp. 418–23 for 19th-century markets and indicators in Britain, and pp. 428–31 for American universities and colleges before 1914.

[20]Raymond Callahan, *Education and the Cult of Efficiency: A Study of the Social Forces that Have Shaped the Administration of the Public Schools* (Chicago: University of Chicago Press, 1962), 19–21.

in the affairs of government and industry after 1910, and in education immediately afterward, was unprecedented.

In the new optics of efficiency, some universities and colleges looked rather good to begin with. In a great city like Boston, a post-secondary fee-for-service dentistry school might rank with the local university department of arts-and-divinity. The dental school ensured workers would stay healthy and productive, entirely in the private sector, raising and lowering tuition fees as the market permitted, and making no demands on the state. The arts-and-divinity school boasted a 0% unemployment rate. There was no way to tell when graduates abandoned preaching (as, for example, Ralph Waldo Emerson), instead fading back into family occupations or using their advanced schooling to take up entirely new occupations, often as school teachers or municipal civil servants.

The new statistics and indicators of the Cult of Efficiency quickly proved far more invasive than their predecessors. A university that looked good in the first flush of the Efficiency movement might soon look bad, as squads of accountants and waves of managerial experts flooded through, turning their attention to matters that had little to do with education as discovery or transformation, and everything to do with increased productivity.

President Webster of Clark University grew weary of it:

> I am tired of scientific management, so-called. I have heard of it from scientific managers, from university presidents, from casual acquaintances in railway trains; I have read of it in the daily papers, the weekly papers, the ten-cent magazines, the fifteen-cent magazines, the thirty-five-cent magazine, and in the *Outlook*.... For fifteen years I have been a subscriber to a magazine dealing with engineering matters, feeling it incumbent on me to keep in touch with the applications of physics to the convenience of life, but the touch has become a pressure, the pressure a crushing strain, until the mass of articles on shop practice and scientific management threatened to crush all thought out of my brain, and I stopped my subscription.[21]

But Frederick Taylor believed in EFFICIENCY (he likely would have capitalized the word): the elimination of waste, bad management, and "soldiering," the last term meaning "poor work habits on the factory floor." Taylor thought management and industrial labour could always be improved, if only managers and owners would give up their traditional and habitual "rules of thumb." There was one, and *only* one, best way of doing any particular job, determined through "scientific" study. It would have little or nothing to do with "the way it was always done in the past." Once determined, the "correct" method should be applied through an "...an almost equal division of the work and the responsibility between the management and the workmen."[22]

---

[21]Quoted in R. Callahan, *The Cult of Efficiency* (Chicago: University of Chicago Press, 1962), p. 24.

[22]F.W. Taylor, *The Principles of Scientific Management* (New York: Harper and Row, 1911), p. 37.

The keys to the method were the stopwatch, detailed studies of movement (time-motion studies), standardization, functional foremanship (the hiring of foremen who could teach effectively the parts of a job), and forward planning ("global" planning). Callahan summarizes a crucial feature of the Taylorist view:

> Taylor, in describing the system, took great pains to differentiate between the basic principles of the system and its mechanics. He pointed out that a person unfamiliar with industry would seem surprised that such a system should be necessary since it would be taken for granted that both workers and management in their own self-interest would be already producing to their maximum. But, he said, this was not the case. In most plants, production was far below what it could have been and should have been.[23]

When managers did their mathematical best to match time, work, material, and people, productivity would rise. When workers stopped "soldiering" —that is, pacing themselves

> to keep time for themselves, to avoid exhaustion, to exercise authority over their work, ...to exercise their creativity, and last, but not least, to express their solidarity and their hostility to management...[24]

—productivity would rise still further.

Applied to elementary and secondary education, the results of Taylorism were predictably grim. The most famous educational applications were those of John Franklin Bobbitt. His 1915 article on "High School Costs"[25] still repays close study.

> Accurate cost-accounting lies at the foundations of all successful business management.... [S]atisfactory instruction in high school English can be had for fifty dollars per thousand student-hours... and those responsible for high-school management have a standard of judgment that can be used for measuring the efficiency of their practices.... Fifty-nine dollars paid in Rockford is the median price paid for algebra and geometry. There is no reason to think that the results obtained in Rockford are in any degree inferior to those obtained in the dozen cities paying a higher price.

By the 1920s, superintendents in Baltimore and Boston were handing out merit pay to Latin teachers based on a formula linking heating costs, salary charges, time-on-task (both teachers' and pupils'), administrative salaries, and examination results. If you lowered the heat to 60° F, gave merit pay for good examination results, and inspected the classroom every second day to be sure no one was wasting time, then... you had an efficient school. Never mind that it had become a prison, that the administration was reminiscent of Genghis Khan (but did the Khan ever have so large a bureaucracy?), that inspection from the centre took no account of people's local circumstances, and that the main point of

---

[23]Callahan, *Cult*, p. 25.

[24]David Noble, *Forces of Production: A Social History of Industrial Automation* (New York: Oxford University Press, 1984), 33.

[25]*School Review*, XXIII (1915 October): 505–34.

education to give people joy in learning, to provide the mental furniture they would need to have permanently interesting lives, to make them into critically-minded inquirers and citizens was utterly lost.

Raymond Callahan's remarkable book describes in its last two hundred pages the impact of Taylorism on school administration and universities. After a wave of detailed time-work studies just after the Great War, universities and colleges succeeded in persuading themselves and others that efficiency studies would not solve their financial and political troubles. For some decades, until the depths of the Depression, they managed to keep the bean-counters at bay.[26] The public schools were not so lucky. Two Lancaster University scholars recently summarized the continuing impact of Taylorism on American education, with the implication that higher education would not be able finally to resist the movement:

> It is easy to identify elements of Taylorism in the operation of many of their [the Americans'] large-scale social and educational programmes. Thus there is a recurrent pattern of centrally devised and standardised programmes, divided into manageable units, aimed at particular target groups, implemented by teacher/workers, who had not been involved in the planning of the programme, constantly monitored by outsiders concerned with efficiency, and finally judged by 'consumers' rather than by 'workers.'[27]

Universities did manage to put off the evil day through a double strategy. First, they went into the business of educating administrators in Taylorist and post-Taylorist management techniques. "If you can't beat 'em, join 'em."[28]

---

[26]We emphasize that Callahan's book does not argue the question of PIs and their long-term effects, concerned as he is with the negative consequences of efficiency-minded education administration on a continental scale. Callahan's evidence, on the other hand, permits our inferences.

[27]G. Helsby and M. Saunders, "Taylorism, Tylerism and Performance Indicators: defending the indefensible?" *Educational Studies*, 19, 1 (1993): 55–77. "Tylerism" is a behaviourist scheme for evaluating teaching and curricula. It calls on those who develop programmes of study to be as precise as possible about the behaviours they aim to produce in students. The clarification of behavioural objectives depends on a prior statement of overall curricular aims. From aims, thence to objectives, one goes on to detailed studies of the scope and sequence of studies needed to produce the desired behaviours. Tyler's major work, *Basic Principles of Curriculum and Instruction* (Chicago: University of Chicago Press, 1949) was welcomed at the time as an improvement over techniques of administration that relied exclusively on PIs and on psychometric and normative testing of all kinds. The popularity of Web-based programmes of instruction in the 2000s is a striking reminder that Tylerism is alive and well, as such programmes usually depend on precise statements of goal, aim, objective, scope, sequence in order to achieve efficacy and efficiency on the Internet.

[28]M.L. Cooke, *Academic and Industrial Efficiency: A Report to the Carnegie Foundation for the Advancement of Teaching* (New York: Merrymount Press, 1910) was a Carnegie-inspired document that aimed to show the broad range of Taylorist management devices available to colleges and universities. The mere publication of this document may have helped to persuade at least some business and government leaders that efficiency was being taken seriously in post-secondary education institutions. We doubt that after 1915, very many administrators or regents found Cooke's schemes

Part of this scheme of resistance was that school boards, and university boards of regents/governors, would hire administrators with advanced degrees in administration and management, complete with courses in statistics and work-analysis. It soon became a *sine qua non* that education administrators would have magistral or doctoral degrees in these fields, as proof of commitment to a Taylorist view of the world.

By implication universities claimed they could be relied upon to develop the theory of efficiency in management, even hiring some administrators who looked as if they believed in the possibility of Taylorist management. But the whole idea was that universities and colleges expected that the theory they promulgated should never actually *apply* to them! Universities now had more administrators than before, more committed to detailed accounting than ever before. Administrators on both sides of the Atlantic simply asserted that this was enough, and for a while government and business agreed. But with the Depression, developments in the social sciences, especially in psychology, together with innovations in industrial control theory, came to reinforce the tendencies displayed in Phases I and II. The transformation of university administration could not now be put off forever, particularly given the rise of behaviourist psychology, with its radical emphasis on visible and testable outcomes.

The second prong of the university strategy was to accept a redirection of the social sciences to the study of measurable outcomes and testing. If all went according to plan, the objects of the new studies would be almost entirely restricted to elementary and secondary schools, and the universities would get off scot free. In higher education across North America, and then in Europe, the fields of psychology, sociology, social service research and practice, criminology, and education became more thoroughly "scientific" and statistical than ever before.[29]

Phase III: Behaviourist Social Science, Electronics, Accountancy, & the Dream of Organizational Control

Behind the scenes, the social sciences were undergoing something of a revolution through the War and into the 1920s (especially psychology, broadly defined to include studies of individuals, groups, and organizations). This revolution was long in coming. Students of the history of psychology point to Francis Galton's curious studies of intelligence in 1880s South Kensington. Galton's work relied on studies of measurable behaviour, such as quickly deciding which of three large objects was the heaviest, or testing how quickly and firmly a person could squeeze

---

appealing, distracted as they were by War, the Roaring Twenties, and the Depression.

[29]Gerald E. Thomson, "Remove From Our Midst These Unfortunates," Ph.D. thesis, University of British Columbia, 1999, provides in Chs. 1 and 2 a helpful description of the rise and rise of statistics and testing in a large Canadian city, and provides extensive references for analogous developments across North America.

Galton's hand. In a larger sense, the origins of the field include Darwin and Lyell, careful observers of behaviour, and pioneers of a science leading to the prediction and control of behaviour.

Following on Galton's studies, Alfred Binet tried around the turn of the 20th century to see if the behaviours of people could be reliably linked to their intelligence. This time intelligence was defined not just as rapid physical response but as a combination of judgement, comprehension, and reasoning. Binet carefully studied his own daughters in these regards, but his techniques soon came to much wider attention when applied to a large population: the thousands of young men who served in the American armed forces in World War I. IQ testing promised a way of sorting large numbers of people quickly and cheaply into categories of competency and ability. It relied on the power of normative statistics to guide the creation of ever more reliable tests. It was an odd but important fact that it did not matter what kind of theory of intelligence a IQ test-writer espoused. What mattered was whether tests were reliably tied to academic and professional success in life.

This background helps to explain the bizarre case of Sir Cyril Burt, a British psychologist who, until his retirement in 1950, built an influential career on the proposition that intelligence was primarily hereditary in origin. His *Factors of the Mind* (1940)[30] and later studies showed, to his satisfaction anyway, that IQ correlated closely with the professional and occupational levels of test subjects. He concluded occupation and social class were decided by people's levels of inherited intelligence. The next and logical step was to use tests to slot people into educational streams and, later, professions and occupations. Views of this sort helped eventually to justify the creation and administration in the United Kingdom of an examination called the Eleven-Plus, so named because children were to be aged eleven years or more at the time they took it.

After 1944 the Eleven-Plus test decided whether children would be admitted to academically-oriented secondary grammar schools, opening onward to university entrance, or to comprehensive high schools. It is hard to overestimate the significance for national life of this testing system. Tens of millions of families thought of little else for years at a time as each of their children approached the crucial testing-time. A great psychometric bureaucracy grew up to administer tests, and a large civil service to distribute educational funds based on results of test administration.

Even though IQ was supposed to be mainly hereditary, it was obvious from the start that this could not possibly be true. There were far too many exceptions to the rules that tied intelligence to class—and increasing suspicion that Burt had fudged his data to produce the results he

---

[30]Cyril Burt, *Factors of the Mind: An Introduction to Factor-Analysis in Psychology* (London: University of London Press, 1940).

wanted.[31] These tests quickly became just as much devices for checking the performance of preparatory and elementary schools as they were for verifying the performance of individual children. Schools *could* make a difference, and thus they began to teach to the test. Parents at once began to vote with their feet, sending their children to those schools, public or private, with reputations for producing high scores on the Eleven-Plus.

Through the 1950s, '60s, and '70s, it became depressingly evident that the tests, as a form of PIs, did not and indeed *could not* work. Not only was the work of Burt and his followers on both sides of the Atlantic successfully discredited, but parents and governing authorities also came to resent a curriculum effectively made by the test-writers, and which rewarded the world-view of a tiny fraction of the British upper-middle-class.[32] It took only a short time to realize that excellent students and first-rate schools, on any criterion, were doing badly on the Eleven-Plus. The test led to serious mistakes in the assignment of children, cost a great deal, relied on faulty theory, but suited the technicist and managerialist inclinations of people in government and in the private sector. By the time the system had been eliminated in most of Britain, thousands of schools and millions of children had paid the price.[33]

The North American experience of standardized testing, including testing in universities and colleges, has been the subject of more extensive historical study than most educational phenomena. From the late 1930s onward, testing went from triumph to triumph, whether it be norm- or criterion-referenced standardized tests of knowledge in subjects as different as history and music and mathematics. At the height of its popularity, testing was associated with what Stanford University historian David Tyack called "the One Best System," that is, a system of schooling and higher education that properly distributed knowledge to all according to their needs, in line with the requirements of economic and social efficiency.[34]

Testing went through a decade or two of public scepticism, but never disappeared, either in Britain or in North America. Even in the progressive 1960s, standardized tests continued to be popular as diagnostic tools. They helped teachers to pinpoint areas of strength and deficiency in the various

---

[31]N.J. Mackintosh, *Cyril Burt: Fraud or Framed?* (Oxford: Oxford University Press, 1995).

[32]See the knock-down treatment of Eleven-Plus in Brian Simon, *Intelligence Testing and the Comprehensive School* (London: Lawrence & Wishart, 1953).

[33]For a latter-day version of state-school testing gone wrong, as chilling in its implications as the natural history of the 11+, see J. Steinberg and D.B. Henriques, "None of the Above: When a Test Fails the Schools, Careers and Reputations Suffer," *Our Schools*, 11, 1 (2001 October): 71–87 [orig. *New York Times*, 2001 May 21].

[34]For a lucid study of testing and labelling in education at all levels, see the recent work of Sarah Deschenes, David Tyack, and Larry Cuban, "Mismatch: Historical Perspectives on Schools and Students Who Don't Fit Them," *Teachers College Record*, 103, 4 (2001): 525–47.

subjects of instruction, and they pointed to various kinds of learning deficits and incapacities. Because educators remembered the excesses of the 1940s and early 1950s, and for other reasons having to do with the cultural circumstances of the day, they were able to keep testing in its properly subservient place for some while. Then testing returned with a vengeance.

The readiness of the British and the North American publics to accept testing and to contemplate PIs in the 1980s and 1990s is easier to understand given these nations' lengthy histories of statisticized and behaviourist social science, and their nearly equally lengthy commitment to standardized testing.[35]

Two more major factors at work in the larger society help to account for the impact of standardized testing in industry and schooling. These were

1 strengthened faith in the powers of *accountancy*, and
2 new developments in *electronics, automatic production control, and industrial practice.*

These help us to explain how higher education could maintain autonomy and a sense of critical judgement, despite contrary forces and factors.

Accountancy

Beneath and behind the growing public interest in measures and devices of all kinds, there was a dream. It was the dream of the statistically-minded social scientists of the 1920s, the behaviourist psychologists and social psychologists, the Taylorists and efficiency-cultists of the period after about 1910, and of social engineers in the late 1940s. It was the dream of education and society as machines, efficient devices for the attainment of high social objectives on one hand, and inculcation of measurable knowledge and marketable skills on the other. It was the idea that a machine-like solution could be found to the ancient problem of assigning the young to their proper

---

[35]*Cf.* Theodore M. Porter, *Trust in Numbers: The Pursuit of Objectivity in Science and Public Life* (Princeton: Princeton University Press, 1995), esp. sec. on "Mental Testing and Experimental Psychology," 209–14. Porter's view of quantitative research is generally friendly (as is ours). But at all times Porter insists on the dangers of searching for quantitative rules, and doing so in secretive or possessive ways. He recommends that scientific communities become ever more open about the transforming truths we call "knowledge." Meanwhile, the communities of science deserve to be strengthened in the name of civility and social progress. At p. 216, Porter writes:

> Insistence on rigorous standards of knowledge has become a strategy of opposition, used by powerful industrialists to immobilize the regulatory agencies. To reject expert judgment, then, is to abandon all hope of constructive public action.... [A reasoned] opposition to methods claiming objectivity, such as cost-benefit analysis, derives also from a sense that they often measure the wrong thing. As an abstract proposition, rigorous standards promote public responsibility and may very well contribute to accountability, even to democracy....The drive to eliminate trust and judgment from the public domain will never completely succeed. Possibly it is worse than futile.

places and professions. It was the hope that a truly scarce good—advanced education—could mechanically and fairly be distributed, through exact testing and accountancy, to every deserving person.[36]

But the dream is older still.

In accounting theory, it has been standard practice to reduce business to financially measurable activities, inputs, outputs, and costs. But as Keith Hoskin and Richard Macve write, that "accounting is an ancient practice with a distinctive modern power." It wasn't just a question of the invention of double-entry accounting, but rather the appearance in the 19th and 20th centuries of Cost and Management Accounting, the rise of the accounting profession, and "systems of accountability." There is an immense and unavoidable difficulty in the history of accounting:

> [T]here has never been a clear link... between accounting's use and the improvement of rational economic decision-taking.[37]

The sheer technicality of accounting, its study in universities(from the 13th century onward!), its specious application to the ranking of military cadets and army practices in the early 19th century, and its recognizably late-industrial applications in the "management-by-numbers" of railways in Europe and the United States: all helped to strengthen the idea that a disciplined body of outside inspectors, and inside managers, guided by numbers, should be given power over social and business activity about which they might well know nothing. Thus modern accounting was not a

> ...practical response of men faced with new entrepreneurial challenges, sensibly devising ways to capture the data needed for rational economic decisions for in that sense, no 'practical' man would have invented modern accounting practice, the outputs of which are not at all what is obviously needed for such purposes.

Accounting has a culture all its own, highly professionalized. Appropriately applied, it is a useful shorthand to help accountants in business talk to other accountants in government or banking or the stock market. How, then, did it become a substitute for practical and participatory decision-making, rather than a useful adjunct to them?

---

[36]In a sense, these ideas are the sisters of an even larger idea: that (as Julie Reuben puts it),

> [s]cholars [in modern, industrial-age universities] hoped that the distinction between fact and value would lead to more reliable knowledge as measured by greater agreement. The subsequent history of academic disciplines in the twentieth century indicates that this hope was illusory.

Julie Reuben, *The Making of the Modern University: Intellectual Transformation and the Marginalization of Morality* (Chicago: University of Chicago Press, 1996), 269.

[37]Keith Hoskin and Richard Macve, "Writing, examining, disciplining: the genesis of accounting's modern power," in A.G. Hopwood and P. Miller, *Accounting as Social and Institutional Practice* (Cambridge: Cambridge University Press, 1994), 67–97, this citation from p. 67.

Public universities and colleges have long depended on systems of governance, rather than flying squads of accountants, to provide accountability to the public, to students, to professorss, and to staff. For a university, accountability is no more or less than the ability, on request, or at legislatively required times and places, to say what it does, why, and how it continues to work to improve the match between its claims and aims, and its actual performance. These are all matters of judgement, not primarily matters of statistics or numbers alone.[38]

Accountants should, therefore, have a minor role to play in assuring a university's accountability. The major roles should go to public bodies that do their business in public, reporting on the teaching, research, and finance of the institution, doing it understandably and often. The senate, the board of governors, administrators, departments, professors, and students, all will have their parts to play in making the university open and accountable. Because the universities are public bodies, some of their aims will come from public authorities, and some of their reporting will be done to and for those same authorities. But the chief work of accounting will be to communicate with the broad public and the many professional communities to which the college and university are responsible.

At the older Canadian and American universities, the wish to make new and more workable systems of self-government was already evident by the 1880s and 1890s. For it was obvious, however paradoxically, that a public post-secondary institution could be truly accountable only if it were largely autonomous. If it were merely a branch of the state apparatus, then free judgement and critical thinking would be impossible, as would be the sciences and the humanities that depend on those things.

So at the University of Toronto, the role of the Senate and the powers of the President were revisited and reformed again and again in the 1890s and early 1900s, partly in answer to a demand for accountability. By this was meant the ability to be able to say what the university's mandate was, and to have the means to carry it out.[39]

By the 1890s, the Ivy League universities of the United States were in the midst of a similar "accountability revolution." There as in Canada, the point was not to improve efficiencies "by the number," but to encourage more reasoned decision-making about curriculum, to accept that scholars

---

[38]The pressure to adopt or to adapt detailed accounting techniques was, of course, unremitting in North American and European universities. Even if post-secondary education institutions were able to resist it with some success, one has to take note of that pressure. For an instance of the pressure, see W.H. Allen, *Self-Surveys by Colleges and Universities* (Yonkers-on-Hudson, New York: World Book Company, 1917).

[39]H. Averill and G. Keith, "Daniel Wilson and the University of Toronto," in M. Ash, *et al.*, eds., *Thinking with Both Hands: Sir Daniel Wilson in the Old World and the New* (Toronto: University of Toronto Press, 1999), pp. 139–210; also A.B. McKillop, *Matters of Mind: The University in Ontario, 1791–1951* (Toronto: University of Toronto Press, 1994).

and the public each had a rightful place and a voice, and to see to it that the necessary means of achieving the mandate were present. Was there a decent library? Were there enough professors so students could hope for personal help and guidance? Were the conditions of research and publication good enough to guarantee that new knowledge would be communicated freely to the world, and taught immediately in the classroom?

The test of accountability lay in a form of governance, in clear mandates, and in a sensible discussion of how to provide the means to achieve those mandates. We do not suggest that the 19th-century university, either in North America or in the Old World, made quick progress on these fronts, but there was, nonetheless, plenty of evidence to suggest that they were trying. The paradoxical fact is that even as university governance experienced a slow-moving reformation which bore fruit only in the 1960s, an entirely contrary movement—Taylorist, behaviourist, and non-accountable—was taking shape and gathering energy. We think that along with the developments in the social sciences we have just described, another contributing factor came from the growth of accountancy, a development that would reach its full flower only in the latter decades of the 20th century.

It would soon become commonplace that governments, think-tanks, and business people would demand that chartered accountants and bean counters intervene directly in post-secondary education. The motives for this demand had and have to do with was the wish to make public institutions less public, as well as cheap and efficient devices for the accomplishment of specific economic goals. But in Phase III of the PIs movement, those motives were not entirely visible or active, and were in any case less noticeable because of the contemporary fascination with the various manifestations of behaviourism. The contemporary growth in popularity of accounting techniques was, similarly, not a direct cause of change in the practice of university administration. But a commitment to new forms of accounting and management was certainly consistent with the statistical and psychological theories already at large in the 1920s and 1930s. These were, therefore, among the foundations of what would later become a full-blown PIs movement.

Electronics, automatic production control, & industrial practice

From the late 19th century onward, punched cards were used to organize large quantities of data, automatic timers to check on workers' entries and exits from labour, and counters to relate data, time, and production quotas to one another. The potential uses of these devices for the detailed management of highly abstract and complex production became intensely interesting to public and military leaders in the run-up to World War II. But as early as 1930, the maturation of electronics led managers and researchers alike to think of new ways to intensify work routines, especially by providing immediate feed-back on sub-routines of which work was said to be composed. Besides, electronics held the promise of detailed surveillance of a kind administrators and managers had until then been able only to dream of.[40] David Noble describes a crucial application of these innovations:

> Finally, working on analyses of radar systems, submarine, ship, and aircraft detection, and other military 'operations,' British and later, American physicists and mathematicians, developed the new field of 'operations research' (OR)....[Operations Research] provided quantitative aids for 'the prediction and comparison of the values, effectiveness, and costs of a set of proposed alternative courses of action involving man-machine systems,' analyses in which 'all human and machine factors are meant to be included.'[41]

Professor Noble's *Forces of Production*, from which this quotation comes, next moves to a chapter called, "Toward the Automatic Factory," followed by a longer discussion of "Social Choice in Machine Design." His detailed argument repays close and repeated study, showing as it does how different schemes of "automatic industrial control technology" made their appearances. These decisions were rarely (if ever) the results of technical or even economic facts and factors. Rather, they were the consequences of an "obsession with control, certainty, and predictability, and a corresponding desire to eliminate as much as possible all uncertainty, contingency, and chance for human error."[42]

Control and planning were nearly always in the hands of bureaucrats and the denizens of think tanks; these features of PIs apply to post-secondary education everywhere in the western world. One might justifiably wonder how supporters of PIs can square their belief in free markets and competitive individualism, with their apparently overwhelming need to dominate and to direct university teaching and research. We think it is too simple to say the desire for control is merely the natural wish of capitalists to ensure universities will do research and teaching that contribute to corporate profits. Nor is it always self-evident that capitalists *have* this need for control, although they readily say that they would like to extend to the whole world the regimes that have worked so well for them in their own industrial practice. The explanation goes deeper even than the phenomena David Noble so ably describes.

We must go to the roots of the need to control, and the desire to deprive universities and colleges of the freedom to carry out their social and educational obligations. Governments generally dislike truly independent teaching and research because it may be critical of them and may disturb the status quo. They have developed mechanisms both in the civilian bureaucracy and in the military to compel the work and the results they want.

---

[40]Noble, *Forces*, pp. 42 ff.
[41]*Ibid.*, 53.
[42]*Ibid.*, 191.

Now they were beginning to have the power to do the same in the universities of the English-speaking world.

∎

We mentioned earlier that on all sides of the Atlantic and the Pacific, universities and colleges were able to resist the worst (or sometimes any) encroachment of standardized testing, whether of subject matters or of psychological capacities and dispositions. How was this possible?

Consider the example of just one American social scientist and university administrator, G.D. Stoddard.

George D. Stoddard (1897–1981) was a child psychologist and longtime director of the Iowa Child Welfare Research Station. He opposed the deterministic, normative views then dominant in the testing movement. It's hard now to imagine how courageous his stand was at the time (between 1925 and 1942). His research and his colleagues' in nutrition, sociology, health, and medicine all helped to show that IQ scores could move as much as one full Standard Deviation under certain social or physical conditions. His work was controversial not just because it disturbed a simple, if deterministic model of human personality and mentality, but because it put Taylorism in doubt. In the heyday of Taylorist management schemes, testing had promised to make education a completely predictable, manageable, profitable, and efficient affair. Without simple-minded testing, what would happen to Taylorist management schemes?

Stoddard's career was given colour by his thoroughly liberal commitment to the New Deal, and by his leadership of several major American universities in the 1940s and 1950s. The point in mentioning him, and by his example a sizeable body of researcher-reformers rather like him, is that he was, as Hamilton Cravens puts it,

> the quintessential New Deal liberal who believed in the promises of professionalism and positivistic science but went a step further than most of his liberal colleagues and argued that the individual can be an autonomous person.[43]

All Stoddard's actions as a major American academic politician, including his presidencies at Illinois and New York University, showed his belief that the autonomy he wanted for individuals should, *a fortiori*, be extended to institutions of post-secondary education. In this sense, his career exemplifies the successful deployment of a strategy that was at least sceptical of PIs, if not outright hostile to them. It was Stoddard's view on the value of private

---

[43]H. Cravens, "Stoddard, George Dinsmore," *http://www.anb.org/articles/14/14-00898.html* [include the hyphen in the name of the site], American National Biography Online 2001 November, from American National Biography, published by Oxford University Press, Inc., copyright 2000 American Council of Learned Societies, Further information is available at *http://222.anb.org*. [This notice, in its entirety, provided under the express requirement of the ANB and of Oxford University Press.]

and communal judgement in education, and his theory that these things were a crucial feature of human and educational development—and views and theories of these kinds—that gave the universities new ammunition in their quiet and continuing struggle for autonomy.

Sceptical non-compliance was by no means the only strategy in play here. The sheer success of university research and teaching in and after World War II played a crucial part in persuading the public and private sectors to leave the universities alone. Nationally-funded university science and engineering made a remarkable difference in the Allied victory and postwar recovery; in war and reconstruction, nothing succeeds like success.[44] University administrators pointed to their institutions' accomplishments as proof there was no need for micro-management by accountants, politicians, or businessmen appointed to boards of governors or regents.

In this third Phase, few governments actually insisted on Taylorist or radically behaviourist schemes for post-secondary education; rather it was a question of "recommendations" made in an atmosphere of considerable economic pressure. University resistance to management-style Taylorism was partly in the spirit of pioneer Upper Canadians and later Ontarians who opposed the imposition of regulated State education systems in place of local and familial arrangements in the early and mid-19th century.[45] That is, universities called on their client communities to remember their best local, familial traditions and roots. Besides these forms of politics, university leaders pointed to the century-long experience of collegial governance in the Ivy League universities of North America, and the ancient universities of Europe, all to raise a barrier to mindless applications of testing and other statistical fads.

Yet another reason universities could and did resist was that even in their more ambitious moments, business leaders and like-minded government officials could not quite see how Taylorist analysis, detailed accountncy, or standardized testing would fit well with higher education, especially in its collegiate and residential forms. To business people, the work of the university was *sui generis*. And anyway, Boards of Governors already had immense residual power—no need for more.

Besides, just as in the latter stages of Phase II, universities and colleges went about offering courses and organizing research in statistics, social work, education, commerce, and all the rest, thus laying to rest (the universities hoped) the objection that post-secondary education was opposed, root and branch, to innovation.

---

[44]For the Canadian case, but with generous reference to the contributions of American, British, and Commonwealth universities, see Donald H. Avery, *The Science of War: Canadian Scientists and Allied Military Technology during the Second World War* (Toronto: University of Toronto Press, 1998).

[45]Bruce Curtis, *Building the Educational State: Canada West, 1836–1871* (London, Ontario: Althouse Press, 1988).

■

Turning to Phases IV and V, we have a list of factors (not necessarily causal) that help to account, years later, for the PIs groundswell in the United Kingdom, the United States, and Canada. These include:

- from Phase I, an abiding fondness for statistical reports as a proxy or a proof of social progress;
- from Phase II, public and private fascination with the application of time-work and other efficiency measures in all facets of public and private life;
- from Phase III, discoveries and opinion-shifts that rapidly intensified the popular faith in the elements already present from Phases I and II , the many uses of testing and normative statistics; the predictive powers of IQ tests, personality inventories, and their like, for individuals and for organizations; new forms of automatic production control; and, of course, a continuing fondness for assured techniques of social and organizational control.

Now add to these cumulative factors a growing body of public and official writing on higher education, its governance and its finance, through the 1930s and 1940s—a body of work in Europe and in North America that hinted very broadly that something like PIs was afoot.[46] Two American writers, R. Novak and D. Leslie, review some 3,000 pages of such work published in the United States by the U.S. Office of Education, the Carnegie Foundation for the Advancement of Teaching, and the American Council on Education. Analogous official documents were published in the 1930s in the United Kingdom, France, Germany, New Zealand, Australia, South Africa, and Canada, *entre autres*, often under Carnegie or Rockefeller auspices.[47] Most of the American documents under review were ostensibly concerned with the question of federal versus state rights and obligations in post-secondary education. But as Novak and Leslie put the matter:

> Four overlapping themes emerged in policymakers' and educators' efforts to make sense of this difficult era for public higher education: 1) power and control (who governs); 2) money, efficiency, and productivity; 3) the inseparability of money and control; and 4) the merits of voluntary cooperation and self-regulation.[48]

That is to say, by 1940 there was already a framework of public policy on which a movement toward PIs could be constructed.

---

[46]R. Novak and D. Leslie, "A Not So Distant Mirror: Great Depression Writings on the Governance and Finance of Public Higher Education," *History of Higher Education Annual*, 20 (2000): 59–78.

[47]See for references, and for its argument on social research/social policy, Richard Glotzer, "The Influence of Carnegie Corporation and Teachers College, Columbia, in the Interwar Dominions: The Case for Decentralized Education," *Historical Studies in Education/Revue d'histoire de l'éducation*, 12, 1/2 (2000 spring/fall): 93–110.

[48]Novak and Leslie, "Not So Distant," 62.

Phase IV: Systems Theory & Management Fads

After 1945 the world economy experienced its greatest-ever expansion. European reconstruction, the fighting and winning of the Cold War and of its sub-wars, the massive expansion of scientific and technical knowledge, and the rising consumption of billions of people—all contributed to the new economy.[49]

Post-secondary teaching and research had been a direct contributor to the industrial and economic explosion of the 1940s and later. Naturally, across the world, university and college teachers and administrators moved quickly to assert that this was so, and to claim a share of the wealth created by expansion.

Universities and colleges continued to do what they had always sought to do in the industrial-democratic era: help construct a new view of community and society. Their work showed how certain attitudes (especially a fondness for open debate and democratic participation), and certain forms of knowledge (above all, what is sometimes called "fundamental" knowledge) were necessary to the social and economic reconstruction of the world.

Just as in Phases I, II, and III, organized post-secondary education was able to persuade the public, the government, and the corporate sector that the Golden Goose would continue to lay only if it were (mostly) left alone.

The difficulty was that from the early 1950s, the size and cost of post-secondary education became great enough to attract sustained public attention. More and more people agreed that post-secondary education institutions should no longer escape the strictures of public policy. There was growing agreement that colleges and universities should listen to or even imitate business practice, and that they should shape their activities so as to match their limited means, and to suit the requirements of public opinion and public policy.

Public opinion was by no means consistent on any of these matters, but about 1980, with the advent of neo-conservative governments in the United Kingdom and the United States, it congealed: what had been vague in the three decades before 1980s became crystal-clear. From then on, the business model was assumed to have a natural *droit de seigneur* in the academy.

The complexity and massiveness of the modern economy, and the movement of much economic activity from the public to the private sphere after the War, encouraged public belief in the wisdom of imposing business models and methods on the public sector. As GDP rose rapidly and with few signs of severe recession, North Americans and Europeans were increasingly inclined to forget that their rising standards of living owed much to public and community effort, not to the ministrations of private corporations and companies. It was the effect of public expenditure for war and subsequent

---

[49]J.M. Roberts, *Twentieth Century: The History of the World, 1901 to 2000* (London: Penguin/Viking, 1999), Ch. 19, "New Economic and Social Worlds," 584–612.

reconstruction in Europe and Asia. It was public expenditure on education, health, social welfare, and pensions that gave a secure basis to prosperity. None of this is to deny the part private persons and companies played in post-War economic history.

The public's enjoyment and fascination with consumer goods—cars, television, new housing, and higher education, all defined as "luxuries" —meanwhile encouraged a slowly-growing belief that management and production techniques borrowed from business should be applied to the management of post-secondary education.[50] Once colleges and universities ran the way businesses did, so the reasoning went, universities and college would produce more student places, more jobs, and further economic growth through useful research.

A vast irony overlies this story. The very businesses that were supposed to serve as models, large or small, had only the vaguest ideas of how to organize their own management, let alone export it to completely different forms of human and social organization. Recent historical studies show that IBM and General Motors, synonymous with massive economic output, had no notion from one month to the next whether their management and production and sales arrangements would see them safely into the future.

Assuming that business models made sense in university administration, college and university presidents across North America and Europe began to talk the way business executives talk. But they did not *walk* the talk. They continued to resist the excesses of business-style accountancy, testing, time-motion engineering, and organizational testing and re-engineering. In Phase IV, despite that pattern of resistance, the daily lives of professors and instructors began to change. The pressure to produce more pages and to acquire more grants, and the rise of client-satisfaction surveys in various forms, combined to give a fillip to university managers and management-as-science. But the sustained application of the theory occurred finally in Phase V.

Meanwhile, in Phase IV (ca. 1950–ca. 1980), one management fad followed upon another. By far the best guide to management fads in post-secondary education is Robert Birnbaum, whose *Management Fads in Higher Education* has found a broad audience since its publication in early 2001.[51] Birnbaum takes us through the three crucial decades ending in 1980 in the earlier part of his book, reminding us often about the central features of these fads. They are, he asserts, the products of consultants and managers who "sell" them to the unwary, using peculiar rhetoric and

---

[50]On consumerism and its political consequences, see the striking remarks of Jacques Barzun, *From Dawn to Decadence, 1500 to the Present: 500 Years of Western Cultural Life* (New York: HarperCollins, 2000), pp. 778 ff.

[51]Robert Birnbaum, *Management Fads in Higher Education: Where They Come From, What They Do, Why They Fail* (San Francisco: Jossey-Bass, 2001).

high-minded theory; they offer narratives of institutional life, and promise magical solutions to the nasty complexities of everyday life; they promise a "scientific" solution to those complex problems, just as Taylor did. In short, a fad is a *political* device. It promises the impossible: permanent solutions to (happily) insolubly complex human problems.

From the early 1950s onward, in Canada, the United States, Europe, and elsewhere in industrialized and developing countries alike, the administrative apparatus of post-secondary education grew in size and form. It looked increasingly business-like, with talk of management-vs-labour, competition for custom, line-item budget analysis, and multi-year planning.

None of this was especially bothersome so long as the traditional distinctions were miantained between the academic and the financial arms of university government. As colleges and universities grew in size and number after 1950, and even more after 1960, most academics would have agreed that a more sustained and systematic approach to administration was called for. They could afford to take that view because management was still seen as a *service to* the university, not its primary activity.

Birnbaum thinks that the very first post-War management fad in post-secondary education was the popularity in the 1950s and 1960s of MIs, management information systems.[52] This combined with the invention of computing systems as a new foundation for detailed and intrusive university administration. Departments and laboratories could no longer hope to have any secrets from the institutional accountants and analysts in the central administration once MIs and computers were in place. High-level administrators could pretend to a kind of omniscience and rationality previously undreamed-of.[53]

We do not disagree with Birnbaum in detail, but would point in Canada and elsewhere to a parallel fad: the popularity in the 1950s and 1960s of economic and political theories closely tied to the behaviourist psychology we described in Phase III. These might loosely be categorized as systems theories, or even as games theories. Theories of these kinds appeared sometimes in conjunction with defence and military research, but also in detailed research on negotiation, including labour-management negotiation.

If one person could be taken to embody the ideas of systems and games theory, as connected to administration, it would be Herbert A. Simon (1916–2001), American social scientist and Nobel Prize winner (1978) in economics. Simon was a pioneer in the closely-related fields of organizational psychology,

---

[52]Birnbaum, *Management Fads*, 27.

[53]Tom Peters, the author of one of the business community's favourite populist books, *In Search of Excellence*, admitted in an interview in 2001 that the statistical data for the book was simply made up. What is perhaps more interesting is Mr. Peters' recommended research methods: ask smart people in your firm and elsewhere, gather and analyze their views, and make your own judgement. It sounds remarkably rational and much like what universities have traditionally done in tenure and promotion judgements. *(Globe and Mail,* 2001 Nov. 23.)

applied statistics, and operations research. It is of more than passing interest that Simon took his 1943 doctorate in political science, a choice that points to Simon's later interest in behaviouristic theories of corporate decision-making. Simon's multiple logics, and his multiple-factor approach to decision-making, led him to a theory of "satisficing." By this Simon meant the reaching of economic and political goals, no matter how complicated the environment, by mapping a rational pathway through complex circumstances, meanwhile minimizing risk. It was partly his techniques of risk assessment that showed Simon to be a calculating behaviourist in the traditions of Watson, Thorndike, and Skinner.[54]

When we think that the presidents of universities as varied as Toronto and Manitoba, Bissell and Sirluck, could be literary men and yet fascinated by the powers of management science *à la* Simon; when places as various as Saskatchewan and Memorial and Sherbrooke could devote significant chunks of scarce cash to management staff, accountants and systems analysts among them: then one is surely in the presence of a management fad.[55]

This first big fad (MIs) of Phase IV was long-running. Indeed, the expensive salaries and office space required by that fad are features of university and college budgets across North America in 2001, forty years later. As we wrote earlier, we see the Phases as cumulative. Universities and colleges the world over are all too familiar with resource allocation models, comprehensive budget analysis, and the like. These things never quite fade away.

Birnbaum labels the next three generations of management fads as:
- Zero-Base Budgeting and Management by Objectives
- Strategic planning and benchmarking
- Total Quality Management and Business Process Re-engineering

---

[54]See Herbert A. Simon, *Administrative Behavior: A Study of Decision-Making Processes in Administrative Organization* (New York: Macmillan, 1947; and many later editions); also his lectures at the University of British Columbia, 1986, on artificial intelligence, expert systems, and information processing (Archives of the University of British Columbia, cassettes 1348, 1351, and 1353).

[55]Claude T. Bissell, *Halfway Up Parnassus: A Personal Account of the University of Toronto, 1932–1971* (Toronto: University of Toronto Press, 1974), esp 109ff.; and Ernest Sirluck, *First Generation: An Autobiography* (Toronto: University of Toronto Press, 1996). Compare John Macdonald, *Chances and Choices: A Memoir* (Vancouver: University of British Columbia (UBC) and UBC Alumni Association, 2000), 116 ff., a sharp-eyed assessment of social forces that also contributed in the 1960s to the growth of large management apparatus including demand for access to post-secondary education and therefore an increase in the overall size of institutions, and an increasing litigiousness in relations among and between academics and administrators. By litigiousness, Macdonald refers to a re-balancing of university governance so as to take more account of university teachers' and students' views in running the institution. He thinks reforms of university governance are partly to blame for the increasing size of administrative apparatus in colleges and universities in North America and elsewhere. None of these autobiographical memoirs shows any systematic awareness of the danger lurking in demands for business-style "accountability" and PIs.

This sequence does not fit the Canadian, European, and Commonwealth experiences of 1980s and 1990s quite as well as it does the American history of university management. We have dealt elsewhere with benchmarking. And because the practices of Zero-Base Budgeting, strategic planning, and Business Re-Engineering have been the pet projects of extra-university bodies in Canada (the Canadian Association of Business Officers, the Canadian Corporate Higher Education Forum, the Association of Universities and Colleges of Canada, the Council of Ministers of Education, Canada, and even the OECD), we leave those to our chapter on Canadian cases.

This leaves us to review MBO, Management by Objectives, and TQM, Total Quality Management. These two will return, but deserve their own, special treatment here in Phase IV.

MBO will strike any student of management fads in higher education as important, but for Canadian and European observers, it has particular interest for its explicit references to behaviourist ideas, and because of its emphasis on observable outcomes. MBO has roots in budgeting schemas popularized in the 1960s by the American Department of Defense and the Rand Corporation, and thus has an American complexion.

But the attractiveness of MBO outside the United States may been even greater than it was inside. The power of standardized testing and of behavioural analyses had been acknowledged in the old Empire and on the Continent, sometimes for unpleasant reasons, very early on, and this gave MBO a certain superficial attractiveness from the start. But then, there was the further point that higher education administrators were visibly arriérés by comparison to the American cousins. It was time to catch up, and this one discouraged a close study of institutions' historical and cultural roots for a more glitzy future. By 1975, it had been used to justify a massive increase in the size of administrations. At the University of British Columbia, under the presidency of Douglas Kenny (1975 to 1983), the numbers of Vice-Presidents doubled, then trebled in five years, while the overall population of the presidential office suite grew by 450%. Kenny's own behaviourism as a professional psychologist may account for his fondness for programme budgeting and MBO, but at all events, his staff, professoriate, and students showed themselves increasingly restive as the years wore on. The management fads that fascinated Kenny were of little or no use in preparing the university for the brutal budget cuts handed down by the Social Credit government of the day after 1982.[56]

Robert Birnbaum levels at MBO the same criticism he does most fads:

---

[56]For the response of colleges and universities in British Columbia to management fad-ism in the early 1980s, see Warren Magnuson, ed., *The New Reality: The Politics of Restraint in British Columbia* (Vancouver: New Star Books, 1984), and edited by the same author, *After Bennett: A New Politics for British Columbia* (Vancouver: New Star Books, 1986).

> Lacking data, advocates relied instead on rhetoric....MBO's use and success in business and government proved later to be exaggerated, as did reports of its use in higher education.[57]

MBO was simplistic, as hinted in our earlier comment about its indifference to history. Worse, it actually "intensifie[d] hostility, resentment and distrust between a manager and subordinates."[58] Still worse, considering the subsequent development of PIs systems, MBO emphasized studies of quantity rather than studies of quality, produced more and more centralization in institutional governance, and undermined university and college account-ability by making it impossible to pay attention to critical judgement and critical thinking in everyday life.

By 1985, MBO was no longer heard of in higher education circles, either in North America or in Europe. Even though rumour had it that Lee Kwan Yeu was interested in MBO, it had little impact even in Singapore. By the mid-1980s, Canadian and American universities and colleges were in any case having to cope with Zero-Base Budgeting, yet another fad with the look of pure rationality. All that was wrong with MBO was equally wrong with Zero-Based Budgeting, and more.

The idea in Zero-Based Budgeting was that a budget must begin from the ground up. No programme or activity would be funded unless its rationale and value were established anew in every fiscal year. But after years of cuts and crisis, there was little fat to remove. All programmes had *prima facie* arguments for continued budgetary support, and besides, Zero-Based Budgeting ignored all the politics and all the history that gave a university, a college, or a country (for that matter) its purposes and its methods of governance.

Leaving Strategic Planning and Benchmarking for later discussion, we turn briefly to Total Quality Management. This fad is alive and well, and co-exists with the Performance Indicator movement. A journal devoted to TQM has reached its twelfth volume, runs eight issues per year, and costs $US 292.00/annum.[59] That journal must, one infers, be both popular and scarce.

Besides its continued representation in academic publishing, TQM has produced offspring. Gloria Lee[60] described in 1996 "the challenge of... demonstrating quality, at a time of an eroding unit of resource.... A way forward is explored through the implementation of Total Quality Management (TQM) and Business Process Redesign (BPR)." It turns out there have been almost no successful applications of either TQM or BPR in higher education, but these schemes continue to have lively political impact, and

---

[57]Birnbaum, *Management Fads*, 50.

[58]Birnbaum, *loc. cit.*, citing H. Levinson, "Management by Whose Objectives?" *Harvard Business Review*, 48 (1970): 125.

[59]*http://www.tandf.co.uk/journals/Leaflets/Ctqm.pdf.*

[60]Gloria Lee, "Whatever Happened to the Ivory Tower? Process Change in Higher Education: From TQM to BPR," *Journal of Business and Management*, 2, 2 (1996): 114–31.

to attract academic inquiry. The reason is that they come very close to being a full Performance Indicators regime.

Proponents of TQM claim it is a flexible and decentralized approach to organizational control. Even so, a TQM adherent will gladly admit the object of the exercise is to manipulate people to comply with the goals and practices of the business. At General Motors, Daimler-Chrysler, or in a Mom-and-Pop manufactory, TQM demands the use of statistics, charts, and flow diagrams, especially to monitor and correct defective outputs. Constant revision and improvement of products and services; a long-haul commitment to quality, partly through on-the-job training, and partly through mutual aid, as in "quality circles"; adoption of modern supervisory technique; an end to numerical production quotas (but no end to sophisticated and "total" observation of production activity): these, along with data collection, are central requirements at every stage. The business must be completely "customer-driven." Workers are not to think of themselves or their work, but rather of customers' wants. Managers will organize teams and focus groups on the factory floor to ensure the customer comes first.

Workers act in networks and function as customers and suppliers to each other. "Through constant communication, goal-setting, and auditing, each supplier works to satisfy the needs of the internal customers (other employees) and the external customers (the public)."[61]

Management is central. It chooses goals, and decides on techniques for measuring and communicating quality. It sets parameters for work and labour. TQM nevertheless leaves the impression of being a kinder, gentler management.

TQM's diagrams, bar charts, diagrams, cost-benefit analyses, flow charts, quality costing, line graphs, and risk analyses lead, of course, to benchmarking, goal setting, and performance assessment. In TQM-style postsecondary education, almost all of this apparatus would remain in place. Work plans would replace quotas, students would evaluate faculty, faculty members would busily evaluate each other at all times (meanwhile assessing student satisfaction, graduation rates, "learning," and so on). One can, with difficulty, imagine the quantities of time and paper required to do all of this; even so, L.E. Coate argued in 1994 that TQM would save money. The close connection between customers and post-secondary "producers" would lead to the disappearance of anything that reduced customer satisfaction. Furthermore, students would not be the only "customers," as industry and

---

[61]T. Beaton, "Performance Indicators and Quality Management in the University," *Humanities and Social Sciences Federation of Canada Research Report*, Ottawa, 1999 [see HSSFC web site].

government must play that role at least as often as students do. All will help to decide quality.[62]

One "natural" outcome of these tightly-controlling "processes" is that universities and colleges who adopt TQM would also accept comprehensive auditing. Under such a scheme, goals and procedures would be established, and an auditor examine teacher/researcher compliance with those goals.

> In the event of non-compliance, the auditor and professor would determine a strategy to remedy the problem and ensure compliance in the future. There would be a direct and recurring interaction between the management and the faculty.... Management, subcontractors and staff would design and develop courses and perform counseling and teaching assessment.[63]

If TQM were in place, it would necessarily mean plenty of market research, post-course evaluation, and frequent audits of research, timeliness, and teaching content, style, and outcome.

Assorted evidence shows the persistence of TQM in Canadian post-secondary education management circles. The Canadian Institutional Researchers and Planners Association (CIRPA/ACPRI) devoted its entire 1993 meeting to TQM. In 2000, the Canadian Association of University Business Officers gave Carleton University in Ottawa its "Quality and Productivity Award" for five process redesign projects, including what CAUBO called "student-centred processes"—registration, fee payments, counselling services, and classroom scheduling. Significantly, KPMG and the Royal Bank of Canada are co-sponsors of the CAUBO Quality and Productivity Awards.

The fads of Phase IV all have features that recall the systems-theoretic innovations with which the phase began. And as before, this phase rolled together the forces and features of its predecessors.

About 1980, the last Phase began.

Phase V: Performance Indicators at Last

In summer 1994, the Council of Ministers of Education, Canada (CMEC) met to work on a Pan-Canadian Education Indicators Programme. Unusually for Canada, chartered accountants worked closely with administrative colleagues and policy-minded bureaucrats to prepare the agenda and background papers.[64]

The presence of accountants, and repeated calls for "accountability" before, during, and after the 1994 meeting, hinted at a sea-change in

---

[62]L. Edwin Coate, "Implementing Total Quality Management in a University Setting" in Harry Costin, ed., *Readings in Total Quality Management* (Toronto: Dryden Press/Harcourt Brace, 1994), pp. 447–83.

[63]Beaton, *loc. cit.*

[64]For a discussion of the CMEC rationale for PIs, see Canadian Education Statistics Council, *Education Indicators in Canada: Report of the Pan-Canadian Education Indictors Program 1999* (Ottawa and Toronto: Canadian Education Statistics Council, 2000), pp. 1–7.

Canadian education. For the first time in Canadian history, political leaders and high civil servants were willing to give up a measure of discretion over students, curricula, and research in public schools and universities. Indeed, they looked as if they were ready to move some types of administrative control directly into the hands of the accountants, and to decide appropriate levels of public funding on the basis of purely statistical measures.

Among the accountants and statisticians of that meeting and others like it in the mid-1990s, there were, of course, moderates. Had they triumphed, the new statistics might have been mere guides to educational policy,[65] or perhaps soporific reading matter for obscure Treasury Board officials.

But moderates by the 1990s were not often triumphant at provincial or national levels.[66] Instead, "true believers" in the faith of numbers-driven-policy acquired more and more influence over public educational policy. Particularly in Alberta and Ontario, claims for performance measures took on a compulsory tone. The dominant theme of discussion from 1995 onward was that public spending on education must be held even, or decline. Further, the entire public post-secondary system should become more "responsive" to private sectors of "the economy" (however defined by the ideologues of any particular day).[67]

New statistics would, so the accountants and their political masters claimed, provide reliable links between teaching and research on one hand, and "markets" on the other. The links they proposed are reminiscent of the "ties" Gulliver experienced as he awoke from his famous shipwreck:

> ...[W]hen I awaked it was just day-light. I attempted to rise, but was not able to stir: for... I found my arms and legs were strongly fastened on each side to the ground; and my hair... tied down in the same manner. I likewise felt several slender ligatures across my body, from my arm-pits to my thighs. I could only look upwards.[68]

That is, no single measure would necessarily, by itself, interfere with university autonomy. Nor would any one measure necessarily undermine provincial government responsibility for higher education. But if

---

[65]See Sid Gilbert, "Performance indicators for universities: Ogres or opportunities?" OCUFA Forum, Spring 1999, at Web site: *http://www.ocufa.on.ca/*.

[66]At the First National Consultation, Counsel of Ministers of Education, Canada, Edmonton, Alberta, 1994, claims for performance indicators were surprisingly muted, especially considering that the meeting took place in a province where Key Performance Indicators already decided at least some of the curricular and administrative structure of work in provincial community colleges. See J. Hodder, unpublished manuscript talk, First National Consultation, Counsel of Ministers of Education, Canada, Edmonton, Alberta, 1994, pp. 1–4, for an illustration of a "soft" approach to performance measures.

[67]For variable definitions of "economy" and "market," see E.G. West, *Higher Education in Canada: An Analysis* (Vancouver: Fraser Institute, 1988), an early and well-written argument for vouchers and indicators in publicly-supported (but not publicly-funded) higher education.

[68]Jonathan Swift, *Gulliver's Travels*, ed. J.F. Ross (New York: Rinehart, 1948), 5.

universities and colleges and schools were directed (at least in part) by the several requirements of labour markets, of financial and service markets, and many more markets yet to come the net effect, the sheer accumulation of market ties would have the effect of tying post-secondary education so tightly to business national or trans-national goals that institutional autonomy would be emptied of meaning.

We know now that CMEC's approach in the 1990s and early 2000s was not born from the forehead of Zeus; it had roots in earlier phases of the indicators movement. But to the earlier and accumulating forces two more factors had been added. The first was the founding and growth of international and national organizations whose *raisons d'être* included the creation of large-scale data sets and performance indicators for post-secondary education. The second was the ideological revolution signalled by the elections of Margaret Thatcher and Ronald Reagan.

European interest in data and numbers for higher education, understood as an element in policy making, and understood as a prerequisite for continent-wide planning, grew quickly after 1955. The creation of the European Community put a seal on this work, much of it carried out in Strasbourg and then in Brussels. Meanwhile, the Organisation for Economic Co-operation and Development was founded by treaty in 1960, and extended the work of the earlier Organisation for European Economic Co-operation set up in 1948. The OECD had among its chief objectives continuous improvement of living standards among its members (which included Canada and the United States in addition to 18 European states).

Closely connected with the International Monetary Fund and the General Agreement on Tariffs and Trade, the OECD at first thought of its work in education in professional, vocational, and technical terms. By 1980, it had become much more ambitious, moving toward publication in the 1980s of a document called *Education at a Glance*, a massive and highly influential volume comparing national performances of member nations on investment per student in higher education, on throughput rates, on employment patterns, and on putative ties between educational attainment and economic production (among many others). Beginning in the 1960s, the OECD published a series of well-researched studies of national educational policy for its members. These latter documents combine nuanced historical and sociological inquiry with hard-nosed PIs-based assessment, and continue to be influential guides in the thinking of all OECD nations. The OECD and its publications have permitted and invited politicians and journalists on both sides of the Atlantic to play the game of competitive comparison, usually in order to justify strong political intervention in university and college affairs.

Ideology is disguised in all of this by endless talk of "neutral and objective indicators," "reliable measures of productivity in teaching and research," and the like. Much of the new language of the Right draws on arguments and ideas we found in Phases I–IV; but some is novel and deeply worrisome, particularly the faith it declares *vis-à-vis* the powers of the market, the unlimited virtue of individual effort, and the enlightenment that necessarily follows from unlimited competition between people...and among their universities.

Public anxiety about corporate and technocratic interests is high, and PIs are not yet quite triumphant. Our discussions of the United Kingdom, New Zealand, and the United States show how the pioneers of PIs began their campaign, but also indicate that jurisdictions which started with the strong commitment to PIs have found them so expensive, so centralist, and so counterproductive that PIs systems are being modified or even abandoned. But in Ontario, Alberta, British Columbia, and Québec, few politicians have noticed what has happened elsewhere, as our chapter on the Canadian case illustrates.

Having laid out these phases, it possible to consider not only the underlying political and philosophical positions of "PI" enthusiasts, but also the way they like to put PIs to work. We turn in the next chapter to the central meanings of "performance," and a critical investigation of seven main arguments for PIs. With that work done—on the politics and the philosophy of PIs—we are in a position to describe the lived experience of PIs in four national jurisdictions, and then to make recommendations for the disposition of PIs.

2

Good Sense & Statistics at War

"Like dreams, statistics are a form of wish fulfillment."
—Jean Baudrillard, *Cool Memories* (1987, trans. 1990)

SEVEN ARGUMENTS ON PERFORMANCE INDICATORS

Performance indicators are chameleons: their protective colouration depends on circumstance and context. To see how these slippery entities connect with larger problems in the history, politics, and theory of public post-secondary education, we turn to seven extended arguments on PIs. We ask:

[1]   Can PIs help build public post-secondary education?

[2]   Could and should PIs help make post-secondary education more "nimble" and "flexible" in face of market demand?

[3]   Are benchmarks a way to assure quality education, or just a way to make it cheap, technically proficient, and materially productive?

[4]   Are PIs a way of making post-secondary education more completely accountable, and if so, accountable to whom?

[5]   Do PIs satisfy Canadians' need to know in detail what is happening in Canadian public post-secondary education?

[6]   How do PIs contribute to the larger phenomenon of "managerialism"?

[7]   Must PIs *always* serve to justify (or to hide) cuts and cost-cutting? What does this mean for the quality of higher education wherever PIs become popular?

1. On Indicators & Public Post-secondary Education

Through the history of democratic practice in industrialized nations, statistics and "indicators" have played an honourable role in social development. At the beginnings of publicly-financed education, the case for public finance *and* public accountability was built with the help of numbers and "indicators." In Canada, as in the United States and Britain, school promoters in the 1850s and 1860s made extensive use of statistics.[1]

It took a century before publicly-supported education at all levels became the rule, rather than the exception. But by the 1960s and 1970s, financial support of secondary-school, university and college provision exploded across Europe, the Americas, and Australasia.[2]

The case for public funding still rests partly on appeals to statistics of various kinds. In the mid–19th century, these were "numbers" about illiteracy, about vagrancy, about citizens without sufficient education to participate fully in democratic society. All helped the campaign for publicly-funded and publicly-accountable education—including, eventually, higher education.

In the dislocation of the Great Depression, social science research drew liberally on statistics, not just on cultural and social studies, to throw light on Canadian society, especially on its class system. A representative and influential exponent was Leonard C. Marsh (1906–1982). Marsh directed a social science research programme at McGill 1930–1941, aimed at understanding Canadian political and social economy during the "hard times," and his publications helped lay the foundation for the Canadian social security system constructed after 1945.[3] The force of Marsh's

---

[1]For discussions of the use of statistics in this early period, see three quite different authors on public education in English Canada: Alison Prentice, *The School Promoters: Education and Social Class in Mid-Nineteenth Century Upper Canada* (Toronto: Prentice-Hall, 1999); Bruce Curtis, *Building the Educational State: Canada West, 1836–1871* (Philadelphia, Penn.: Falmer Press, 1988); and (almost entirely on the rise of publicly-funded and publicly-accountable higher education) A.B. MacKillop, *Matters of Mind: The University in Ontario, 1791–1951* (Toronto: University of Toronto Press, 1994). On the uses of statistics in the American campaign to build public systems of education at all levels, see E.N. MacMullen, *In the Cause of True Education: Henry Barnard and Nineteenth-Century School Reform* (New Haven: Yale University Press, 1991), esp. 66–7, 98–101. Notably, the figures gathered by school and university reformers of the day were not in any sense compulsory; they were, instead, drawn together by participants and supporters of public education, who believed the public interest was at stake and at risk in a system where educational opportunity was distributed exclusively under free-market rules and market conditions.

[2]*Cf.* Arthur Marwick, *The Sixties* (Oxford: Oxford University Press, 1998), esp. Ch. 6, "Acts of God and Acts of Government," 247–87; Doug Owram, *Born at the Right Time: A History of the Baby Boom Generation* (Toronto: University of Toronto Press, 1996), 180–4.

[3]See esp. Leonard C. Marsh, *Report on Social Security for Canada* (Toronto: University of Toronto Press, 1975, repr. of 1943 report for the Federal Committee on Post-War Reconstruction), but also the same author's *Canadians in and out of Work: A Survey of*

arguments stemmed from detailed and exhaustive social descriptions, some statistical in character, of income levels, production figures, and state expenditure. This was empirical research directly in service of community and of the public interest. It did not identify the interests of industry with the interests of the public. Neither did it deny the value of economic activity. It simply refused to see the one as the same as the other, as PIs typically do.

Marsh thought social "security" formed the only viable foundation for a strong economy.[4] This implied an energetic programme of public expenditure and institutional expansion. In short, Marsh used statistics as "indicators" of Canadian society, but did so in the service of social objectives, and on the basis of social principles, not accounting principles. He was in no way interested in forcing detailed management practices on anyone, nor in compelling community institutions to conform to the demands of accountancy.

A similar outlook helped shape two large inquiries on education and culture in the 1950s: the [Hope] Royal Commission on Education in Ontario (1950) and the Massey Commission on the Development of the Arts and Letters in Canada (1951).

Ontario's Hope Commission,[5] faced with a demographic crisis as the post-War baby-boom arrived in the province's public schools, found it had also to tackle problems in the governance of education (there were literally thousands of school boards, providing service of uncertain quality), and in resolving questions of taxation, especially for the Roman Catholic separate schools.[6] A good deal of the Commission's work on these matters was necessarily statistical in character.

In extending compulsory attendance, and offering public support to more diverse forms of secondary education, the Commission implied there would be much-increased support for public post-secondary education. The Commission's position was buttressed by statistical evidence in the form of "indicators" about society and its schools. As the creation of many new universities and colleges in the 1960s and 1970s would show,

---

Economic Classes and Their Relation to the Labour Market (Toronto: Oxford Unversity Press for McGill University, 1940); and his *Health and Unemployment: Some Studies of their Relationships* (Toronto: Oxford University Press for McGill University, 1938).

[4]More than a half-century later, Marsh's ideas appear in new linguistic dress, but with little logical difference, in Edward Broadbent, ed., *Democratic Equality: What Went Wrong* (Toronto: University of Toronto Press, 2001).

[5]Ontario, Royal Commission on Education, *Report* (Toronto: Baptist Johnson, King's Printer, 1950), xxiii+933 pages, of which about fifty are committed to statistical description.

[6]For a more complete discussion, see Eric Ricker, "Teachers, trustees, and policy: the politics of education in Ontario, 1945–1975," PhD thesis, University of Toronto, 1980; and on questions of demographics and demand for education, R.D. Gidney, *From Hope to Harris: The Reshaping of Ontario's Schools* (Toronto: University of Toronto Press, 1999, Ch. 2, " The Education System at Mid-Century, 1945–1960," 9–36.

the foundation laid in the Hope Commission was a strong one. That foundation included extensive statistical argument that demand for post-secondary places would not soon fade, and indeed, would *never* fade. If these numbers were in any sense PIs, their import was that the province underestimated demand for public post-secondary education, and had not fully realized that Ontario's history pointed to the necessity of broad access to university education.

The Federal Royal [Massey] Commission on the Development of the Arts and Letters, particularly in its Technical Reports published 1949–51,[7] made use of simple statistical tables to conclude that the arts and sciences were far too marginal in Canada's publishing, communications, cultural, and political worlds. The Commission started with a number of assumptions, and used "indicators" to make points arisng from them. It did not pretend to be doing pure social science research,[8] and accepted that Canadian history and politics had clear implications for government policy in culture, science, and post-secondary education.[9]

A supporter of PIs at their narrowest might argue the Commission's proceeding was contrary to the true spirit of indicators, whose message is neutral, and should be untainted by human judgement or by history. On this view, the statistics on employment contained in the Royal Commission Reports should have led immediately to more funding for applied science, since the performance of applied science in the labour market was fine, and the performance of the arts miserable.

A moment's reflection will show how silly the Commissioners would have been to use indicators this way. Their outlook included their ethical and political orientation, their nationalism and their frankly progressive views, a theory of culture and society, and most of all, the view that their job was to make informed judgements—not to adopt simplistic numerical characterizations of their nation or its political economy.

The mid–20th century argument insisted that the social and political complexities of late-industrial societies required an ever-better-educated populace. The writers of the Commission accepted that argument, as one of many contributing views, not the *only* view. Indeed, they saw the

---

[7]Canada, *Royal Commission on National Development in the Arts, Letters and Science*. Briefs and Royal Commission Studies, 1949–51 (Ottawa: King's Printer, 1949–51), 2 vols. In the *Studies* volume, see esp. K.F. Tupper, "The Teaching of Applied Science," 337–52, replete at pp. 340–1 with detailed statistics on the national picture of employment for applied science graduates.

[8]It is significant that a strong reason for appointment of the Royal Commission was the sustained lobbying of the Canadian Arts Council and the Canadian Music Council after 1944–45. See Keith Macmillan, "National Organizations," in A. Walter, ed., *Aspects of Music in Canada* (Toronto: University of Toronto Press, 1969), 300.

[9]Paul Litt, *The Muses, the Masses, and the Massey Commission* (Toronto: University of Toronto Press, 1992). See also Maria Tippett, *Making Culture: English-Canadian Institutions and the Arts before the Massey Commission* (Toronto: University of Toronto Press, 1990).

argument as one having to do with public demand and the public interest, not the requirements of the economy, or of Taylorist[10] efficiencies in universities and provincial ministries.

There can be no value-free PIs. To use numbers in a societal context, you must be open and honest in declaring the values that motivate you. The Hope and Massey Commissions, where they made use of numbers, did so.

By the 1960s, the numbers were being used to portray rising demand for access to post-secondary education, a demand rooted in immediate post-World War II adjustments but expanding with the population, and finally exceeding even that growth factor. After about 1968, a broad spectrum of public opinion held that the inequitable distribution of money and power in society—not least the inequitable place of women in society—must be remedied, however partially, by fair and equitable access to higher education. Numbers played their rightful part in this analysis.

However, throughout the century leading to the rapid growth of universities and colleges in the 1960s and early 1970s, a second stream of essentially conservative belief and argument opposed government spending on principle and also the egalitarian politics of the sixties, demanding the "invisible hand" of the market be allowed free play. In the midst of social upheaval, rapid economic change, and neo-conservative ideology, older ideas of competition and efficiency in the provision of education became freshly attractive.

On occasion, the argument for market efficiency took multiple and punitive forms. In the 1980s, for example, the Southam press chain published a series of articles on what it termed the "literacy crisis" in Canada, asserting that literacy levels in Canada were alarmingly low, and that our schools, colleges, and universities had failed.[11]

Then came the great fiscal crises of the 1970s and 1980s. For reasons not yet entirely understood, deepening fiscal difficulties radically narrowed the public's understanding of accountability in higher education. Accountability came to be defined as a means to minimize the costs of higher education, to reduce the role of government, and to transfer costs as much as possible to students so taxes could be reduced. Statistics would show how well universities responded to these crises. Gone was the view that faculty and students should help analyse social and political problems, or that the universities should work to improve accessibility for women, disadvantaged minorities, and the poor.

By this time we have journeyed far—alas, too far—from the original purposes and uses of statistics and detailed indicators in public higher education. The original indicators may never have been neutral or purely

---

[10]On Taylorism, see Chapter 1.

[11]John Willinsky, "The Construction of a Crisis: Literacy in Canada," *Canadian Journal of Education/Revue canadienne de l'éducation*, 15, 1 (1990 hiver/Winter): 1–15.

descriptive; but they were redeemed by their social and political purposes. PIs in the 1990s and 2000s no longer have those purposes, but instead aim at the reduction of post-secondary education to marketable commodities, lowered public financial commitment, and new forms of centralized control over teaching and research. This is a case where we would take the old over the new.

2. PIs and the Construction of "Accountable," "Nimble," & "Responsive" Universities and Colleges

PIs are merely one device in the toolbox of modern administrative practice. Institutions claim that with the help of this device, they can detect outdated structures and practices, and through market discipline will become more flexible and nimble in the face of rapid shifts in demand for educational products. Quick and continuous change in programmes will compel universities and colleges to accept innovation and "reform."

One way to tie post-secondary education to the market is "incentive" funding, linked to PIs. Sometimes (as in the state of Colorado) an "incentive-oriented" PI is about reaching "bypassed student populations," or accomplishing some other, similar social objective.[12] More often the "incentive" demands that one's institution, department, and staff show they are making "ever better" use of the physical plant and of working hours, and thus serving the state's or province's economy (that is, more education for less money)—or suffer punitive cuts in future funding.[13]

A common PI in Canadian and American jurisdictions is "grant and industry funding/tenured faculty member/year." In order to ensure maximum success in finding grants and contracts, universities and colleges have established campus Industrial Liaison Offices, often supplemented by Research Offices and Patent Offices, to encourage faculty members to match industrial and government demand as closely as possible, in order to attract funding.[14] Significant short-term benefits accrue from responding quickly to shifts in government research policy and changes in industrial need. Post-secondary institutions have shown they can be as clever and quick as their counterparts in the private sector in searching for these funds.

Unfortunately, maintaining new bureaucracies in the areas of research, industry, and patents is very expensive. Further, as more and more

---

[12]Kit Lively, "Incentive Financing for Colorado's Colleges," *Chronicle of Higher Education*, 49, 2 (1994 March 02): A22.

[13]Sheila Slaughter, "From Serving Students to Serving the Economy: Changing Expectations of Faculty Role Performance," *Higher Education*, 14 (1985): 41–56; and for a Canadian perspective, Tom Pocklington, "The Marketing of the University," in T.W. Harrison and J.L. Kachur, eds., *Contested Classrooms: Education, Globalization, and Democracy in Alberta* (Edmonton: University of Alberta Press and Parkland Institute, 1999), 45–55, but esp. 48–52.

[14]Pocklington, "Marketing," p. 55, gives a list of 24 Canadian universities with Industrial Liaison offices in 1999.

university personnel in medical, applied science, and other professional schools become dependent on the "soft" money that grants , patents and markets bring, their appointments are not tenured in the usual ways, and many positions become part-time or sessional.

The truly experimental powers of the university, its most innovative and far-sighted work on behalf of the community, depend on its reliable base budget, its stable core. But in the medium and even the short term, the core of the university shrinks as the enterprise of grant-getting expands in scale and importance (for the sake of better PIs, but also in order to make up for declining public finance). PIs-driven grants have the unexpected and contrary effect of reducing the university's ability to experiment, to think and to speak critically, and to make long-range plans. In the only sense that counts, the university that wants to be nimble and responsive is the university with strong and reliable public funding, for which it must be openly and publicly accountable.

PIs instead encourage a pattern of obscurity and secrecy in industrial liaisons, since no one knows just how many contracts actually are out there. Furthermore, they push universities and colleges towards compulsive patent production and sales, and of research shrouded in secrecy. More money may be made in routine testing or undemanding and safe experiments than in risky cutting-edge scientific research. We believe post-secondary education under such a regime becomes *less* flexible and inventive, and much more open to short-term manipulation and loss.

We have made the point that PIs have the effect of narrowing and limiting post-secondary education so that universities and colleges are restrained in their ability to make significant and deep changes in the public interest. We want to ask now if they may have a further, closely-linked effect: a reduction in the ability of universities and colleges to be fully accountable for what they do. PIs may and do lead post-secondary education to become less flexible and effective; could PIs make it less accountable, too?

The answer, alas, is "Yes!"

3. Can Benchmarks Save PIs?

Benchmarking is a popular variant of classical PIs. Mid-sized and larger industries were supposed to identify good administrative and production devices used in similar or parallel organizations; to accept the best of them; and to adopt the leanest internal organizational structure that would enable their full application. This approach to management has self-evident correctness: of course one should learn from good ideas developed elsewhere. But that is not what benchmarking means.

A chief attraction of benchmarking was the implied requirement that organizations seek to match their purposes and ends to the means available. Practitioners first listed an organization's "deliverables"—what customers expected to get. The next step was to determine which of the organization's "processes" (considered separately and in groups) would or should produce those deliverables. The third stage was to find the best way of organizing and carrying out this activity: the "best practice' for achieving the organization's objectives. One moved backward and forward between means and ends and the processes that tied them together. In business circumstances this at least gave management the *appearance* of rational bases for its decisions.

The same did not hold in public post-secondary education. The practitioners of benchmarking in industry are typically managers, accountants, and their administrators, doing their jobs as best they can, with the single clear goal of increasing profits. Universities and colleges are openly-governed communities of teaching and inquiry with a variety of educational, scientific and public policy objectives. How does one weight these various goals, much less measure them?

Our country has generally aimed, at least until recently, to build independent and critically-minded university communities, open to public scrutiny and debate, and driven by high standards of teaching and research in the disciplines and in the professions. The main purposes of post-secondary education have been notably consistent: the transformation of students and their teachers, engaged in the life of inquiry, the development of independent research and high standards in the professions, and the stimulation of informed debate about public issues including the mandate and work of the university itself. It is hugely difficult to see how a commitment to benchmarking could possibly help in achieving these aims—and very easy to see how it might subvert some of them.

It may be argued benchmarking could be useful in certain of the purely technical aspects of the administration of the university, such as the functioning of ancillary enterprises, accounting practices, and the like. For instance, the Ontario Universities' Application Centre received a best practices award from the Post-secondary Electronic Standards Council in Washington D.C. for its electronic transcript system. The Centre handled 35,000 transcripts, distributed $281,872 to Ontario universities in transcript fees, and eliminated the cost of paper records and mailing. Students might well benefit in the long-term if it made applications and transfers simple and cheap. This development, however, had nothing to do with raising educational standards or any other educational goal, but rather a technical-material objective. The question is, are all benchmarks like this one?

Indeed, cumulative success in these technical areas persuades university administrators and civil servants that benchmarking is valid for *all* aspects of the university. So one finds benchmarks for applications of technology to teaching (sometimes defined as the number of credit hours delivered on the screen), the proportion of funding from industry (which inevitably favours universities with medical schools because they have some of the most expensive research and are, in any event, greatly favoured by donors who all know that one day they might die), the number of times your book or article is cited (which may be an index of how bad it is, not how good it is, or may illustrate the proliferation of journals in your field compared to others, and is, in any event, manipulable by the unscrupulous) or the number of students employed six months after graduation (despite that in the short-term this is heavily dependent on the economy—witness the problems of computer science graduates in 2001 compared with 1999—and that statistics in all advanced countries show that in the long run virtually all university graduates are gainfully employed and on average earn considerably more than the rest the community). Despite this latter point, vast amounts of administrative time are devoted to measuring "employability." Indeed, bureaucracies invent new ways of increasing their size—now they must measure whether the job directly relates to the university degree of the individual employed. In other words, more bureaucrats must be employed to rate all the jobs in the country which might be filled by graduates.

Some benchmarks have an evidently perverse effect. One of the most popular is to measure whether students complete their course in the fixed number of years allotted. This takes little or no account of the number of mature students holding other jobs, or of the great increase in part-time employment by undergraduate students as a consequence of governmental decisions to increase fees, thus ensuring that they devote less time to their studies. Québec universities, for example, promised the provincial government to improve this benchmark, in some cases substantially, in a short period of time (see Ch. 6, final section). We know anecdotally that in many universities this produces enormous pressure from the deans to increase the pass rate regardless of merit. But the benchmark goal will be met. What is in the United Kingdom called "the tick culture" will have triumphed.

Furthermore benchmarking usually assumes there is one best way of doing things. This is rarely true in post-secondary teaching or research. For example, technology is more generally useful in some areas (bio-medicine) than in others (philosophy). That does not make bio-medicine better than philosophy, merely different. Some teaching practices are indeed better than others, but distinctions between good, bad and better do change over time and are not uniform across the university. The criteria must depend in the final analysis on continuous and open debate among committed practitioners of the discipline who should be prepared to rationally defend their criteria inside and outside the university. It is, for example, the whole community of practicing historians, including historians outside the academy, who are the guardians of demanding standards in teaching and research in that field. Hence our recommendation in the final chapter about the use of external departmental reviews. Best practices in teaching, research, and community service cannot be the automatic result of numerically-driven, managerially-imposed indicators, but must result from open discussion and experiment.

Benchmarking also requires the gathering of vast amounts of statistical information at great expense, particularly when this is done by a central authority—see the section below on the United Kingdom. It also requires that most aspects of the university be reduced to numbers regardless of how absurd this becomes. Those that cannot be measured have to be ignored. But what do the numbers mean? As Henry Miztberg suggests:

> Anyone who has ever produced a quantitative measure—whether a reject count in a factory as a surrogate for product quality, a publication count in a university as a surrogate for research performance, of estimates of costs and benefits in a capital budgeting exercise—knows just how much distortion is possible, intentional as well as unintentional.[15]

Benchmarking is open to the same type of abuse as another popular management fad—Management by Objectives. Both require the institution to set its own goals, because companies and institutions vary so much in size, clientele, and mission. The temptation is to set the goals low so that one always gets the highest marks, rendering any comparative tables meaningless.

Benchmarking is simply an expensive detour from the real world of the academy where difficult decisions about merit, quality and the like have to be made by real professors and administrators. Benchmarking is a mirage persuading academics that automatic formulae can substitute for informed and fair judgement. But like the victims of the mirage in the desert, civil servants and university administrators continue irrationally to pursue it.

Benchmarkers pay close attention to the economy, and to business practices. They often say that this is a way of making their universities and colleges more directly accountable. They don't always say to whom the universities and colleges would be accountable, or why, but they do insist that using benchmarks tightens the connection between the economy and the university. They make many other claims for benchmarks, as we have seen, but this one—the claim about instant accountability—deserves a closer look.

4. PIs & "Deep" Accountability

Since the late 1980s, Applied Science departments across North America have found themselves struggling to invent new programmes of teaching and research, valiantly trying to keep up with industrial development. Departments must make inventions and register patents,[16] maintain grants

---

[15]H. Mintzberg, *The Rise and Fall of Strategic Planning: Reconceiving Roles for Planning, Plans, Planners* (New York: Free Press, 1994), qu. in Birnbaum, 79.

[16]For an example, see *Patscan* (Vancouver: University of British Columbia, occasional publication), a regular if jokey listing of patents and profit-making ventures produced/created by academics and commercial researchers at the University of British Columbia. A recent summary of patents filed and issued may be found at: *www. budgetandplanning.ubc.ca/factbook/factbk97/rsearch3.htm.* This leads to a summary of "Gross License Royalty Paid to UBC and Equity," at *www.uilo.ubc.ca/General% 20Information/Reports%20&%20Presentations/Review/...* Equity had risen from $2m to $12m in the five years ending 2000, while royalties hovered between $1.1 and $1.3m annually. Although these sums are small by comparison to the Gross Operating Budget, they are significant because of the health PI they produce, and also because

from public and private sources,[17] and publish ever more pages in refereed journals (an equally pernicious PI).[18] Meanwhile, discussions of basic science and broad principles of scientific education are relegated to the background, displaced by economic necessity, the pressures of industrial liaison, and the publish-or-perish syndrome.

Worse: suppose a system of PIs has convinced our imaginary Applied Science department to build a significant new scientific research team only to find that the economy has collapsed, and demand has temporarily disappeared. Even though the economy is to blame, it is supremely indifferent to teachers, professors, staff and students—not to mention quality. *The Department pays the price.* Grants disappear, enrolment declines, and government withdraws support from the university and/or the department concerned—all with the justification of PIs. Meanwhile, those who introduced the PIs get off scot-free, and move on to make new PIs for new victims in new jurisdictions.

Proponents of PIs will still argue that under their ministrations, the victims become pliant, nimble, and with the help of funding cuts and ever-tighter market control, more accountable. It is painfully clear the victims are in no way more accountable under this regime, but instead, *less* accountable. No, post-secondary education is not more accountable under PIs. Instead, it is simply more... controlled.

It is especially galling when critics say PIs are justified because universities and colleges resist change. This charge is a slightly-modified re-write of the demand that post-secondary education be more accountable, but this version relies on a peculiar interpretation of recent university history. On that interpretation, post-secondary institutions never act quickly.

Universities and colleges do indeed take their time about making changes in curriculum and research. It took years to develop the profile of the human genome, and it will take time to evaluate its impact on research and science teaching. It took more than a decade for literary people (professors, students, and interested members of the public) to evaluate those features of the post-modernist outlook that might be helpful in a BA English degree. These are momentous changes. It *should* take time to accomplish them. Thus the

---

they are typical of figures just like them at the top 100 research universities in the English-speaking world. For more on this question, see Chapters 7–8.

[17]For an example in recent Canadian university history, see Eric J. Damer, *Mechancal Engineering at UBC, 1915–2000* (Vancouver: Ronsdale Press, forthcoming 2001), esp. Chapter 4, which includes extensive discussion of grants and the politics of grants-manship in this Applied Science department after 1950.

[18]Australian universities and colleges, strongly "encouraged" by DETYA (Department of Employment, Education, Training, and Youth Affairs, Australia) support numerous departments and institutes concerned with "bibliometric" measures of "excellence" (that is, number of pages published/tenure-track academic/year, and the like). See esp. the work of the Research Evaluation and Policy Project at the Australian National University (*http:// repp.anu.edu.au/themes.htm*).

argument that PIs will make universities more rapidly responsive to outside change rings not just hollow, but *dangerously* so.

A balanced account of higher education since 1970 shows Canadian universities and colleges *have* reinvented themselves, responding to changing social conditions and the development of whole new inter-disciplinary fields of study, serving ever-larger numbers of students of all ages and from all parts of society, carrying out valuable research work on an unprecedented scale, and reluctantly adjusting to ever-shrinking public financial support.[19] Canadian public higher education is doing far more, with ever fewer means, than ever in history.

Some critics of higher education argue *both* that universities are resistant to change *and* that they are too pliant when faced with demands from left-wing critics.[20] Others claim they have been too pliant, period, and have undermined quality education.[21] However, since a key element of PIs is student demand (the market), it is inevitable that critically important areas that have never attracted large numbers of students, such as mathematics, higher level physics and chemistry, the less glamorous reaches of engineering, and most modern languages with the cultural studies that go with them will be pushed out—not to mention fine arts, music and the like. These all combine a minority demand with high costs in staff or equipment. There is no escape—PIs lead to mediocrity and to the philistine.

Supporters of PIs nevertheless insist public higher education has not been responsive to industrial and economic "change." In the late 1980s, Edwin G. West argued for a voucher system in public higher education and for modified performance indicators (for instance, student opinion surveys, before and after graduation). His view was that market discipline was essential because public universities and colleges had responded sluggishly, if at all, to changing economic times.[22] In the 1990s, these ideas

---

[19]For a documented survey of the growth Canadian post-secondary education, particularly research work, see *Realizing the Potential: A Strategy for University Research in Canada: Report* (Ottawa: Royal Society of Canada, 1991). Among the more vociferous critics of Canadian universities (and it is easy to find analogous works for all the OECD countries), see D. Bercuson, R. Bothwell, and J.L. Granatstein, *Petrified Campus: The Crisis in Canada's Universities* (Toronto: Random House, 1997). Bercuson *et al.* are hard to follow at the best of times, but here the charge against Canadian post-secondary education is that it is not responsive to markets, but on the other hand far too responsive to "left-wing" demands for equity, openness, fairness, and the like. That is, the critics want it both ways.

[20]For instance, Martha Nussbaum, *Cultivating Humanity: A Classical Defense of Reform in Liberal Education* (Cambridge: Harvard University Press, 1997).

[21]Allan Bloom, "The Crisis of Liberal Education," in his *Giants and Dwarfs: Essays 1960–1990* (New York: Simon and Schuster, 1990), 348–64.

[22]Edwin G. West, *Higher Education in Canada: An Analysis* (Vancouver: Fraser Institute, 1988), and his later *Higher Education and Competitiveness* (Kingston, Ont.: Government and Competitiveness, School of Policy Studies, Queen's University, 1993). Similar proposals for primary and secondary education, including a call for various kinds of "marketization" and "privatization," form the core of Stephen Easton's *Education in*

were taken a step further in books and articles that claimed universities, by themselves, *can never be responsive enough*, never *obedient enough* to their number-crunching critics.[23]

Although West's facts are weak, his remarks help us to see the objective: PIs devotees want to *compel an unending chain of responses* to economic change, but *only change that PIs enthusiasts think important*. The goal is not to improve educational practice, nor to respond to public objectives. Rather, the idea is to make graduates as employable as soon as possible, to make it easier to justify reduced public expenditure for higher education, and thus indirectly to force changes in teaching and research and practice. Universities thus become cheap training centres for industry which will not spend its own money to do this work. This has little or nothing to do with education, but everything to do with markets and management.

Universities' hunt for grants and supplementary funding is easily explained by the thirty-year-decline in public funding in public higher education throughout the OECD countries. But the experience of individual universities and departments under pressure to perform by doing well in grant acquisition (increasingly grants from the private sector) is that PIs bear most on those people and departments that can easily increase those very PIs, and quickly.[24] The consequence is mission-oriented research, whose mission is set not by the public interest, but by private interest.

Canada: An Analysis of Elementary, Secondary, and Vocational Schooling (Vancouver: Fraser Institute, 1988). For a critical study of West's 1988 volume, see W. Bruneau, "British Columbia's Right Wing and Public Education," *Our Schools, Our Selves*, 1, 4 (1989 August): 94–106. On the question of privatization, see W. Bruneau, "Privatization in School and University: Renewal or Apostasy?" in M. Charlton and P. Barker, eds., *Crosscurrents*, 3rd ed. (Toronto: ITP Nelson, 1998), 472–83.

[23]For an extensive, but critically-minded catalogue of these claims, see James Turk, ed., *The Corporate Campus* (Toronto: James Lorimer, 2000), *passim*; also, J. Currie and J. Newson, *Universities and Globalization: Critical Perspectives* (Thousand Oaks, California: SAGE Publications, 1998), but esp. Part III, pp. 141 ff.

[24]Toward the end of 2000, then Vice-President (Research) Bressler of the University of British Columbia [UBC] sent a letter to colleagues in health sciences to indicate that UBC's "performance" in acquiring Medical Research Council of Canada and Natural Sciences and Engineering Council of Canada grants, was bad and getting "worse" (e-mail November 2000, Bressler/Colleagues, in the authors' possession). Evidence for Prof. Bressler's view is publicly available at *http://www.pair.ubc.ca/research/mrc98.htm*, which compares UBC "performance" against 14 other universities with medical schools. These documents should be combined with the annual financial reports of UBC for 1995–2000, which indicate with varying precision the amount of private funding attracted to medical, dental, and pharmacological research at that University. The two sets of statistics operate, it would seem, to influence the administrative policy and practice of the University, but even more to put pressure on individuals and departments to maintain programmes of research and development, whether or not they conform in publicly verifiable ways to the larger mandate of the institution.

G.K. Chesterton once advised: "Don't criticize Christianity too harshly; after all, it hasn't been tried yet." We might say something of the sort about public higher education. Its aims have to do with making critical thinkers of people, developing the logical, the moral, and the practical powers essential for active citizenship. When things are going as they should, this is what happens in classrooms, where every idea and every assertion is open to critical discussion, and what happens in open meetings of senates and boards of governors, where the same critical thinking is applied to decisions about degree programmes and university finances.

Canadian universities have not yet met these high standards. They should, and must be held accountable if they do not. The meaning of that word "accountable," weighs, as it must, heavily on the souls of university and college people. We used the term "deep accountability," rather in the way some speak of "deep ecology," to help in seeing the dangerous superficiality at play in the world of PIs, but also to point to the forms of accountability that seem to us essential in Canadian, but really in *any* democratically-responsive higher education system.

A public university or college is, we assert, truly accountable when it ensures members of the public can readily survey teaching, learning, inquiry, and governance. It is accountable when open to scrutiny, open to participation, open to criticism, and demonstrably committed to critical thinking, critically-minded teaching, and intensely-conducted learning and research (so far as circumstances permit). It is accountable when it has senates, boards, committees, newsletter writers, and communicators hard at work, happily telling anyone who will listen just what it is the university or college is doing. It is accountable when the contracts it makes with the private sector are easily accessible (on the Web, if at all possible). It is accountable when professors' lifetime records of teaching and publication are similarly available on the Web or other media. It is accountable when it can show it understands its mandates, and interprets them in the light of both history and current social need.

It would be hard to imagine a sharper contradiction than between *(a)* accountable and responsible government, and *(b)* authoritarian management.[25] Yet the rise of PIs as a tool of government policy and administrative

---

[25]In a revealing 1995 briefing book, the British Committee of Vice-Chancellors and Principals (abbreviated in the United Kingdom as "CVCP") wrote:

> During discussion it became apparent that the proposed indicators might be better described as management statistics rather than performance indicators. Institutions could, if they so wished, convert these statistics into performance indicators. Close attention must be paid to the missions of institutions before management statistics can be converted to relevant measures of performance.

Committee of Vice-Chancellors and Principas, *Higher Education Management Statistics: A Future Strategy* (London: Committee of Vice-Chancellors and Principals, 1995), para. 1.8.

In British universities and polytechnics in the 1990s, fine distinctions between "performance" and "management" were lost in the rush of central government to

practice has made it hard to see or feel that difference and that contra-diction. It is not just a question whether PIs invite scholars to cut ethical corners, so grant numbers look good at year's end. Rather, the question is, who is finally responsible in a PI-driven institution?

Proponents of PIs argue their statistics are reliable scientific guides to policy making.[26] Thus, the accountants and managers who dream them up are the servants of the numbers, honest agents of objective and applied social science. The makers of PIs say they must not be held responsible for decisions and policies that flow from their numbers. In an odd twist, the responsibility for mistakes (and benefits) flowing from PIs are to be assigned to the victims, that is, the professors, students, and staff who do the work of public higher education. PIs thus combine the worst features of your average hit-and-run accident with reasoning that assigns blame to victims. A familiar and analogous story in the 1980s was the assignment of blame for unemployment to the jobless.

5. On PIs & the Public's Need to Know

Canadian universities and colleges have shown themselves quite willing to live by high standards of accountability. In fact, since the mid–1960s, and the reforms of senates and boards of governors of that time, post-secondary education in Canada has become more open and answerable than ever. With publication of the Duff-Berdahl report and adoption of at least some of its recommendations,[27] nearly all Canadian universities of the 1960s and

---

control, and then to privatize as much of the system as possible. By 2000, fifteen years of life with "league tables" (see Chapter 3) showed that PIs encouraged a managerialist, rather than a participatory, view of university government.

[26]In Canada, the best-known proponent of PIs as "guides to policy" was the late Professor Sid Gilbert of the University of Guelph. See esp. his "Search for Education Indicators," *Education Quarterly Review* (1994): 44–53. At p. 51, Prof. Gilbert defined

> An education indicator [as] a policy-relevant statistic that provides strategic information about the condition of education: reporting where progress is being made and where it is not, identifying emerging issues and informing the debate on policy considerations. Indicators have a comparative dimension or reference point. This may be an absolute standard, a past value, or a comparison across schools, regions or countries. Indicators permit value judgements about education systems or some of their key aspects.

Prof. Gilbert's restrained language and sensible limitations on the use of PIs are helpful in seeing how such statistics have been and could yet be contributors to the invention of accountable public post-secondary education. But Prof. Gilbert's want of interest in matters of university governance, his vagueness about the meaning of such terms as "quality," and his determined (and disingenuous?) refusal to list the "values" that drive PIs, show the limits of his approach.

[27]James Duff and R.O. Berdahl, *University Government in Canada* (Toronto: University of Toronto Press, 1966); and E. Benjamin, G. Bourgeault, and K. McGovern, *Government and Accountability: The Report of the Independent Study Group on University Governance* (Ottawa: Canadian Association of University Teachers, 1993), 4–24, and *passim*.

1970s saw members of the public, the professoriate, staff, and student bodies join boards of governors and senates. A desirable and almost immediate effect of this new openness was the willingness of some administrations to open their financial records, and to lay bare at least part of their financial dealings; sometimes this was accomplished through the preparation and publication of numbers, statistics, accounts, and tables.

Even so, the promise of broad accountability of Canadian public higher education to the public interest has not yet been fully realized. Accessibility is not what it could be, or should be. Nor are our colleges and universities in a position to act as powerhouses of social and cultural change, in the ways required if Canada is to thrive as an open and democratic community. Ann Dowsett-Johnson, writing in the 2001 edition of the annual *Maclean's Guide to Canadian Universities and Colleges*, says that demand for places in higher education is likely to rise by 40% in British Columbia and Ontario by 2010, and 20% Canada-wide.[28] Yet when *Maclean's* created its annual ranking of Canadian universities in 1991, the results were attacked as:

- ■PARTIAL to institutions that could most easily report measurable outcomes,
- ■SUPERFICIAL, because they paid so little attention to the "lived experience" of higher education (including the way inquiry and research can best be communicated to students, educationally significant "face time," and so on),
- ■DUBIOUSLY MOTIVATED, as rankings would encourage senseless competition on the 22 criteria in the *Maclean's* measures, whether or not these can or could ever be linked to transparency in governance, clarity in curriculum, strength in research, or the possible tie between the work of the university and the mandates laid out in relevant legislation,
- ■OVERLY DEPENDENT on the views of business leaders and university CEOs and others who have not darkened the doors of a classroom in decades (we agree it is useful to know the opinions of CEOs, if only because such persons are powerful people; but of course their views can say little about the quality of institutions), and
- ■FAILING to rate the provinces in terms of adequate funding of higher education.

Attacks on the *Maclean's* indicators from the academic community have fallen off over time. The annual *Maclean's* guide still sells, but by the first year of the new millennium, it attracted only a brief flurry of anxious comment by university presidents. These were presidents unable to raise their institutions' *Maclean's* ratings, year over year.

We think the survival of *Maclean's* indicators suggests general conclusions about Canadian universities and colleges and their account-

---

[28]Ann Dowsett Johnson, "Measuring Excellence," *Maclean's Guide to Canadian Universities and Colleges* (Toronto: Rogers Media, 2001), 10–15, esp. 12.

ability. First, the *Maclean's* guide fills a void that administrators through their organizations, the Association of Universities and Colleges of Canada, and the Canadian Association of University Business Officers have been unable to do.[29] Nor have university and college teachers and students found the resources needed to fill the "information gap." Would-be university and college students must still turn to *Maclean's* for a particular, superficial, but still general survey of the system. Sociological evidence suggests that few students change their minds about their likely destination for advanced study after reading *Maclean's*; their decisions are based on considerations of funding, proximity, programmatic necessity, and so on, just as they have always been.[30]

The closest Canadians have come is the Alternative Federal Budget [AFB], an annual project of the Canadian Centre of Policy Alternatives and Cho!ces, a Winnipeg-based social justice coalition. AFB brings together representatives from a wide spectrum of Canadian civil society, including representatives of student and university teachers' organizations. AFB is released just before the announcement of each federal budget. Its surveys of public opinion, and its reliance on the views of people with direct experience of post-secondary education, make it a useful guide to public interest in teaching and research.

In 2000, the AFB made a plea for sustained funding of post-secondary education, partly to increase accessibility, and partly to support quality research and teaching. The AFB noted that the Federal government's boutique funding of research, including the 21st Century Chairs of Research Excellence and the Canada Foundation for Innovation,

> will push the universities to sacrifice humanities and social sciences scholarship, undergraduate education and teaching as a whole. The small increases in the research councils budgets are inadequate to address the pressures which universities face in paying for direct and indirect research costs associated with the new investments in infrastructure and personnel.[31]

---

[29]For a compendious review of programmes of study, administrative structures, and so on, see Association of Universities and Colleges of Canada, *Directory of Canadian Universities* (Ottawa: AUCC, 2001), and AUCC, *Trends* (Ottawa: AUCC, 1999), annual. These publications are popular among guidance counsellors and administrators, but have not caught the public's fancy. The Canadian Association of University Business Officers published in 2000 its *Financial Statistics of Universities and Colleges, 1998–1999* (Ottawa: CAUBO, 2000), but these numbers must be combined with dispersed information and data in the Association's various related publications, in order to draw any "performance" conclusions from the data.

[30]L. Andres and H. Krahn, "Youth Pathways in Articulated Post-secondary Systems: Enrolment and Completion Patterns of Urban Young Women and Men," *Canadian Journal of Higher Education*, 29, 1 (1999): 47–82; and L. Andres, "Rational choice or cultural reproduction? Tracing transitions of young Canadians to higher education," *Nordisk Pedagogik*, 18, 4 (1998): 197–206.

[31]At segment on Alternative Federal Budget, *http://www.policyalternatives.ca/*.

AFB shows, in other words, that a mission-oriented view of teaching and research has become a worrisome pattern across the Canadian system. That mission has to do with industrial growth and profit, not with the political and cultural requirements of Canada, and certainly not with quality in teaching and research, or with access to universities and colleges. Although any supporter of public post-secondary education is likely to applaud the work of the AFB, the AFB could not, even so, be considered a satisfactory vehicle for discovering and communicating the goals and the present circumstances of higher education in the country.

To press the point a little further, the absence of a university- or college-based source of information suggests that Canadians (and most other OECD systems of higher education) have a considerable way to go in making clear to their publics how they understand the public interest, how they serve it, and how they carry out the public mandate with which they are entrusted and for which they are (under)funded.[32]

We suggest that in the absence of informed comment from universities and colleges, too many Canadians, Americans, Britons, and so on, conclude it's all right to measure "quality" and "accountability" by *Maclean's* numbers, or worse, by numbers of the invasive and manipulative kind described earlier. There is another, more acceptable vision of quality and accountability, based on clear definitions of the public interest, including equitable distribution of knowledge, broad access to post-secondary education, and high standards of openness in the transaction of university and college "business." This would be a campaign to offer the public, across all the OECD countries, a view of what an adequately-funded system of public higher education could do to revive civil government, to renovate social structures, and to give the professions a vital foundation in ethics and learning. Meanwhile, alas, the information void has been well exploited by supporters of PIs. In Canada, those supporters say the nation's colleges and universities are unable or even unwilling to show what they do. In Alberta, after 1993, the provincial government announced it was dissatisfied with the extensive statistical descriptions of universities and colleges provided in the past, and insisted on new PIs across the board to determine at least some of the funding universities and colleges in that province could expect to receive in future.

We can see a little of the critics' point, and even something of the reasoning that led Premier Klein to act as he did. It *is* true that universities and some colleges have difficulty describing and communicating the contribution they would like to make to the public interest in Canada, and showing how their material and social circumstances affect their ability to carry out their public mandates.

---

[32]Organisation for Economic Co-operation and Development [OECD], *Education at a Glance: Education Indicators 2001* (Paris: OECD, 2001), esp. Chapter "E" : *http://www.ocde.org/els/education/ei/eag/chE.htm.*

But if universities and colleges are having trouble acting as they could and should, it's not all that hard to see why. Among other things, they have not been helped by the arrival of PIs, a source of distraction and worse. We have illustrated how PIs undermine any strong sense of quality, accountability, or excellence in the system. To that point, we would now add another: that the language and criteria of PIs confuse the issue fundamentally. In face of that confusion, universities and colleges have, by and large, retreated. Their academic senates are weaker than they have been since the early 1960s, partly because they no longer have the power to debate publicly, and then to *act* according their means and mandates.

6. How PIs Encourage Managerialism

The difficulties of our academic institutions, underlined by cuts and intensified by PIs, invite further explanation: how universities and colleges in the late 20th-century are *managed*. The last fifty years have seen an unprecedented proliferation inside universities of large and frequently opaque bureaucracies.

The size and outlooks of these management systems, have discouraged public scrutiny and public participation. Nor do they encourage proper working of open academic senates and departments. The rise of PIs has strengthened the hand of administrators, accountants, and business consultants who claim management to be the answer to the problems of post-secondary education.

It is ironic that in the name of accountability, we have entrenched exactly the kinds of management that make it hard to work for the public interest. When the University of Toronto allowed vicious industry-based attacks on the academic freedom and scientific integrity of Dr. Nancy Olivieri, a distinguished researcher at the University of Toronto's affiliated Hospital for Sick Children, the University's management acted in a controlled and controlling fashion to isolate Dr. Olivieri from collegial and institutional support. Critics argued that a contributing factor to that depressing series of events was the anxiety of management to maintain external research funding, thus maximizing a crucial Performance Indicator (total amount of external research funding/faculty member/ year). Thus a PI fortified a non-accountable management in its outlook and in its practices. That is, PIs helped to make the University less, not more, accountable. Certainly they did nothing to restrain the lamentable behaviour of management officials in the Olivieri case.[33]

Universitas 21, an international consortium of universities including UBC and led by the Thompson media group, serves to make a further point

---

[33]Jon Thompson, Patricia Baird, Jocelyn Downie, *The Olivieri Report: The complete text of the report of the independent inquiry commissioned by the Canadian Association of University Teachers.* A CAUT Series Title. Toronto: James Lorimer, 2001.

about management styles under PIs.[34] How U21 helps UBC to achieve its goals and mandate in British Columbia and in Canada is utterly unclear; nor is it clear how UBC, faced with the financial difficulties common to all Canadian universities, will be able to carry out course-development in U21. But when the deal was presented to the UBC Senate, it was already *fait accompli.* The documents had been signed, and the Senate was provided with copies only on the very day of the meeting to approve the whole U21 plan. This was, one might justifiably conclude, managerial highhandedness at its worst. But... it may be that UBC's PIs—especially its increasingly precious intake of foreign cash, and the number of courses it provides electronically—will look better after U21. The Senate had no opportunity seriously to consider how U21 is to be accountably linked, with appropriate assurances of intellectual quality and rigour, to UBC's mandate.

The reader will by now wonder how management tools have acquired so much influence. Why have entire provinces (Alberta, Ontario, and British Columbia among them) and states (in the United States, but also in Europe and in industrially-advanced countries in Australasia) accepted them? One reason is money or rather, its absence.

7. Cuts, Costs, & Quality

Behind the rise of PIs lie thirty years of cuts in public financial support which have sapped the entire public higher education system. With the help of PIs, government bureaucrats and private-sector critics maintain the decline in funding was desirable. The cuts reduced the overall size of government, for one thing, which in turn allowed tax cuts, but also permitted private interests to have much more direct involvement in decision-making at the individual faculty member or student level.

PIs—all sorts of numbers, mostly about "productivity"—are useful devices when government is looking for ways to cut the system, and to cut some parts more than others. In Alberta, one persistent theme in the early days of PIs was *differential* cuts. The idea is to encourage sharp competition between institutions.

This idea rests on an historical error: the belief there has never been much competition among Canadian universities and colleges. The record says the exact opposite since the 1850s. Competition was fed at first by religious and political factionalism, but soon we acquired the arrangement we have today: institutions of all kinds do their best to acquire students, public funds, and private endowments, to some degree at the expense of other, sister institutions. Every, so often a politician or high civil servant would say that competition was wasteful and unhelpful. Finally, in the 1970s, several provinces created arm's-length bodies to serve as intermediaries between government and post-secondary institutions—honest

---

[34]David Beers, "The New Global-Cyber-University, Inc.: UBC is Buying In, But Not Without Opposition," *Vancouver Sun,* "Mix" Section, 2001 May 12, H6.

brokers in decisions about who should get most or least public funding, where new programmes of study and new buildings might best be located, and how libraries and laboratories might share their resources. The idea was that collaboration and cooperation would reduce redundancy, encourage efficiencies of scale, and maximize access.

Under the stress of cyclical cuts in public funding, these bodies disappeared by the mid–1980s. Competition among public institutions, and between public and private entities, returned with a vengeance. By this time Margaret Thatcher (UK) and Ronald Reagan (USA) had been elected, in 1979 and 1980 respectively. With their elections came a massive attack on public institutions, on public expenditures of all kinds, and on the idea that the community should be guided by the public interest. Their regimes gave new energy to the idea that market discipline must apply to public institutions, if necessary by sale to the private sector, or through PIs, in order to ensure responsiveness and efficiency.

Neo-conservative ideas and practices help explain the popularity of PIs and PI systems in some provinces, states, and regions across the OECD. We return to our opening questions: How should we define accountability and quality in the early 2000s? How ought we to teach and do research on a basis of autonomy? How can we most persuasively show students, members of the public, university and college teachers that only autonomous, free institutions can best serve the public interest? And what about "quality"?

■

In the 1990s quality was a persistent theme in PIs discussions. At first, the new emphasis on quality assurance seemed an improvement over the PIs of the mid–1980s, especially those of Sir Keith Jarrett and his followers in the United Kingdom.

An example of a "quality indicator" in the new wave of PIs would be "ease of student access to professors." This PI helped justify the creation of large and expensive computerized instruction laboratories and web-based learning "systems." We'll give this particular PI a name: "SPTT" —Student-Prof Time-on-Task.

By 1990, advocates were suggesting that PIs systems had moved beyond the "output indicators" of the 1980s, and could take proper account of "process" and "inputs." SPTT and similar measures would mean more funding to ensure enough profs to go around, and necessary electronic means in place, so that SPTT could only go upward, year on year, measured in minutes per prof per student. This looked, at first glance, like a PI that would push up funding, and increase what American business analysts call "face time" (face-to-face encounters between teacher and student, whether in the office or on screen). How wrong the optimists were!

In 2000–2001, American professors and student at Boston University found this friendly-looking PI was not at all friendly—nor did it have much to do with quality. SPTT actually meant "number of phone calls required to contact directly a professor," and number of office hours/week/professor. The Dean of Faculty and the President announced a scheme requiring professors spend eight hours per day behind their desks.[35]

It quickly transpired that if professors stayed in their offices and classrooms for the same eight hours/day their secretaries did, those professors would no longer move freely to and from their libraries and laboratories, nor work underpaid, overtime hours at home, nor attend meetings and conferences, nor maintain close contact with the community. (By the way, students turned up for office hours in the numbers they always had, no more, no fewer.) The new policy would have satisfied the requirements of one PI at the immediate expense of excellence, community relations, and quality. The Boston University administration quickly withdrew its scheme.

SPTT at Boston University had not been debated in the academic Senate, nor had its implications for professorial work-load been considered at the bargaining table, nor had it been demonstrated that SPTT would show the University was accomplishing its public and private objectives as an independent university enjoying significant public funding.[36]

What *should* count as proof that an institution has high "quality"?

We see a "good" university or college as one that has *at least* the following characteristics:

- iron-clad **assurance of academic freedom and tenure**; without these cornerstones of critical thinking and inquiry, quality is impossible

- **senates, faculties, and departments** where *(i)* the criteria and the standards of good teaching and good research are persistently and publicly debated—and decided; *(ii)* equity and fairness can be taken into account in every aspect of the university's operation, and connections between research and teaching are consistently strong (that is, what you find out in the lab or the library assuredly make their way into the classroom); and *(iii)* the public mandate of the institution is discussed, revisited, and reinterpreted as often as possible

- **public financial support** to ensure that *(i)* tuition is kept low enough to permit and to encourage broad access; *(ii)* teachers' salaries are high enough so the university or college can attract able scholars and researchers; *(iii)* there are enough regularly and permanently available teachers to ensure that students can see and hear them regularly; *(iv)* there is a sustained basis for research and development

[35]Mark Clayton, "Pressuring professors to put in more face time," *Christian Science Monitor*, 2000 November 07.

[36]James F. Carlin, "Restoring Sanity to an Academic World Gone Mad," *Chronicle of Higher Education*, 1999 November 5, p. 8; and Charles Zappia, "The Private Sector and Public Higher Education," *Perspectives* (2000 May): 34–44, and also by Zappia in the same periodical, "Politics and Standards," 51–59. Carlin is frank in his estimate that Boston University's only mistake in the debate on "face time" was to have picked a clumsy PI, and that next time, B.U. would "get it right." Zappia offers an argument wholly opposed to compulsory ties (through PIs) to "markets."

work, and this means good libraries and laboratories as well as funds for research assistance; and *(v)* the physical setting of the institution is healthy—and encouraging of teacher-student communication

- **openly-agreed and fair collective agreements** between administration and staff, whether teaching or non-teaching, so that standards of promotion, tenure, and discipline are fair and transparent; high quality teaching and research are impossible when those standards are secret and/or arbitrary

- **administrative arrangements that support** the above items, with open and competitive appointments of administrators to their posts, open evaluation of administrators (at least as demanding as the kind that teachers and students routinely face), and insistence that administrators manage less and lead more. By this we mean, for example, that administrators ensure students have the information they need to make choices, that the public have routine access to information about business contracts and other financial information in university or college records, that the public have good reason to think its mandate for public post-secondary education has been observed and met.

At the end of this book we provide a list of PIs that have acquired popularity across the world. The only PIs that come close to encouraging quality are about money and finance, that is, various "input indicators." It would take a supreme act of imagination to see how output PIs could offer even *indirect* assurance of quality in post-secondary education.

To give still more force to the claim that PIs have little do with quality, and worse that PIs *undermine* it, think of the "employability" PI. We offer below (figure 2) an Alberta variant of this PI from that jurisdiction's provincial government. The province drew on a fifteen-year old tradition of "employability" PIs in the United Kingdom, and profited from advice given in 1993–5 to the Ontario government by Edward DesRosiers and Associates, consultants, for an "information framework" (that is, a PIs system) to measure the economic utility and "impact" of public post-secondary education in Ontario.[37]

---

[37]Edward DesRosiers and Associates, *An Information Framework Linking Eductional Outcomes to Economic Renewal* (West Hill, Ontario: Edward DesRosiers and Associates, 1993 October 15), pp. 34; see also G. Grant Clarke, E. DesRosiers, and Stephen Hawkins, *An Information Framework for Higher Education in the Maritimes* (West Hill, Ontario: Edward DesRosiers and Associates, 1995 October 18), p. 49. Compare Council of Ontario Universities, *Report of the Committee on Accountability, Performance Indicators and Outcomes Assessment* (Toronto: Council of Ontario Universities, 1994), p. 43; revised 1994 May 15. Although Chapter 8 provides a more detailed examination of the DesRosiers reports, it will be useful to say here that the 1993 and 1995 documents recommended that funding for Ontario and Maritimes post-secondary education be dependent on measures of the direct economic "impact" of schooling. Not only that, the 1993 document proposed that various fields of study be connected to graduates' eventual employment in the primary, tertiary, and secondary sectors of the economy. That is, a PI on employability would test not only how rapidly a graduate was

Figure 1: Employablity of Graduate: Alberta

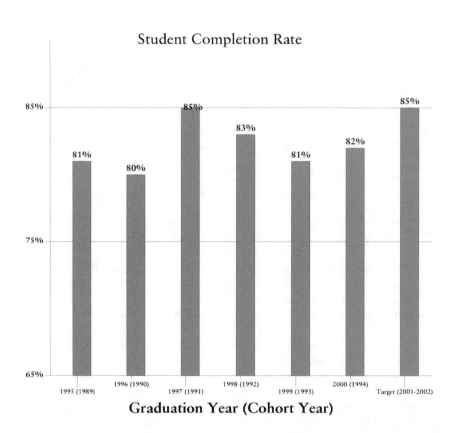

Student Completion Rate

Graduation Year (Cohort Year)

Sources: Statistics Canada; Canadian Association of University Teachers

The data depicted show that the Government of Alberta performance indicators are about the employment of graduates in the fields for which they were educated, no matter the economic conditions of the times, or the requirements of personal educational development that may have influenced the professional choices of graduates.

In Alberta, as in the state of Oregon in the United States, PI writers decided simply to *define* employability as a term proving there is "quality" in higher education (not to mention accountability and cost-effectiveness), and the Alberta system leaves the impression they have followed that same path.

---

employed, and not only if the graduate was employed in the field for which she had been prepared, but also whether the "trend-line" of her employment was appropriately directed to the primary, the secondary, or the tertiary sector.

Our point about all this is of the simplest: this PI is about the economy, and about the kinds of choices adults sometimes make. It has next to little to do with post-secondary education. On the other hand, anywhere from 93% to 97% of university graduates are employed, and that might well be considered a remarkable indicator of the attractiveness of a post-secondary education in these changing times. But this kind of PI is at best an indirect way of talking about "quality" in post-secondary education. More likely, it is a distraction, or worse.

Three main points about PIs:

1. PIs have moved from curiosity to compulsion, mainly since 1980.

2. As PIs became more popular, public funding of post-secondary education in Canada, the United Kingdom, Australia, New Zealand, and parts of the United States, dropped. In Canada, the drop was sometimes precipitous. Between 1994 and 2000, Federal cash transfers to public post-secondary education fell by $3 billion, this after sharp cuts in 1984, 1986, and 1990. In the seven years ending 1997, Federal support for university research fell by 15%.[38] Even as funding reached a plateau, outside intervention in university and college affairs has gone up.

3. As public funding declined, new agencies and offices of assessment and accountability grew.

For the sake of completeness, we provide on page 71 a summary of recent(1990–2000) public funding for public post-secondary education in Canada. Questions of comparison quite apart, the table is a useful backdrop to the recent history of PIs.

As PIs have become compulsive and compulsory in one Canadian jurisdiction after another, public funding has declined. In the United States and the United Kingdom, as in Australia and New Zealand, the same pattern is noticeable for the last two decades of the twentieth century. It is tempting to suggest not just a correlation between these two developments, but a causal linkage.

PIs were never about quality. They were and are about cuts and control.

■

---

[38]See Denise Doherty-Delorme, "Research, innovation, and prosperity," in Denise Doherty-Delorme and Erica Shaker, eds., *Missing Pieces II: An Alternative Guide to Canadian Post-Secondary Education* (Ottawa: Canadian Centre for Policy Alternatives,

We end with the observation that *not one* of the usual arguments for PIs holds water.

Having looked at the history of PIs, few readers will be surprised that PIs fail the test. But then, the proponents of PIs spend little time reading history, and in any case, it unwise to rely exclusively on history to decide on high post-secondary education policy. That is why we thought it important to review the main arguments used by supporters of PIs, without considering the historical background.

We've asked just what PIs are, and whether PIs can or will produce the results they are supposed to do. We've offered conceptual and empirical evidence to show that they cannot and will not.

Our next step is to describe national and regional experiments with PIs, following them from start to finish. We begin with the United Kingdom.

Provincial and Territorial General Government Revenue and
Expenditure: Financial Management System Basis

FY Year Ending	Current $ PSE Exp	Constant Total Expend.	Total PSE Exp	Expenditures	Inflator	% of prov. exp.
2000	10,985,137.0	190,405,637.0	10,985,137.0	190,405,637.0	1	5.77%
1999	12,309,313.0	194,124,550.0	12,520,966.3	197,462,438.2	1.01719457	6.34%
1998	10,061,998.7	178,195,840.6	10,326,069.3	182,872,473.5	1.026244344	5.65%
1997	9,870,568.9	175,724,328.9	10,281,470.5	183,039,549.8	1.041628959	5.62%
1996	10,513,117.3	178,850,788.7	11,112,507.7	189,047,711.5	1.057013575	5.88%
1995	10,234,821.6	176,276,374.5	11,022,115.5	189,836,095.6	1.076923077	5.81%
1994	10,184,648.7	172,399,415.4	10,986,517.0	185,972,944.0	1.078733032	5.91%
1993	10,800,462.6	171,263,505.9	11,826,750.9	187,537,413.7	1.095022624	6.31%
1992	10,563,549.9	165,362,985.3	11,710,722.7	183,320,956.6	1.108597285	6.39%
1991	9,533,953.8	150,559,157.1	11,017,972.0	173,994,609.7	1.155656109	6.33%
1990	8,956,951.0	138,580,854.8	10,699,706.2	165,544,550.5	1.194570136	6.46%

Part II: Case Studies

3

The United Kingdom: Assessment Without End... Amen

"From Gradgrind to collectivization—statistical dogmas bring forth monsters."
—Christopher Hitchens, "Against Sinister Perfectionism," *Times Literary Supplement*, 26 November 1999

"Enter the inquisition, exit loyalty."
—Noel Annan, *The Dons: Mentors, Eccentrics and Geniuses* (London: HarperCollins, 1995), 295

United Kingdom Glossary

AAU   Academic Audit Unit, set up by university administrations; superseded by HEFC

AUT   Association of University Teachers. Union representing academic and other academic staff in the older universities of the United Kingdom

CNAA   Council for National Academic Awards. Formerly responsible for awarding degrees and carrying out inspections in the polytechnics

HEFC   Higher Education Funding Council. There are separate funding councils for England, Wales, and Scotland. Northern Ireland falls under the HEFC (England)

HEQC   Higher Education Quality Council; predecessor of HEFC

ILT   Institute for Learning and Teaching

LTSN   Learning and Teaching Support Network

NAFTHE   National Association of Teachers in Further and Higher Education. Represents academics in the former polytechnics

OFSTED   Office for Standards in Education, officially the Office of Her Majesty's Chief Inspector of the Schools in England

QAA   Quality Assurance Agency. Contracted by the HEFCs to carry out academic audits of universities across the United Kingdom

RAE   Research Assessment Exercise. Carried out across the United Kingdom every four years

THES   *The Times Higher Education Supplement*

TQA   Teaching Quality Assessment

SCOP   Standing Committee of Principals

SQA   Scottish Qualifications Authority

UNIVERSITIES UK

Formerly the Committee of Vice-Chancellors and Principal (CVCP). Represents university administrations.

Over the last two decades the United Kingdom has moved rapidly away from its traditional, decentralized system of university education. Where government formerly provided block grants to universities based mainly on student numbers, the new centralized system puts heavy emphasis upon performance indicators and quality assessment. Before the Thatcher years funding was channelled through the University Grants Commission (UGC), a body formed in 1917, recognized by a Treasury minute in 1919, and dominated by Oxford, London, and Cambridge.[1] The Thatcher government was deeply hostile to the old Oxbridge elite—particularly the senior civil service, which it accused of managing the United Kingdom into a state of genteel decline—profoundly suspicious of professionals, and coldly disdainful of academics. Its solution to the nation's problems was downsized government and reliance on market forces to determine efficient and accountable outcomes. The result for universities was inevitably the opposite: increased government control, with more bureaucracy and less funding.

The central government started to cut funds in the early 1980s, and continued in fits and starts through the next two decades. Meanwhile student numbers rose dramatically, from 574,000 full-time equivalent in 1979 to 1,122,000 in 1994 and then to 2,081,664 full-time students in 1998–9, 235,000 of them in further education colleges. Recurrent spending per student in the eighties dropped from £6,090 to £4,537.[2] The unit of resource (student fees plus government grants) fell from an index of 100 in 1970 to 40 in 1990.[3] Thatcherites saw this as a triumph for "efficiency"—more for less.

The government washed its hands of the consequences, insisting it would naturally never interfere in how universities managed their own affairs. Simon Blackburn, then editor of *Mind* and a don at Oxford, remarked in 1989: "This disclaiming of responsibility is about as edifying as

---

[1]For a short but critical review of the UGC system, see David Crevier, "The British University Grants Committee," CAUT *Bulletin*, March 1974. The UGC was appointed by the Secretary of State for Education and Science, with the largest group of members from the universities. Building grants were determined by the UGC and it acted as a facilitator in national bargaining over salaries. It made quinquennial visits to universities. After 1946 it was also responsible for collecting information and advising the Secretary of State over such matters as manpower planning. Despite the block grants, it could be quite *dirigiste*, especially in its latter days before it was abolished by the Thatcher government. The current buffer bodies are the Higher Education Funding Councils (HEFC) for England, Wales, and Scotland. See Bahram Bekhradnia, "Buffer body with a good track record," THES, 1994 May 27. For details of current HEFC policy for England, see website: *www.hefce.ac.uk*.

For events in 2000 and 2001, the authors are heavily indebted to the *Times Higher Education Supplement* (THES). We have footnoted only direct quotes and references to editorials. The THES web site is *www.thes.co.uk*.

[2]Association of University Teachers, *Higher Education: Preparing for the 21st Century* (London: AUT, 1995); THES, 2000 September 29.

[3]Noel Annan, *The Dons*, 292.

driving a motor car at someone and disclaiming the responsibility for the injuries."[4] In 1995 the capital programme was cut by 31 per cent, accompanied by a drive to casualize academic labour. Tenure on the British model was abolished in the 1988 Education Reform Act.[5] Casualisation grew quickly through the nineties. Between 1980 and 1990, the United Kingdom was the only EU country with real negative growth in pay (minus 3.8%) for academic teachers.[6] Lord Baker, the former Tory Education Secretary, estimated academic salaries rose one per cent in real terms between 1981 and 2000, against a 40 per cent increase for all workers in the same period.

For political and economic reasons—desire to break the power of the older universities, to increase access, and at the same time to control and cut expenditures—the government re-christened the polytechnics as universities, increasing their number to more than a hundred.[7] The new universities quickly demanded equal treatment with the old ones, particularly in regard to funding and to research opportunities, and especially since all institutions would be assessed by the same criteria, thus creating winners and losers.[8] The polytechnics were much more familiar with central government control and the audit culture through the Council for National Academic Awards (CNAA), which controlled the awarding of degrees and carried out inspections along with Her Majesty's Inspectorate of Schools.

The government aimed to create a market in higher education, giving preference to practical subjects, and to ensure universities were efficient and accountable by replacing collegial governance with centralized performance indicators and managerial control. It needed to forestall any

---

[4]Debate between Simon Blackburn and Robert Jackson, the Minister responsible for Higher Education, *TLS*, 1988 30 December–1989 5 January (hereafter *Blackburn*).

[5]Tenure in the UK allowed for dismissal for cause but did not allow for lay-offs for financial reasons or as a consequence of planning decisions. The resulting arrangements were more like the Canadian situation.

[6]L. Dominelli and A. Hoogvelt, "Globalization, Contract Government and Taylorization of Intellectual Labour in Academia," *Studies in Political Economy*, 49 (1996), qu. in Janet Atkinson Grosjean, Garnet Grosjean, Donald Fisher, Kjell Rubenson, *Consequences of Performance Indicators in Higher Education: An International Perspective* (Vancouver: Centre for Policy Studies in Higher Education and Training, University of British Columbia for the Humanities and Social Sciences Federation of Canada, 1999).

[7]See David Watson and Rachel Bowden, "Why did they do it? The Conservatives and access to higher education, *Journal of Education Policy* 14, 4 (1999): 243–56.

[8]The Conservative Party appears to have reversed its position. In 2000 Theresa May, the shadow education secretary, stated that the change had resulted in the dilution and sometimes destruction of what had made the polytechnics effective and popular. The Conservatives have put forward a plan to divide the universities between those which would be privatized and receive a substantial endowment, and those which would continue to be financed by the state—thereby, in effect, recreating the binary divide without actually saying so. *THES*, 2000 September 8, editorial 2000 October 6. The Labour government is currently considering the creation of an elite tier of research universities, *ibid.*, 2001 November 23.

potential counter-revolution, and in particular to prevent students from opting out of science and engineering (as happened in the market-driven system of New Zealand, and later in France). These requirements meant more, not less bureaucracy telling academics and students what they might and might not do.

> Education policy exhibited the distinctive new-right pattern of marketisation and bureaucracy. This was quite predictable since transaction costs, duplication of services and the creation of measurable indicators to mimic price signals all require form-filling, the multiplication of administrative posts and the creation of a world safe for the accounting profession.[9]

By the late 1990s education had become "a mainly state-funded, centrally driven system, governed by common rules and regulations set down by central government agencies but managed locally."[10] The centralizing approach dictated by the Treasury was applied to many other areas as well. In an article otherwise flattering to Thatcherism, Simon Jenkins complained the Treasury had imposed "some 680 ridiculous performance measures" on local government in its drive to control every detail of administration.[11] The regime imposed on universities was every bit as detailed.

The primary emphasis had become skills training for industry. Gone was the vision of the Robbins Report in 1963, according to which universities were for

> instruction in skills, the promotion of the general powers of the mind, the advancement of learning, and the transmission of a common culture and common standards of citizenship... [with] the encouragement of a high level of scholarship in the arts, humanities and social sciences [as] an essential feature of a civilized and cultured country.[12]

Indignant academics, however, sometimes forget commercial values were never wholly absent from the traditional university.

Ironically, those politicians in the United Kingdom most hostile to membership in the European union have transformed its relatively decentralized higher education system to one that more and more resembles the centralized educational bureaucracies of the continent.

Lord Baker, who did much to create the system under Thatcher, now describes it as a nationalized industry with all the drawbacks and few of the benefits, an academic version of the Polish shipyards under communist rule. The Conservatives (together with some in the Labour party) seem wedded

---

[9]Eric Shaw, "A look at mediocrity in the extreme," THES, 2000 June 2. Shaw is senior lecturer in politics at the University of Stirling.

[10]See *Blackburn;* also David Farnham, "The United Kingdom: End of Donnish Dominion," in David Farnham , ed., *Managing Academic Staff in Changing University Systems: International Trends and Comparisons* (London: Society for Research into Higher Education and the Open University Press, 1999), 212 [hereafter Farnham]. See also Gaither, *op. cit.*

[11]Simon Jenkins, "Farewell at last the sick man of Europe," *The Times*, 2001 March 6.

[12]*Farnham*, 211.

to the view that British universities used to be private and should be returned to that state, forgetting that the civic universities of northern England, the University of London, the Scottish universities, and the national University of Wales were civic universities, not created or run by the central state and most definitely *not* private business corporations.[13]

There was a widespread assumption that privatization meant the UK would follow the supposedly superior path of the United States. In fact, the major American expansion since World War II has been in the *public* sector. The state universities of California, Wisconsin, Michigan, and Illinois, for example, have now become fully competitive with elite private institutions.

Nor did the UK trend towards central government control change much with the election of a Labour government. Labour has proved even more enthusiastic than the Conservatives about measuring and counting.[14] As Noel Annan observed, "Oxford and Cambridge were to learn that whereas the previous government had chastised them with whips, the new government, like Rehoboam, would chastise them with scorpions."[15] During its first two years in office, Labour continued Thatcherite cuts to the general revenues of the universities under the guise of "efficiencies." At one point schools, colleges and universities had the lowest share of national revenue since 1962.[16] In 2000, the government announced increases for that year and, subsequently, for 2000–04, effectively ending thirteen years of cuts in real terms in the "unit of resource" without restoring previous funding levels. The Labour government prefers to spend its money on one-off projects considerably cheaper than increases in general funding of universities. This allows it to maintain endless competitive bidding, which frequently costs universities a substantial percentage of any funds received.

This new education policy required, in the eyes of the government, new central agencies to replace the old Universities Grants Commission which in the view of the Thatcherites had been captured by the academics. In 1992 the government passed the Further and Higher Education Act, creating three higher education funding councils for England (including Northern Ireland), Scotland, and Wales. Since political home rule in Scotland extended to higher education, structures would sometimes be different north of the border (and potentially also in Wales and Northern Ireland).

The government saw a lack of agreed standards, since many of the new universities were clearly not in the same academic league as the more estab-

---

[13]Letter of Lindsay Paterson, University of Edinburgh, THES, 2000 June 30. Speech of Lord Baker, THES, 2000 June 16.

[14]TLS, 1999 December 3. Annan advised academics to distrust all politicians.

[15]*Annan*, 299.

[16]Howard Glennerster, professor of social administration at LSE and advisor to the Labour government, THES, 2001 September 7.

lished institutions. There were as well a few internal and external scandals. The nub of the matter, however, was that the United Kingdom had moved dramatically into the era of mass higher education, with an initial goal of enrolling 30% of all young people between 18 and 21. Labour has revised that goal to 50% of those under 30 by 2010. How, in such circumstances, could one maintain quality, particularly while cutting the budget for higher education every year? The answer was more education for less money, using performance indicators to measure quality and output. This would have the effect of transferring blame for the consequences of overcrowding and under funding to the university administrations and their academic staff.[17]

The Thatcher government and its successors believed assessment should no longer be attempted through the traditional modalities of marking[18] or of looking at the input factors in education (the size of the library collection, the number of computer stations per student, faculty with doctorates, and so on) but should instead emphasize outputs. In ever greater detail throughout the eighties and nineties, the government articulated this new approach in such measures as manpower need, accessibility, time for completion of degrees, and first destination of graduates.

The vice-chancellors attempted to keep some control of the process by creating their own agency, the Academic Audit Unit (AAU), and their own performance indicators (which by 1992 numbered 69). These were mainly statistical, and criticized by the bureaucracy for their inability to deal with quality and outputs.

The 1990s saw a steady march away from this model toward a state-run and state-controlled national inspectorate of universities, culminating in the creation of the Quality Assurance Agency for Higher Education (QAA). The funding councils were legally responsible for quality assurance in the universities but contracted for the inspection with the QAA which was, most explicitly, an agency not of higher education but rather of the central govern-

---

[17]See Elizabeth C. Stanley and William J. Patrick, "Quality Assurance in American and British Higher Education: A Comparison," in Gerald H. Gaither, ed., *Quality Assurance in Higher Education: An International Perspective* [New Directions for Institutional Research, Number 99] (San Francisco: Jossey-Bass, 1998).

[18]Marking in the UK prior to the Thatcherite reforms was not purely individualistic. The ideal involved end-of-year exams, double marking, a cohesive examination group, an inclusive examination board and a scrutiny meeting, where examiners decided their framework. Pat Leon, "Trying to box clever," *TLS*, 2000 March 31, quoting Alison Wolf, Institute of Education, University of London and Executive Director of the International Centre for Research and Assessment. It also involved a system of external examiners in the subject area. Maurice Croft, "External Examining: A review of its rationale and mode of operation," paper presented, Conference of the International Network of Quality Assurance Agencies in Higher Education (INQAAHE), Montréal, May 1993.

ment.[19] University administrators and academic staff reluctantly accepted centralization, perhaps thinking, with some justification, that they could learn to play the game and outwit the bureaucrats. Their tactics did not take into account the enormous costs involved, and the life of grunge imposed on the academic staff. The central bureaucracy seemed invincible until March 2001, when revolt broke out in some of the older universities and turned back the tide of detailed centralized assessment, although the final result was not clear at the end of 2001.

THE RESEARCH ASSESSMENT EXERCISE

The centralizing approach has, in turn, led to two major drives to assess quality in research and in teaching, both of which rely on implicit and explicit performance indicators. The first of these is the Research Assessment Exercise (RAE), begun in 1986. The guiding principle of the RAE is selectivity, partly to ensure excellence, partly because of the limited amount of money available for university research. There have now been four of them, with the fifth due in 2001. Their main purpose has been to produce quality ratings on which the funding councils could make decisions. Their form is attuned to the external examiner system with which British academics are familiar. In this case, however, there are no visits to the universities. All material relating to the research exercise is submitted in a standard statistical and narrative form. The only information for the academic panels is, therefore, documentary. There are sixty-nine areas of assessment, including medicine and dentistry, with a seven point, criterion-referenced scale based on national and international levels of excellence. As time has passed, there has been increased emphasis on research publication in the time period after the previous research assessment exercise. As a consequence, publication in refereed journals in the time period reviewed has become the main performance indicator.

The consequence has been to concentrate research funding in the older universities in the United Kingdom. For example, those universities with medical schools secured 72% of all research grants and 74% of those from the research councils.[20] The Higher Education Funding Council for England published a study in March 2000 showing funded research overwhelmingly concentrated in a few of the older universities, particularly Oxford, Cambridge, and London (especially Imperial College, King's College, and University College). "As funds have become more concentrated, so the output of the most active universities has both increased and improved: they are

---

[19]Most QAA documents can be read on the agency's web site at *www.qaa.ac.uk*. Although the QAA was incorporated as a limited company with the bodies representing the institutions as legal owners, the majority of the directors were either nominated by the government's funding councils or independent members.

[20]*THES*, 2000 March 14. See also AUT, *Higher Education, preparing for the 21st century*, UK, 1995.

delivering more and better research." The report concluded that "the shift in selectivity is primarily attributable to the RAE process." The interim report on selectivity and excellence, which is part of the review, "shows that in the past 15 years the effectiveness and productivity of the UK research base has increased significantly."[21] Nevertheless there were repeated warnings during 1999 and 2000 that under funding was seriously eroding important areas of British research.[22] The Chancellor of the Exchequer responded that the government would spend £1.2 billion over four years, starting in 2000, to improve science laboratories and to fund graduate students in science and engineering. The Wellcome Trust added another £348 million. These grants helped universities restore the funding for capital expenditures brutally cut in the mid-1990s, but little was done to alleviate the salary differential between British and American scientists, although funds were provided to lure "stars" from aborad and to encourage British academic to return.[23]

The Royal Society warned against the continuing trend to concentrate research in a few institutions, advising that diversity was one of the keys to continuing excellence: "The health of the UK science base depends on the high quality of research across the country." It noted, for example, that members of the Royal Society are to be found in thirty-four institutions outside the Oxford-Cambridge-London triangle. The Royal Society did not oppose selectivity but wished to moderate its effects.[24]

Research assessment exercises have created a more organized and efficient approach to research, especially in the sciences, in United Kingdom universities. They have increased publication. They can provoke other reforms as well, such as in research training. The HEFC (England) has announced assessment will now be linked to the quality of research training either in the RAE or with a separate funding scheme, a development supported by the AUT.[25]

Not everyone is a fan of the RAE. The newer universities are especially unhappy with a system they claim rewards those who already have and, except in a few niche areas, excludes new competitors. The National Association of Teachers in Further and Higher Education (NATFHE), which represents academics in the new universities, is particularly hostile. "[I]f research is supposed to go hand in hand with teaching," argues Tom

[21]Claire Sanders, "Research-rich elite wins cash", *THES*, 2000 March 24, quoting a report by Jonathan Adams, head of the higher education policy unit at Leeds University. The survey was based on bibliometric data.
[22]See for instance, "Resource starvation threatens UK physics," *THES*, 2000 May19, and for geology, "Science projects suffer in squeeze," *THES*, 2000 May 5.
[23]*Chronicle of Higher Education*, 2000 July 6; *THES*, 2000 July 17.
[24]John Enderby, "Excellence comes through diversity," *THES*, 2001 February 2.
[25]Alison Godard, "Research elite risk losing stars,"*THES*, 2000 April 21.

Wilson, head of higher education for NATFHE, "why does 90% of research funding go to universities that teach only 10% of students?"[26]

Critics have pointed to over-emphasis on short-term publication at the expense of long-term and fundamental research.[27] Since the RAE considers only the period since the previous assessment, academics are encouraged to break research up into ever smaller but more numerous articles in order to satisfy the bean counters—what David Cannadine memorably called "battery chickens on overtime laying for their lives."[28] This, in turn, necessitates creation of ever more academic journals in which to print the required articles. Critics argue this discriminates against collaborative and fundamental research. Interdisciplinary research suffers because no one department can claim exclusive credit for it.[29] Marianne Elliott, who has been a departmental chair, professor of modern history, author of five books, and head of the Institute of Irish Studies at the University of Liverpool, writes in her most recent book: "In view of the current audit culture—a virus-like infection spreading through every aspect of British higher education, a culture which actively penalises long-term research projects such as this book—I am somewhat in despair about my ability to embark on such a major project again."[30]

Moreover, this encourages game-playing, with energy devoted to the game at the expense of research. For example, some universities poach academics with high publication records in order to boost their RAE standing without actually conducting any further research in their own institution. Frequently they can do this only by seriously distorting their own salary structure. Some move academic staff from one department to another to improve RAE standing. Others have been charged with questionable reporting in order to improve their standing—the creation of a "virtual" research university instead of a real one. The RAE hopes to counter that possibility by publishing those parts of the submissions that contain factual data and textual information about research activity while omitting personal and contractual details or future plans.[31] It also challenges the assumptions about staff poaching and inter-disciplinary research.[32]

---

[26]Tom Wilson, "That's one for me, 14 for you," THES, 2000 May 26. See also in the same issue, Phil Baty, "Union prepares to fight for the abolition of RAE."

[27]Lewis Elton, "The UK Research Assessment Exercise: Unintended Consequences," *Higher Education Quarterly*, 54,3 (July 2000).

[28]Gordon Marsden M.P., "Ban Battery Methods", THES, 2000 January 21. The RAE responded to this criticism by limiting the number of articles that each individual within a department could put forward.

[29]*Annan*, 295.

[30]Marianne Elliott, *The Catholics of Ulster: A History*, New York: Basic Books/London: Allen Lane, 2001, xxix.

[31]Letter of John Rogers, Manager RAE 2001, THES, 2000 June 9.

[32]See HEFC web site. The HEFC argues that national statistics do not show a significant increase in mobility in the year before the RAE exercise, although this does not negate the existence of poaching at the local level.

Noel Annan, no fan of the complacency of English universities during the fifties and sixties, has pointed out one of the paradoxes produced by the RAE and its equivalent in teaching:

> Vice-chancellors said openly that if swinging cuts were imposed, standards would fall. Now that they had been imposed no Vice-Chancellor said openly that the quality of teaching and research in his university had fallen. To admit to a decline would be to invite outside inspectors to recommend that some departments should be closed down. Yet how could standards not have fallen when fewer academics taught vastly more students? Whitehall, however, presented this as a triumph of 'higher productivity' and 'efficiency gains.'[33]

The RAE has produced a number of individual scandals. The case of Avril Henry, a researcher of international standing at Exeter University, shows how the RAE machine can crush individuals. Ms. Henry was given a university grant to complete an interactive computer application for an explanatory catalogue of the sculptures of Essex Cathedral. When it was discovered she would retire before the next RAE exercise and therefore could not be counted for it, the project was canned. The comments of the administrators are revealing. The acting director of research said: "I'm sure the project is worthwhile in itself, but the awful truth is that we can't get any RAE joy from it, and the money could be spent on something more 'returnable.' I wish I could feel that the university had higher, holier motives for encouraging research." The head of the school acknowledged the university should advance research and that the "… project is of international standing and support of it would further that aim." But the money was available solely for the purposes of improving the school's standing in the RAE:

> On academic and moral grounds your case is extremely strong; but the officers of the university and the school have an obligation to maximise the benefit to the institution of the funds devoted to them. I find that they have acted in accordance with the managerial briefs they hold, and I therefore have to uphold the decision against you.

The Vice-Chancellor refused to set up a grievance committee to hear the case, and a spokesman for the university upheld his decision as valid under the university statutes. Ms. Henry and the AUT appealed to the Queen as Visitor, who ordered a grievance committee of the university to hear the complaint. Ultimately, the Lord Chancellor, acting for the Queen, found in favour of Ms. Henry in a scathing judgement. The university then negotiated a mutually agreeable settlement.

Exeter was involved in another questionable tactic: removing some staff members from the payroll during the RAE and paying them a lump sum in lieu of salary. The Exeter spokesman said: "Every university is having to review its arrangements to maximise its RAE return."[34] John Rogers, who manages the RAE for all the funding councils, claimed this tactic was point-

[33]*Annan*, 294.
[34]*THES*, 2000 May 19.

less because the RAE assesses the university only on the number of staff they return for the exercise, so the percentage of staff entered for assessment has no bearing on the results. Was Exeter confused, or using the RAE as an excuse to discriminate against the academics in question? Or was John Rogers disingenuous, since the HEFC notes in its performance indicators the percentage of staff put forward for the RAE exercise?

University administrators may actually punish academics who are not put up for the RAE exercise, pressing them to retire or transfer to non-research contracts. *The Guardian Education* cited Lancaster University as conducting this type of selection on a major scale.[35] Other academics may find themselves dead in the water, not because they have failed to produce the required number of articles, but because their research does not fit the scheme the department wishes to present to the RAE. In other words, lone wolves and dissenters beware—orthodoxy has a new tool.

In the spring of 2001 the AUT annual meeting heard allegations of systematic exclusion of active researchers through non-accountable management procedures. It was alleged that the research performance of individual universities was falsified, and managers led to exclude academic staff whose work was not thought to fit with what was considered most likely to impress RAE panels. Universities were following the lead of Oxford, which in 1996 reduced the number of staff entered for the exercise and, as a consequence, received more money than Cambridge—a case of academic games-playing *par excellence*. The meeting demanded the executive audit the RAE to discover the extent of the game-playing, and campaign for rules to prevent such abuse.

Critics suggest the RAE encourages conservatism in the choice of research topics and in recruitment. Centralized research management is likely to prefer the safe to the controversial or the unproven. Others fear emphasis on publication in prestige journals, rather than dissemination to end users, creates the risk of "the academic world... talking only to itself and so sterilising its work." McNay's study suggested only 34% of academics considered the RAE had improved the quality of their research, while the majority thought it had little or no effect "apart from the stress and time-loss associated with the administration of performance reviews."[36]

The HEFC is considering another complaint from some quarters: that it is absurd to keep assessing the top research departments over short periods of time because this diverts funds from research to game playing and bureaucracy. The head of the research policy section at HEFC said in April 2000 that "where a submission gained a grade 5 or 5* for two earlier RAEs, there may be some benefit in prolonging the planning and

---

[35]*The Guardian Education*, 20 February 2001.
[36]I. McNay, "The Paradoxes of Research Assessment and Funding," in M. Henkel and B. Little, *Changing Relationships Between Higher Education and the State*, London, quoted in *Consequences of PIs*.

funding horizon." Another problem is that RAE funding is tied to *improvement*. A consistently top-rated department, because it cannot improve its standing, will never receive more money. The 1996 review therefore gave more generous funds to lower-rated areas which had improved, rather than to the best.

Others suggested the RAE discriminated against women because it was based on male patterns of working and on male networks, taking no account of pregnancy or parental responsibilities. A tribunal ruled against the London School of Economics for denying a woman an academic job because another candidate was considered to have more RAE potential. After this case, the AUT called for a halt to the RAE because of "inherent discrimination" and demanded that procedures at the local and national level be subjected to "rigorous equal-opportunities audit" overseen by the Equal Opportunities Commission. The HEFC retorted that the workings of the RAE were even-handed between men and women, and regulations for the 2001 RAE made it explicit that the situation of staff who have taken maternity leave or other career breaks would be taken into account. It then set up a staff sub-group to explore gender and related people issues—a move welcomed by the AUT despite the permissive nature of an earlier report on this matter.

McNay surveyed departmental heads and found 71% of them said the RAE had a positive impact on research, while 62% reported a negative impact on teaching. Research centres ban otherwise "free" staff from teaching responsibilities to increase research productivity. An HEFC seminar discussed whether or not the fascination with research damaged teaching. Roger Brown, Principal of Southampton Institute, argued "People have started to realise that research can damage teaching quality...."[37] However, it turns out that United Kingdom research is heavily subsidized by the unpaid overtime of the academic staff who prefer not to cut into teaching time.[38] The RAE persuades academic staff to devote their own unpaid overtime to research rather than to teaching, indicating where most academics locate the system's priorities.

Sally Brown, Deputy Principal at Stirling University and chair of the 2001 RAE panel on education, noted the dilemmas created by the exercise:

> If universities get poor RAE ratings, they get less money. This leads to more routine teaching and the abandonment of research. If the RAE results are good, researchers are brought in to spend time on research. There is a gradual separation of research and teaching with teaching done by part-timers and postgraduate students... The irony is that the students never get to see the 'stars' who attracted them there in the first place.[39]

Academic staff excluded from the RAE find themselves assigned heavier teaching duties, which negatively affect their research time and undermine

---

[37]*THES*, 2000 February 25.
[38]Alison Godard, "Unpaid slog sustains research," *THES*, 2000 May 12.
[39]*THES*, 2000 June 16.

their careers. In such circumstances teaching becomes a punishment—a curious result of performance indicators.

Universities would also have to submit staff development plans as part of the RAE. Meanwhile, however, the HEFC recognized any serious staff development plans might have the "unintended consequences" of reducing casualization. As a consequence, this part of the performance indicator plan will not be particularly prescriptive (that is, not treated seriously).

The report recognized that impact information and citations might be less useful in subjects such as history, where longer-term scholarly activities might be recognized, and that in general a broader range of evidence should be considered by RAE panels. It noted that if improvement in RAE grades continued at past rates, the likely result of the 2001 exercise would be to require an increase in research funds of £60 million a year. Was anyone surprised that later in the year the HEFC announced that the cash was not available to pay those who had improved their standing? Perhaps in 2003, said the Council. But perhaps not. Vikki Goddard, the head of planning and development at Liverpool, said: "It raises a number of questions about why we have gone through this year's RAE in the first place."[40]

Critics said the HEFC was also narrowing the definition of research by excluding scholarship and creating a total divorce between research and teaching. Said Stephen Rowland of the Higher Education Research and Development Unit at University College:

> This move would disqualify from research funding those scholarly activities that most closely inform teaching. Moreover such a narrow definition of research would also disqualify many critical studies in the arts and humanities.[41]

On the other hand, Universities UK, which represents university administrations, strongly supports the RAE. It considers the criticisms either unfounded or not fundamentally serious. The system is similar, it suggests, to many other countries, and better than any other model yet proposed. It claims British university research ranks second in the world in terms of international prizes, refereed publications, and citations, and first on a per-capita basis. It ascribes this success, at least in part, to the RAE.[42]

COMMERCIALIZATION: A NEW RESEARCH APPROACH

The central government is obsessed with the view that converting university research into commercial activity would end the dismal British record of industrial research and development. But if one searches for the source of the lag in British research and development, the answer is obvious. With important exceptions, British industry (just like its Canadian counterpart)

---

[40]*THES*, 2001 October 5.
[41]Letter of Stephen Rowland, *THES*, 2000 November 10.
[42]CVCP, *Briefing Note: Research in Universities*, 1999 summer.

does not invest much cash in research and development as distinct from testing. British industry spends half of that invested by companies in the United States. This arises from a culture which focuses on short-term gain and shareholder value rather than long-term development based on science, technology, and engineering. But it is more convenient for the government to bad-mouth academics than private companies. The Office of Science and Technology is considering diverting funds to another stream to finance commercial spin-offs despite the failure of an earlier scheme ("Realising our Potential Awards") which allegedly simply financed second-rate research.[43] This year the government created a new programme whereby £34 million was distributed among eighteen universities to establish eight enterprise centres promoting university-industry links.

Another tack has been to fund joint British-American academic alliances. This is a particular enthusiasm of the Chancellor of the Exchequer. The first of these was the funding by the Treasury of a joint Cambridge-MIT institute to promote industry-academic links with £68 million over five years. This was done without competition or consultation with the academic community. In the end most of the money is going to Cambridge Massachusetts rather than to Cambridge England. Other universities are lining up for similar grants.[44] These grants introduce a new, albeit somewhat imprecise, performance indicator—negotiation of alliances with universities in the United States. Presumably this involves money which might have gone to the research councils to distribute for peer-reviewed research funded through the RAE exercise.

The Department of Education and Employment provided £8 million for some 50 two-year projects to improve links between universities and employers, although the actual grants seemed to have more enlightened goals than the title of the programme might suggest. For example, Coventry University received £188,000 to develop an on-line mentoring service for disabled graduates.

Speaking for the Conservative opposition in the House of Lords, Lord Baker attacked the "the incessant trivial intervention" tactics of the government which, he alleged, were combined with under-investment in libraries, laboratories, and computer facilities, without recognizing which government had invented these tactics.[45]

Emphasis on links with industry can pose significant problems. Scientists seem likely to lose much of their autonomy as science and engineering become less collegial, more attuned to the production line, and thus less creative.[46] This approach undermines the idea of the university as a place of disinterested and independent scientific research—an idea whose

---

[43]Michael Rennie, "A waste of good ideas," *THES*, 2000 March 17.

[44]Lee Elliot Major, "Bridging loans," *THES*, 2000 February 8. Dr. Major is deputy editor of *Research Fortnight*.

[45]*THES*, 2000 June 16.

[46]Review by Philip W. Anderson, Nobel laureate, *THES*, 2000 October 27.

importance was made clear by the report of Lord Phillips on mad cow disease and variant CJD in the United Kingdom.

Other problems may arise. Glasgow University has one of Europe's largest staff engaged to promote commercial research. Some administrative staff engaged as consultants, not as employees, stood to make millions out of the work of university researchers. The AUT branch noted that niversity should be rewarding the people who do the research, not the administrators.[47]

Universities UK welcomed funding for commercialisation projects but warned multiplication of funding competitions was wasteful and should be reviewed. It pointed out that the arts and humanities were frequently and unfairly overlooked by the government in the commercialization exercise.[48]

Universities UK recognizes that university teachers will, as a consequence of the importance of commercialisation, now be judged on three criteria—teaching, research, and the amount of money they attract to the institution. The latter becomes a new performance indicator for academic staff. Universities UK admits this will discriminate against academics in departments with only minor commercial activities, but argues that the negative effects on these departments are offset by the budgets of the research councils, which spend three times as much on traditional research as on entrepreneurial projects. It rejects the view that this approach will encourage routine but profitable exercises such as drug testing at the expense of more fundamental and perhaps in the long term more commercially useful research, arguing that academics will recognize the difference when they judge their peers. In other words, prestige will trump large but routine commercial contracts in the decision-making process on promotions and the like. One does not have to be a cynic to doubt this, particularly if the indicator is to be simply the total amount of cash brought in. Peer evaluators who do not follow the indicator will probably see their judgements overturned on appeal.[49]

One university certainly saw the likely future. Deciding to face reality, the University of Central Lancashire secured a £30,000 grant to teach its academic staff how to win commercial business contracts.

QUALITY ASSURANCE: FROM AAU TO QAA
The Arrival of the QAA

Quality assurance is the device by which the government hopes to ensure efficiency and accountability in the provision of higher education in the United Kingdom. The idea has gone through several mutations over the past decade and is much more controversial than the RAE, mainly

---

[47]*THES*, 2000 October 27.

[48]Universities UK, *Commercialisation funds good news, but could be more efficiently spent*, press release, 2001 April 4.

[49]Interview, *Universities UK*, 2001 March.

because of its onerous bureaucratic demands on academic staff and university administration, and because there is a suspicion the government has wanted to create and to dictate a national curriculum in each subject, thus treating undergraduate education as a three-year extension of secondary school. The definition of quality inevitably becomes the most significant performance indicator for higher education teaching.

Before 1990 there was a patchwork of accrediting agencies—professional accreditation in certain professions, regional accrediting consortia, inter-institutional subject-based networks, an external examination system, and internal quality controls. The polytechnics had their own system. In 1990 the vice-chancellors created the Academic Audit Unit, designed to ensure universities had arrangements to maintain their own quality goals. This plan did not imply direct subject audits. It was too little too late, and a succession of new state agencies appeared.

The work of the AAU on institutional review was taken over by the Higher Education Quality Council (HEQC) which audited institutions, as distinct from departments or faculties, for their quality assurance mechanisms. The HEQC remained under the control of the universities. Subject audits, however, were undertaken by the Division of Quality Audit of the HEFC. It focussed on departments and subjects through the Teaching Quality Assessment (TQA) scheme. TQA proved massively unpopular with individual academics and with university administrations, who argued that the costs in time, cash, and game-playing far exceeded any benefits. The vice-chancellors agreed that the dual nature of quality assessment was cumbersome and should be replaced by a single agency.[50] They got their wish with the creation of the Quality Assurance Agency (QAA), but this has merely provoked more serious attacks.

In 1996 the Conservative government launched a major inquiry into higher education with Sir Ron Dearing (later Lord Dearing) as chair, which reported in July 1997.[51] The Dearing Committee dealt with a great variety of subjects. the most publicized being student fees. It also paid particular attention to performance indicators and quality assessment.[52] The report marked a key change of emphasis from concern with the quality of the educational "process" to concern with outcomes. It recommended threshold standards to specify intellectual characteristics for particular programmes; these would be the new performance indicators. The Dearing Committee wanted common standards, specified and verified through a strengthened external examiner system, but at the same time sought to reduce bureaucratic pressures on the universities. It recommended standardized nomenclature for awards, agreed and common credit points at relevant levels, and inclusion of recognized stopping off points. It did

---

[50]In 1994 and 1996 the HEQC published reports entitled *Learning from the Audit*, which reveal some of the controversy.

[51]*The National Committee of Inquiry into Higher Education* (London: Queen's Printer, 1997) (hereafter *Dearing*).

[52]See *Dearing*, recommendations 22–26.

recognize that the different arrangements in Scottish higher education precluded a completely centralized system of qualifications. Whitehall is just learning the joys of federalism.

There followed significant changes in assessment arrangements. The QAA took over the audit process, thereby eliminating the dual structure. This agency was controlled by the HEFC. It took over the TQA, which became the "subject review,"and subsumed the HEQC's institutional audit functions. It decided to focus on outcomes, as Dearing had recommended, and thereby significantly changed the relevant markers for performance funding.

Performance Indicators and the Code of Practice

The HEFC nevertheless continued to be responsible for the development of performance indicators, which would then become indicators for assessment of institutional merit by the QAA. It set up the Performance Indicator Study Group (PISG), which dismissed the earlier emphasis on descriptive statistics as useful to management but unable to measure performance. It stressed participation of under-represented groups, student progression, learning outcomes and non-completion, efficiency of learning and teaching, student employment, research output, and higher education links with industry. It included a wide range of factors: institutional context; institutional systems and arrangements for quality assurance; design, approval and review of programs of study; teaching, learning and the student experience; student feedback and quality enhancement; faculty appointment, development and promotion; promotional materials for academic programs; validation, franchizing and other forms of collaborative program provision.[53]

In 1999 December it published *Performance indicators in higher education* for the years 1996–97 and 1997–98. The volume dealt only with undergraduates and covered working class access, drop-outs and drop-ins, completion rates, and share of research output per share of research input weighted by cost centre. The intention was to provide greater transparency and to measure performance "… with respect to widening access, student progression, outcomes of learning and teaching, learning and teaching efficiency and research output." The survey covered 175 institutions. It involved extensive consultation with the sector and two years' work by the Performance Indicators Steering Group. This was to be an annual series to which additional indicators will would be added.

The authors recognized that British higher education was so diverse "that no single measure can adequately describe an institution." They hoped that the indicators would, therefore, be taken as a whole, and would identify "good practice." Some of the performance indicators only spell out the obvious. Is anyone surprised that only one per cent of Cambridge undergraduates drop out without getting their degree while the drop out

---

[53]PISG, *Performance Indicators in Higher Education, First Report,* HEFCE, 1999.

rate is 36% at the University of East London? Others are more controversial, such as the assumption that the higher the number of students who complete a programme in the designated period of time, the better and more efficient the education. Critics allege this encourages dumbing down to improve the results. The Dearing Report also noted the difficulty of treating completion rates as a performance indicator: "Non-completions will become an increasingly difficult concept to measure if more students undertake higher education programmes in a flexible way, over a long period of time."[54] It becomes more difficult still if the full-time students need to work ever more part-time hours to earn money for their fees.

In the same year HEFC published *Profiles of higher education institutions,* which listed FTEs by mode and subject group, finance and staff resources, assessment of teaching between 1995 and 1999, and the assessment of research in 1996 with the proportion of the academic staff selected for the exercise, and printed each university's mission statement. Reading these one after the other is not only mind-numbing but suggests that universities quickly learn the language of mindless bureaucracy.[55]

The QAA gradings were based not on absolute standards but on whether the institution met its own self-generated standards. This looked reasonable, since it made little sense to compare Luton and Cambridge, but it meant comparative tables using QAA data could be misleading—for example, giving a premium to those departments which did not aim too high.

The statistical results are not just of interest to the relevant government departments but also form the basis for the various league tables published by British newspapers. These were copied from the United States (where they began in 1983) and are now published by *The Times, The Sunday Times, The Financial Times, The Times Higher,* and *The Guardian.* Despite the disdain of the bureaucrats at the HEFC, they are the most widely publicized indicators in the United Kingdom.

Subsequently the HEFC has developed other performance indicators—for example, on the first destination of graduates. The vice-chancellors strongly objected to the first iteration of this proposed performance indicator. Universities UK noted an institution's reputation affects its graduates' employment rates even if their programs are identical in quality with other institutions. Further, employability is highly dependent on the economic health of the economy in general and the job market in particular, factors beyond the control of the universities and colleges. The bureaucracy also decided that not any job would do. This led to an exercise whereby jobs would be rated by their under-employability.

Nor did a focus on employment six months after graduation take into consideration many students' need to take short-term high-paying jobs to

---

[54]*Dearing,* 3.3.2

[55]Afficionados of mission statements should visit Dilbert's mission statement-generating machine on the Web. See also Scott Adams, *The Dilbert Principle* (New York: HarperBusiness, 1997), 36–7.

pay off debts incurred under the new student fee regime, or that some children of the middle class take more than six months off after graduation. It ignored as well the long-term statistics showing that university graduates did very well in terms of employment, even if they settled for inferior jobs or were unemployed in the short-term. Even in the short-term 94.1% of all graduates were working or in further study or training.[56] In other words, much effort was directed into an exercise which had little real meaning. Neanderthals no doubt hoped the statistics would show serious unemployment for graduates in the humanities, the social sciences, and the fine arts, thus justifying a continuing attack on those subject areas. If so, they were generally disappointed by the results.[57]

The QAA wants to standardize degrees. Said John Randall: "We need a clear framework of qualifications that everyone can understand."[58] In particular, it has criticized many MA arrangements, arguing some have too many undergraduate courses and others (such as certain MAs from Oxford and Cambridge) are purely honorific.[59] Research with employers found a good deal of confusion about what degrees actually meant. It has therefore set up a framework for degrees listing qualifications in various categories from a general BA to a PhD. The QAA claimed the new structure was not a straightjacket, but all universities must adhere to it.

In Scotland this ran into the rock of Scottish nationalism. Six universities use the MA as an undergraduate degree, one year longer than in England and Wales. In the face of attacks of "creeping anglicisation," the QAA retreated and allowed the Scots to set their own arrangements. At the undergraduate level, it wanted to set firm equivalents for all diplomas, and it equated the new two-year foundation degree with an ordinary three-year university degree. There was a vigorous counter-attack, and the QAA withdrew the framework for a month's reconsideration. Ultimately it adopted a revised version, more in harmony with the desires of Universities UK. Some critics suggested that as universities in the United Kingdom moved away from the system whereby graduates are given only a final standing to

---

[56]*The Guardian*, 2001 April 12. These figures did not include those who graduated with diplomas in nursing, midwifery and health visiting as well as in teacher training where graduate employment rates are close to 100%. Letter of John Cater, Director and CEO, Edge Hill College, *THES*, 2001 April 13.

[57]They did, however, indicate that black and ethnic graduates had more difficulty in securing jobs than whites. HEFC, *First set of employment performance indicators show only 6 per cent of graduates are unemployed*, 2001 April 3; AUT, *Academics welcome report on graduate employment*, press release, 2001 April 4; Universities UK, *Employment prospects good for graduates of all universities*, press release, 2001 April 5. Universities UK noted that 86% of graduates between 30 and 34 years of age were employed in professional level occupations.

[58]News release, National qualifications framework for higher education, QAA, London, United Kingdom, 2000.

[59]Oxford and Cambridge argued that since their MA degrees did not involve either teaching or research, they did not come under the jurisdiction of the regulatory authority.

the North American model of student transcripts covering all course work, the need for this framework would considerably diminish.

The QAA developed eight documents to form an all-encompassing Code of Practice for the Assurance of Academic Quality and Standards in Higher Education, adopting 168 rules called "precepts." The QAA argued these were not prescriptive, but insisted that universities will be named and shamed for not following the precepts. The nine areas are:

- university procedures for setting up and monitoring new academic programmes
- student assessment
- collaborative provision
- external examining
- postgraduate research
- complaints procedure
- disability programme approval and monitoring
- career education
- student placements

Institutional reviews, as distinct from subject reviews, would be guided by these precepts.

Accessibility

The Labour government decided to highlight one particular performance indicator: accessibility. Why is it that only that only nine per cent of young people from semi-skilled and unskilled manual backgrounds in the United Kingdom want to go to university? And what can be done about it? That has provoked vigorous but inconclusive debate. So too has the cognate problem—how do you dramatically increase access *and* maintain standards?[60] In this context it seemed ironic that a Labour government should bring in tuition fees and replace student grants with loans (despite a pledge not to do so). Baroness Blackstone, the Labour Minister of State for education and employment, argued imposition of fees had not changed the class structure of the student body, that improved quality in the state schools should increase working class participation in the universities, and that it should be possible to augment working-class access just as it had been possible to raise the number of female students.[61] She noted that from September 2001, 50% of students will not have to pay fees, and that overall students pay only 10% of the costs of their

[60]See for example the debate between Frank Furedi, who argued that attempting to attract students with no interest in higher education undermined quality (THES, 2001 June 29), and Alistair Ross, who said it is unacceptable that 17% of the population from the managerial and professional backgrounds commandeer 60% of university places, and that Universities should strive to ensure that they socially represent the society they serve (THES, 2001 July 6).

[61]Testimony of Baroness Blackstone to the Education and Employment Committee, House of Commons, 2000 July 25, 26.

education.[62] Baroness Warwick, Chief Executive of Universities UK, riposted that although the universities had been successful in dramatically increasing the number of young women from the middle class, they had been much less successful in attracting and keeping students from deprived backgrounds. Widening access, she said, could not be left solely to the universities but required substantial government assistance.

Two studies suggested the problem was not just one of access. Newcastle University concluded that disadvantaged students had to work part-time, resulting in lower marks and decreased socialization, thus further disadvantaging the students.[63] Another difficulty, said Mantz Yorke, professor of education at Liverpool John Moores University, is a rising problem of drop-outs, currently at 17% nationally, which could be solved by increasing grants to the poorest students.[64]

In autumn 2000, the government provided special funds for universities which meet its access targets. The Excellence Challenge Programme added £131 million over three years to the £20 million already promised. David Blunkett, Secretary of State for Education, urged universities to seek private funding as well for bursaries and hardship grants.[65]

Scotland leads the rest of the United Kingdom in widening access. It increased its overall intake for 2000–2001 at a greater rate than the UK average. In part, this comes from the decision of the Scottish government to scrap up-front fees for a contingency repayment scheme and to introduce needs-based bursaries. This in turn suggests that performance indicators for universities are heavily influenced by government policy, and that some of the PIs should be applied to governments rather than higher education institutions.

That the Labour party is schizophrenic on this matter was illustrated by the Chancellor of the Exchequer, who almost simultaneously excoriated Oxford and Cambridge as elitist, then held up Harvard and MIT as models, and provided extra research funds in a manner guaranteed to maintain the elite nature of the major British universities.

By the election of 2001, the Prime Minister seemed to have recognized that the government's policies on accessibility were a failure. This led later in the year to a reconsideration by the government of the fee system and the possible restoration of maintenance grants.[66]

The government also failed to consider the consequences of its combined decisions to set up rewards and penalties for universities depending on their enrolment figures, and to allow the older and richer universities to over-subscribe their intake by four per cent. Not surprisingly, this produced an enrolment crisis in a number of the newer universities,

---

[62]Letter of Baroness Blackstone, *THES*, 2000 December 1.
[63]Robin Humphrey, "Working is a Class Issue," *THES*, 2001 January 19.
[64]*THES*, 2001 January 19, February 2.
[65]*THES*, 2000 December 1.
[66]*THES*, 2001 September 28.

which the government considers to be one of its major tools for increasing accessibility. English universities and colleges alone will lose £35 million. Six have been placed under emergency funding supervision and were required to submit immediate survival plans likely to involve closure of programmes and lay-offs. One of the victims among the older universities was the Imperial College of Science and Technology of the University of London. It is difficult to see how an engineering and science college could substantially increase its intake when the percentage of secondary school studying science and mathematics is declining. The Universities and Colleges Admission Service noted in 2001 a general decline in applications for most areas of science, engineering and mathematics other than in computer science.[67]

Subject Assessment and Benchmarking

Meanwhile the QAA adopted a new approach to subject assessment for 2000 –2001 in Scotland and 2002 January in England and Wales. One aspect of the new system involves benchmark statements for each subject. These were to indicate the aims of each subject and show good practice. Such statements have been created for twenty-two subjects. They represent general expectations about standards for the award of qualifications at a given level, but not the listing of specific knowledge in a subject.

Benchmarking is

> … about the conceptual framework that gives a discipline its coherence and identity; about the intellectual capability and understanding that should be developed through the study of the discipline to the level in question; the techniques and skills which are associated with developing understanding in the discipline; and the intellectual demand and challenge appropriate to study of the discipline to the level in question.

It includes a checklist of skills to be ticked off by the assessors. In philosophy, for example, students should have the "ability to use and understand properly specialized philosophical terminology." In accounting they should demonstrate "skills in recording and summarising transactions and other economic events."[68] The PISG admits such performance indicators in higher education are "complicated and often controversial" and " interpretation of indicators is generally at least as difficult as their instruction."

There is a conundrum here. The more precise benchmarks become, the more they resemble a legislated national curriculum, with all that implies for political orthodoxy; the less precise they are, the more they look like academic hot air.

---

[67]*THES*, 2001 September 7.

[68]QAA, *Benchmarking Academic Standards*, UK, 2000; *THES*, 2000 May 5. There are statements in 22 subject areas. Most QAA documents can be read on the agency's web site at *www.qaa.ac.uk*. See also Helen Smith, Michael Armstrong,and Sally Brown, eds., *Benchmarking and Threshold Standards in Higher Education,* (London: Kogan Paul, 1999) [hereafter *Benchmarking*].

The Times Higher noted that this approach torpedoed the demand by some ministers for a national undergraduate curriculum imposed by the government. It concluded that the subject statements "… are long on things that are largely unmeasurable" and would provide "huge scope for wrangles." The new system would give comfort to the government, enabling ministers to say that standards are being monitored and maintained and that fees are not being wasted. "But the price of providing this comfort in terms of academics' time is truly enormous."[69]

The Association of University Teachers had given a cautious approval to the QAA in 1998, provided it produced "…a significant reduction in the stifling paperwork and administration that is currently wasting the time of our members and the limited resources of their departments and institutions." It suggested there had to be a reasonable balance between development of a national system and the need to protect institutional and professional autonomy as well as academic freedom. It noted that quality and standards can only be maintained if institutions are properly funded, and that the agency would only succeed if it worked on the principle of consensus. It held the initial proposals of the new agency "could provide a more acceptable alternative to teaching quality assessment (TQA) which is over-bureaucratic, unfair and opaque, and which has failed to gain credibility and support among our members."[70] It suggested the governing board of the QAA should be more representative of the higher education community (which did not take place). By the autumn of 2000, it was changing its mind. In September it noted: "The amounts spent on university administration and the amount of red tape is genuinely suffocating good teaching and research…." It protested against the centralization and homogenization of university work inherent in the programme of the QAA.[71]

Others were more scathing. Alison Wolf, one of the leading researchers on assessment in the United Kingdom, said: "Government, industry and quangos all put considerable amounts of money into the idea, and still do. Yet all the research shows it is wrong. It is too top-down, too bureaucratic, too much work and becomes an endless process of rubber stamping rather than learning."[72]

The Conservative Party joined in the opposition, labelling the QAA a hugely bureaucratic agency in need of reform. Others deplored the demand of the QAA for the abolition of honours degree classifications. Still others suggested minimum standards would become maximum standards, with

[69]*THES*, editorial, 2000 May 5.

[70]AUT, *Association response to the Quality Assurance Agency consultation on the New Quality Agenda*, 1998 May 19.

[71]*THES*, 2000 September 8; Stephen Court, "A tale of hard times that is worthy of Dickens," *THES*, 2000 November 17.

[72]Pat Leon, *THES*, 2000 March 31.

everyone teaching to the syllabus,[73] or that benchmarks "might constrain UK higher education to a conventional and outdated approach."[74] Can benchmarks accommodate the idea of changing and improving standards without a significant bureaucratic enterprise to make these judgements? Yet any system must recognize that standards do change, that the standards of the year 2000 cannot be those of 1950 or 1900. Would university departments not learn more from working with two or three other departments in the same field than by appealing to rather vague benchmarking statements?[75]

Difficulties surfaced almost immediately. Both the history and English literature panels refused to adopt the checklist approach, arguing it was too crude for measurement of success in their subjects.[76] In the history world, a Universities Defence Group formed, arguing that this new structure was the beginning of an imposed national curriculum and an attack on autonomy, and that the process trivialized the subject.[77] Roger Brown, Principal of the Southampton Institute and former head of HEQC, agreed that the benchmarks raised questions about diversity and autonomy. University College London announced that it would boycott the process. It was lured back only when promised the QAA would use a "light touch" in assessing established institutions such as University College.

Meanwhile there was considerable criticism of the subject reviews published by the QAA since January 1999—2,460 grades in 410 reports. There were huge variations between disciplines. The QAA gives each university department a grade out of four in each of six aspects of provision, and an aggregated score out of 24. Scores of 22 or more are rated as excellent. The proportion of departments ranking "excellent" varies from 100% in some disciplines to zero in others. Half of all departments are ranked excellent. Excellence is widespread in psychology, physics, and astronomy, as well as in pharmacy and pharmacology, but much rarer in nursing, communications and media studies, dance, drama, and cinematics. The number of high scores has increased dramatically over time, 50% scoring 22 out of 24 points, up from 34% in 1996–98. A study by Harvey Woolf of Wolverhampton University revealed dramatic variations in methods used by different universities to calculate classifications.

---

[73]Sinclair Goodlad, "Benchmarks and Templates—Some Notes and Queries from a Sceptic" in *Benchmarking*, 79.

[74]Armstrong in *Ibid.*, 28.

[75]*Ibid.*, 25–6.

[76]*THES*, 2000 May 5. For a detailed discussion of benchmarking, see Norman Jackson and Helen Lund, eds., *Benchmarking for Higher Education*, Society for Research into Higher Education and the Open University, UK, 2000, and Smith, Armstrong and Brown, *Benchmarking*. Jackson takes the view that benchmarking is inherent in earlier forms of PIs.

[77]*THES*, 2000 June 9. N.Y. Fletcher of the History Department at Essex is the convenor. "It is now clear," he said, "that they [benchmarks] will be used as just the starting point, with explicit programme specifications to follow. There is a risk that this could all become terribly prescriptive." See also letter, *Ibid.*, 2001 April 20.

He put the same set of exam results through different university systems and found variations up to 15%.

In the QAA's subject reviews, only four departments were judged to be failing—the medicine department at Derby, nursing at Liverpool, and the art and design departments at St. Helens and at Wigan and Leigh. These four failures amounted to 0.6% of all reviews. The minimal failure rate suggests the system lacked any sense of proportion. Eyebrows were raised when the QAA gave the Derby programme in pharmacy and pharmacology a perfect score, eighteen months after recommending its closure. "Many critics believe [the increase] is because universities are learning how to impress, or even deceive, peer reviewers."[78] In other words, universities are devoting resources to spin doctoring which might instead go to teaching and research.

Similar results were found in a report commissioned by *The Times Higher*. 60.5% of departments received a grade of excellent in 1998–2000, compared with 33.9% in 1996–98 and 24.8% in 1995–96. The report suggested that, although there had been improvement in standards, much of the increase in grades was the result of improved gamesmanship by the universities, and grade inflation had generally nullified the validity of the TQA. The author noted: "[S]ince the whole process is set against self-created aims and objectives, it has to be vulnerable to the impact of institutions learning how to write these so as to maximise their grades." The report suggests institutions can simply buy top marks through hiring consultants and the like. "It is the triumph of exam technique over genuine ability," said Geoffrey Alderman, a former pro-vice-chancellor for quality at Middlesex University, a TQA reviewer, and now a consultant who provides training to institutions on how to maximise quality grades. "The TQA has given rise to a quality assurance industry, of which I am a part," he wrote. "It's become outdoor relief for underpaid academics."[79]

The combination of the RAE and QAA systems strongly pushes universities to abandon smaller departments, even when their quality is unassailable. Contrary to the view in some political circles that this affects only "fringy" subjects such as fine arts or sociology, it also impacts on such departments as chemistry, physics, advanced mathematics, and many modern languages which do not have nearly the drawing power for private funds enjoyed by the biomedical sciences. Some twenty-one university physics departments have closed in the past seven years.[80] In 1999–2000 a series of universities withdrew language degrees.[81] A

---

[78]*The Guardian Weekly*, 1999 December 9–15.
[79]*THES*, 2001 March 30.
[80]Report of the Institute of Physics 2001, quoted in *THES*, 2001 October 5.
[81]Michael Kelly, "Forget the cultural stuff, just give them the lingo," *THES*, 2000 July 7. Michael Kelly is professor of French at the University of Southampton and Director of the Centre for Languages, Linguistics and Area Studies in the UK Learning and Teaching Support Network.

Nuffield-financed inquiry headed by Sir Trevor MacDonald reported in May 2000 that language teaching in the schools and in higher education was in a woeful state, despite the obvious fact that development of a world economy gave an edge to those who read and spoke more than one language and understood more cultures than their own. The events of September 11th 2001 reinforced the importance of such knowledge. Furthermore universities which evinced an interest in modern languages tended to emphasize speaking skill rather than a rounded knowledge of the language and culture, without which the learning is apt to be ephemeral. The Higher Education Funding Council for England has responded by creating a Minority Subjects Fund which distributed £2.9 million to departments where there were less than 100 specialized students in all of the United Kingdom. These provided small grants mostly in areas involving ancient civilizations and certain languages such as Turkish, Czech, and Norwegian. It did nothing for the main language areas such as Japanese, Chinese, Arabic, Hindi, German, or Russian. The School of Oriental and African Studies (SOAS) at the University of London is the subject of a separate inquiry.

Roger Brown, former head of the HEQC, noted another possible perverse result: in order to avoid duplication and cost, universities may be forced to abandon their long-standing external examiner regimes and rely solely on the QAA, even though one of the express goals of the QAA is to strengthen local procedures rather than undermining them. He argued there are real questions about whether the material gathered will be useful to students in choosing a university course, one of the justifications of the audit culture. The data will *not* be useful, he suggests, because the information will be rapidly out of date, of questionable value, and at such a level of generalization that it will not help those wishing to choose a particular course. Prospective law students in 2009, for example, will have to rely on data gathered in 2002.

Others pointed out the QAA lacks a proper complaints and appeal structure, and has no mechanism for regular independent review of its own operations. In the United States, universities who challenge serious negative findings by accreditors can secure arbitration through the Council for Higher Education Accreditation.[82]

In Scotland another problem developed: how to administer a system of external reviews in a highly competitive but small university system where everyone knew everyone else. In 1997–98 there were 140,000 full-time equivalent students in twenty-one higher education institutions, thirteen of them universities. The system relies on both Scottish and "foreign" examiners.

---

[82]Letters of Andrew J. Morgan, and Andy Ross, *THES,* 2001 January 19, letter of Geoffrey Alderman.

[The use of Scottish examiners] has heightened the competitiveness issue because such individuals have been assessing operations and programs in institutions with which their own institutions are in competition for students... it is, after all, only human nature to be somewhat reluctant to concede competitive advantage by awarding higher grades to direct competitors...

Exclusive use of foreigners would be prohibitively expensive. On the other hand, Carter and Davidson noted:

There is little doubt that the introduction and implementation of such procedures in all Scottish higher education institutions has done much to generate an explicit concern with the quality of teaching and learning, and has resulted in greater recognition that all institutions are accountable for the quality of the educational experiences they offer.[83]

Geoffrey Squires, reader in education at the University of Hull, argued the reviews had indeed reduced sloppy administration and classroom work but put the emphasis on "organisational tidiness and pedagogical explicitness," thereby losing touch with the real object of teaching, namely learning.[84]

John Randall, head of the QAA, replied to the critics:

Academic review is the product of extensive consultation involving the participation of thousands of academics and the canvassing of the views of employers and other stakeholders. I believe that we now have a system that is capable of commanding confidence both of the academic community and of the wider society that it serves.[85]

He was backed by Education Secretary David Blunkett, who said:

We have published a great deal of valuable information, and I pay tribute to the work of the QAA. It has rightly attracted international respect."[86]

Academics such as David Sadler, head of politics at Simon De Montfort University, defended the process, arguing the benefits were substantial, "that the quality of the student experience has gone up in reviewed departments," and that the process needs to continue, and not just for departments with low scores.[87]

The QAA has responded to some of the criticisms by announcing replacement of the numerical judgements by three categories—failing, approved, commendable; within the latter category reviewers may identify specific features deemed exemplary. Some hoped that this would make it more difficult to construct misleading league tables but that hope is probably ill-founded.

One area where the QAA has taken vigorous and useful action is with the extensive overseas operations of British universities. It warned Staffordshire University that a review of its partnership with the Dublin Institute of

---

[83]Chris Carter and Alan Davidson, "Quality Assurance in Scottish Higher Education," *New Directions for Institutional Research*, 99 (1998 Fall).
[84]Geoffrey Squires, "Inspectors' lives after Woodhead," *THES*, 2000 November 10.
[85]*THES.*, 2000 May 5.
[86]*THES*, 2001 March 30.
[87]*Ibid.*

Technology in Ireland showed its academic standards were safeguarded more by chance than by design. It criticized examination arrangements of Exeter University for a programme in Spain, and investigated the operations of the University of Derby in Israel. In addition, the National Audit Office has critically examined Hull University's business school including arrangements for courses in Malaysia. *The Times Higher* has recognized that "[A]a desperate hunt for additional revenue led a number of universities into overseas ventures that were poorly managed."[88] All this suggests that the QAA should play a significant role in overseeing the academic ventures of British universities overseas, in order to protect especially vulnerable foreign students and to maintain the prestige of British degrees. However, a code of ethics for foreign student advisers came not from the QAA but from the United Kingdom Council for Overseas Student Affairs and the Association of International Student Advisers.

The Life of Grunge

One of the main overall charges against the combined system of QAA and RAE is the life of grunge it creates. Academics, *The Times Higher* noted in May 2000, are part of the over-work culture "with all the grunge of grant applications, teaching assessments, diary exercises, etc." Stephen Court of the AUT wrote about a revival of the spirit of Thomas Gradgrind—the inflexible, dry and dictatorial system described by Dickens in *Hard Times*, now applied to the universities.[89] The government had inadvertently helped to prove the point by demanding universities separate teaching and research in their accounting. Preliminary results of a detailed survey of academic staff time showed most academics worked a six-day 55-hour work week in term time and 53 hours a week in working vacations; these figures rose to 70 hours at the top end, excluding "thinking time" away from the desk or office. This demonstrated that "unpaid slog sustains research," quite the opposite of what the Treasury wanted to prove, and indicated the damage that may be done through disaffection among researchers.[90] This ever-growing bureaucracy is being installed while universities face limited increases to their operating expenses, after more than a decade of vigorous cuts, and while academics find that their salaries fall further and further behind those in other sectors. As Lord Dearing told the House of Lords: "You cannot exploit people indefinitely and continue to be world class. We have exploited our past and our people."[91]

---

[88]*THES*, 2000 June 16.

[89]*THES*, 2000 November 12.

[90]*THES*, 2000 May 12. In order to respond to the Treasury view that teaching and research are separate matters that should be separately funded, the HEFC commissioned a report from JM Consulting showing that research and teaching in the university were integrally connected. *THES*, 2000 June 2; a survey of 2,600 academics in 15 universities in Australia found much the same workload results, *THES*, 2000 July 14.

[91]*THES*, 2000 June 16.

The most remarkable symbol of the audit culture was the decision to require many academics to keep 24-hour diaries of their activities. Would the QAA ultimately regulate the hours of sleep of the academic staff? These diaries are an old Treasury manoeuvre first used in the 1870s at the Royal College in Dublin in order to divide the scientific staff. The UGC resurrected the idea in the 1970s, but since the diaries showed lecturers averaged 50 hours per week, no more was heard of this approach until the QAA came on the scene.[92] Some NAFTHE branches refused to carry out the exercise, arguing it was a violation of their terms and conditions of work.

Another aspect of the life of grunge for many academics is casualisation of university labour. British universities more and more resemble the doughnut beloved of business schools—a small core of permanent managers within a large circle of casual labour. For example, for all staff in employment in 1995 and appointed before 1990, 86% were on permanent contracts, 13% fixed term, and 1% hourly or casual. But for staff appointed in 1994–95, 22% were permanent, 74% fixed term, and 3% hourly or casual.[93]

As THES noted, abolition of the British form of tenure was supposed to make British universities more likely to give people permanent jobs (because it would be easier to make them redundant in hard times). It did not work out that way, and university management chose the route of casual labour rather than axe courses, close departments and declare redundancies. It is simply easier in administrative terms, even with the powers the new legislation gave the management, to use casual labour than to close programmes. The editors noted higher education is second only to catering in the proportion of non-permanent staff employed.

Exploitation has in turn persuaded more and more able young people to turn to careers where they are treated better. Women are disproportionally affected by casual status. So too is the work of departments. Those hired to teach by the hour do not stay around to consult with students or to do the administrative work of the department, which falls on to the shrinking core of permanent academic staff. Casual teachers rarely have offices, email, or a phone, and are thus uncontactable. Nor are they paid for preparation time or, in some places, for supervising exams and marking. Unpaid labour does not pay the rent.[94] The government will soon be in contravention of the European regulations for fixed term workers. This European directive aims at ensuring that fixed term employees are treated as fairly as permanent employees. It requires terms and conditions for such workers no less favourable than for permanent employees, unless objective justification can be provided; that successive renewals should be restricted;

---

[92]Letter of H.C.S. Ferguson, THES, 2001 May 18.
[93]Stephen Court, "Memories of Jobs for Life," CAUT Bulletin, 1998 March.
[94]THES, 2001 April 27. THES noted the case of Clare Goodess of the Climatic Research Unit at the University of East Anglia who had had 54 contracts between 1982 and 2001 before getting a permanent appointment.

and that employers should inform fixed-term employees of permanent jobs available and provide access to appropriate training. This directive would make a useful performance indicator for the university world, but no one expects the Blair government to do anything other than water it down or ignore it. It is hard to see, said one lecturer, how one can dedicate oneself to motivate students for lifelong learning when one's own opportunities are not even career-long.[95] By the end of 2001 the research councils had noted a significant drop in postgraduate student enrolment and were wondering what to do about it since this had serious implications for the future supply of British researchers.

Meanwhile the government is in another difficulty in the college sector, where its incentives persuaded some institutions to lower quality. NAFTHE has charged colleges with recruiting students beyond their capacity to win recruitment funding, then allowing demotivated and disruptive students to remain in class so the colleges can collect retention cash. NAFTHE contended that the new philosophy was "bums on benches brings us banknotes," noting as evidence that new workload rules at the University of Lincolnshire and Humberside meant faculty will have five minutes to mark each post-graduate exam script where the old rule allowed twelve minutes. The consequences for staff morale are obvious. The Vice-Chancellor strongly objected to NAFTHE's criticism, saying the new rules were open to negotiation. A social democratic government committed to Thatcherite principles should not be surprised at how the market works.

There are worries about how to find persons willing to do external reviews and to mark external exams. Indeed, the head of the Scottish Qualifications Authority, Ron Tuck, speculated at his annual meeting that computers would have to replace individuals as markers and assessors. As a first step the Scottish Qualifications Authority (SQA) wants to create large banks of pre-tested assessment material in all subject areas, on which staff designing exams could draw. Can standard machine-marked exams be very far away? And ossification be very far behind?

Hugo Radice, director of Leeds University Centre for Russian, Eurasian and Central European Studies, suggested the British model more and more resembled the old Soviet command economy:

> Our activities take place within a rigid hierarchy than runs up through the head of department to the school, faculty, the university as a whole, and thence to the Higher Education Funding Council for England, the functional equivalent of Gosplan, the high command of the Soviet planning system.... Our task is not to generate high quality of learning and teaching but to satisfy the current demands of the quality inspection system, which means producing a Potemkin village, paint scarcely dry on the walls, for the week of inspection by the Quality Assurance Agency.[96]

---

[95]Letter of Kathryn Ecclestone, University of Newcastle, *ibid.*, 2001 May 4.
[96]*THES*, 2001 March 2.

THE COST OF THE REGULATORY REGIME

The cost of all this remains a controversial matter in both England and Scotland. There has been a growing volume of complaint not only about the actual cash costs involved but about the amount of time demanded of everyone to comply with a variety of quality exercises. Are "vibrant and highly successful universities being buried in paperwork or strangled in red tape designed primarily to bind the feet of a few villains?"[97] The expansion of the university system raised the question of whether the external examiner system could be effectively maintained without external examining itself becoming a major industry. Although the AUT welcomed "any serious attempts to improve the quality of teaching and research in UK higher education," it suggested the government's concern was brought about by its repeated cuts to higher education spending. It questioned whether the cost of regulation should continue to be top-sliced from the money which would otherwise be spent on teaching and research.[98]

The last RAE exercise for the United Kingdom cost £27 million, not including local staff time. In August 2000 the HEFC published an outside report on costs which showed the quality bureaucracy costs £250 million a year.[99] This does not include non-quantifiable behavioural costs such as institutional game-playing for audits and multiple research bids, planning uncertainties, and staff stress. A single subject review by the QAA costs between £40,000 and £200,000, not including time spent by department-based subject teams. The report noted the subject structure of the QAA did not sufficiently take into account the problems raised in inter-disciplinary programs. "With some 'subjects' crossing schools and even faculties (e.g. subjects allied to medicine), large costs are incurred in attempting to align the various components of the artificially simulated subject areas." The report included a dramatic picture of the wall of paperwork required for a single subject review at the University of Leeds.[100] Unsurprisingly, the QAA cast doubt on the reliability of the figures in the report, dismissing them as "guesstimates" and saying the institutions themselves may be to blame for excessive costs.

The HEFC report agreed accountability was necessary but argued the current system was characterized by duplication, confusion, and conflicting demands. It suggested a less interventionist approach based on an investor/partnership model with the universities whereby both the universities and the central agencies could see benefits. It applied the "Modernising Govern-

---

[97] Goodlad in *Benchmarking*, 79.

[98] Association of University Teachers, *Higher education: preparing for the 21st century* (London: AUT, 1995).

[99] PA Consulting Group 2000, *Better accountability for higher education,* HEFC, UK, 2000; Phil Baty, "Millions go down drain in audit fiasco," *THES*, 2000 August 4.

[100] The report notes that all undergraduate programmes at University of Leeds are reviewed annually at a cost of £1 million a year in staff time because that is demanded by the QAA, whereas it would prefer biennial reviews, thereby saving £500,000.

ment agenda" by suggesting the current arrangements be reviewed on the basis of four principles:

- measure what matters
- clarify relationships
- seek mutual benefits
- add value

One suggested result was that the central agencies would place greater reliance on the management controls of each university, provided the universities created appropriate and transparent internal assurance mechanisms. Would this mean a return of the original terms of reference of the AAU in 1990? That would indeed mark the arrival of Thermidor after a decade of Jacobin excess.

At virtually the same time the HEFC published another report, *Diversity in Higher Education,* which acknowledged that the homogenizing and conservative effect of the accountability process lessened both diversity and risk-taking in the sector.[101] This is directly at odds with government policy as stated in its science white paper *Excellence and Opportunity*: "We want to see a diversity of excellence in universities, with universities adopting a variety of missions building on their strengths." This is difficult to square with the government's enthusiasm for highly centralized and ever more detailed performance indicators set out in league tables.

The report noted the cost of bidding grew because the government preferred to supply funds for an ever-increasing series of special projects rather than general funds. This resulted in "positional planning," defined by one vice-chancellor as follows:

> The strategic plans submitted to HEFC are not the strategic plans of the institution. They are bidding documents to position ourselves in anticipation of when the inevitable 'special initiatives' come around.

The Vice-Chancellor of Leeds Metropolitan University noted the increased use of competitive bidding for ever smaller sums of money—a process which he suggested was not cost effective. The report noted the costs of game-playing created by the RAE exercise, for example, "tactically shifting research staff between departments to optimise RAE scores." Other vice-chancellors alleged that it sometimes cost more to bid for particular programs than they in fact received.

At times one side of the Department of Education knows not what the other is doing. At the primary and secondary school level, the Labour government has discovered that the time-consuming bidding process for funds it imposed on the system encouraged schools to spend their money on spin doctors rather than teachers. As one head teacher commented:

---

[101]*THES,* 2000 August 11; see also Richard Brown and Gareth Williams, "A reason to play to strengths," *THES,* 2000 August 18; Sheldon Rothblatt, "Of Babies and Bathwater," *THES,* 2001 January 19.

Among my concerns is the fact that, too often, we are forced into a time-consuming bidding process, which leads many schools to employ consultants in an effort to maximise their chances of being successful... That really can't be right.[102]

As a consequence the Chancellor announced in the 2000 and 2001 budgets that schools would receive direct cash grants worth £100 million in 2001 to spend however they wished, provided the funds go broadly to raising standards in spending on books, equipment, and staff. The Education Secretary seemed to recognize this in April 2001, when he decided that the £330 million promised to the universities the previous November could be distributed as the institutions saw fit—including pay raises. This contradicted the original announcement that the money was to be used to improve human resources structures, and the publication by the HEFC of yet another bidding competition for funds designed for training, equal opportunities, and to meet the cost of performance indicators.

The report on costs noted that universities must submit detailed information to the quality audit of QAA, supply increasing financial statistics to HEFC, and student statistics for the Higher Education Statistics Agency as well as meeting the growing demand for data from research councils, the Teacher Training Agency, European Union agencies, the National Health Service, and external stakeholders. It reported a "lack of mutual understanding and trust" between the universities and the central agencies. In fact, many commentators have noted that universities now regard all requests from such authorities as preludes to another attack, and have learned to play the game so that all data is minutely massaged at considerable cost to ensure the best possible face put upon them—spin doctors come to the universities, with all the costs such visits entail. The report noted how the central authorities demanded reporting in the most minute detail despite the infrequency of administrative lapses in the sector and the "minor nature of those problems which have occurred." "[D]o the tangible results," the report asks, "justify the cost of reforms?" Sir Alec Broers, Vice-Chancellor of Cambridge, argued in a speech in Australia that the existing British assessment system depressed morale by introducing an atmosphere of distrust.[103]

Roger Brown, former head of the HEQC, argued one of the depressing features of the long quality debate was the failure not only to estimate real

---

[102]*The Guardian,* 2001 March 8.

[103]*THES,* 2000 September 15. Peter Knight, the Vice-Chancellor of the University of Central England, argued there was an unholy alliance between Universities UK and the Labour government whereby the vice-chancellors would not whinge about student debt or bureaucratic overkill in the regulatory schemes, in return for introduction of the recommendations of the Dearing Report. When the time came, the government cherry-picked the Dearing Report so that the government got what it wanted but the vice-chancellors did not. The government additionally failed to answer the questions of student debt and regulatory bureaucracy. Peter Knight, "What's in a name?" *THES,* 2000 December 1.

costs including opportunity costs (mainly staff time), but also to consider whether the costs are justified by the benefits or whether they have raised or even protected quality and standards.[104]

John Randall told the House of Commons education select committee it was naive to expect those subject to scrutiny to welcome it, but admitted there were some valid criticisms which the agency would try to correct. He noted that the universities estimate a review of a single department could cost £250,000. He promised a new, integrated system with visits spread over time, reviewers who would deal with naturally-arising evidence rather than artificial assembly of evidence, and external reviews timed to coincide with internal reviews. However, he suggested, complaints about bureaucracy are frequently a smokescreen for objections to the whole scheme of evaluation, and labelled most critics "elitists."

To reduce unnecessary bureaucracy, the QAA said it would concentrate its resources on institutions that officials deemed at highest risk while treating the best universities with a "light touch." Previously published subject reviews, institutional audits, and other relevant available information would establish the scrutiny to which each institution would be subject. For 2001 it would prepare a profile of each institution, to be shared but not published, which will form the basis for negotiations with individual institutions concerning scrutiny. Critics fear secret deals will invalidate the reports. Roger Brown, former chief executive of the QAA's predecessor, warned: "Judgments will be made by agency officials against criteria that are not yet clear, using reports that were written for a different purpose, which are at best historical, and many of which fail basic tests of validity and reliability."[105] The rapidity with which the QAA responded to the boycott by University College London by promising a light touch for that institution only increased academic cynicism about the process.

THE IDES OF MARCH

Open revolt broke out in March 2001, the only surprise being that it took so long. The temporizing steps of the QAA noted above completely failed to anticipate the scale of the unrest. The London School of Economics led the way, but the signs were already there in the contretemps between University College London and the QAA. Then King's College London disowned its QAA report, claiming the agency failed to engage intellectually with the college. LSE decided simply to leave the system. Its Academic Board passed a resolution stating the QAA had infringed academic freedom, imposed its own bureaucratic and pedagogic agenda, neglected student intellectual development, and used incompetent and unprofessional reviewers. It called the new benchmarking regime an insult which would exacerbate the

---

[104]Roger Brown, "The New UK Quality Framework," *Higher Education Quarterly*, 54, 4 (2000 October).

[105]*THES*, 2000 May 26.

problems and increase emphasis on bureaucratic models favoured by the agency. It proposed, if necessary, that the older universities form their own quality assurance system. Within a few weeks, LSE was joined by University College London, Oxford, Cambridge, Edinburgh, and Birmingham, who engaged in discussions to set up their own quality assurance mechanisms and to secede from the QAA.

Lewis Elton, professor of higher education at University College London, was one of the academics who provided the intellectual framework for this rebellion. He had argued for some time that universities should return to a modified form of the original academic audit set up by the vice-chancellors, one owned and managed by the universities. The "quality processes" of universities should be audited externally and "audit trails" used to investigate what suspicions might arise. A new audit arrangement of this kind could include such matters as well-funded and benign appraisals; associated professional development arrangements, with sanctions for those who show they cannot be trusted to take advantage of them; encouragement of innovation; effective change management; and rewards for teaching excellence. These steps would avoid the problems of earlier audit arrangements set up by the vice-chancellors, which proved too ready to accept the status quo. The new arrangement would not only be cheaper and less intrusive but would be based on trust. "It gives academics the responsibility for maintaining and improving quality and discourages the undignified but increasing compliance culture in universities." The audit would be used mainly where this trust was abused.[106] Elton suggested this regime might actually be tougher on departments than the existing compliance regime of the QAA.

HEFC and the QAA went into damage control mode. John Randall, chief executive of the QAA, claimed the agency had committed itself to a lighter touch. It proposed to cut burdens by working more closely with existing local quality assurance arrangements and by varying the intensity based on the institution's record. The HEFC said that it was negotiating its contract with the QAA to ensure a lighter touch. It turned out that exempted departments would still have to prepare new self-evaluation documents to be judged by QAA inspectors. All universities would remain subject to the QAA's institution-wide audits, which will involve 200 new rules in eleven quality assurance codes of practice, impose a strict new qualifications framework, and will make universities conform to programme specifications and subject benchmarks.

The AUT called the QAA changes too little, too late. It asked the Better Regulations Task Force to review the quality audit structure. David Triesman, general secretary of the AUT, said quality assurance was a suitable subject for review by the Task Force and that the QAA would be unlikely to survive a review in its current form: "The task force has five government-

[106]Letters of Lewis Elton, *THES*, 2001 March 30, April 6.

backed principles of good regulation, and the QAA does not adhere to a single one of them." "The degree of bureaucracy," said the AUT, "is out of proportion to the issues it is designed to address," since, after more than 2000 visits to academic departments, the quality observed was with very few exceptions either excellent, satisfactory, or approved.

The AUT demanded "a process which combines a strengthened version of the long-established external examining system with a national system of quality audit," with the latter using a sampling approach. Support came from the editors of *The Times Higher*.[107] The House of Commons select committee on education and employment issued a report which highlighted the burden of QAA inspections and noted casualisation meant lecturers had much less time to devote to students, particularly outside of classroom hours.

NAFTHE joined in, announcing a proposal for the boycotting of "all QAA and QAA-related visits and procedures" would be put to its annual conference in May 2001.

Soon after the QAA announcements, Education Secretary David Blunkett said he had decided the so-called "light touch" was not sufficient and had ordered the QAA to cut inspections by 40%, even though the results of the trial run in Scotland of the new system involving bench marking had neither been completed or evaluated. All departments receiving good scores would be exempt from the next round of inspection, though there would still be sampling in order to provide a benchmark of good practice. Blunkett took these steps without consultation with the QAA, and appeared to be making a concession to the older universities who had recently lost their battle with the central government over top-up fees. The intervention of the Education Secretary was decisive, providing the cover for the HEFC and Universities UK to demand the QAA abandon universal inspection.

John Randall, the QAA chief executive, warned the new system could be open to judicial review, and would lack legitimacy if it were rushed through. The Chair of the QAA wrote to HEFC: "I will not conceal my disappointment at the latest turn of events."[108] A second letter made it clear that the QAA would continue with the existing arrangements well into the next year, held that new dispensation applied only to England, and raised a host of questions and problems about the new approach.[109] The bureaucracy was prepared to fight back.[110] Later in April the Board of the QAA put a good face on the matter, announcing it had all along intended

[107]*THES*, 2001 March 30; see also AUT, *At the heart of the UK: speaking up for higher education*, AUT election manifesto, 2001, recommendation no.2

[108]Christopher Kenyon (QAA) to Brian Fender (HEFCE), 2001 March 26; *THES*, 2001 March; for the implementation of sampling, see HEFCE website for HEFC, Universities UK, SCOP, *Quality Assurance in Higher Education: Delivering Lightness of Touch*, March 2001, HEFCE web site.

[109]John Randall (QAA) to Stephen Marston (HEFCE), 26 March 2001, QAA website.

[110]For the view in detail of the bureaucracy, see QAAHE, *Future Strategy*, 2001 April 1. This is a background document of 14 pages prepared by the staff for a meeting of the QAAHE Board.

in the medium term to shift away from universal review, but grumbled that "there was a flavour of self-interest over public interest in some of the comments that had appeared in the educational press."[111]

Universities UK welcomed the announcement as a step in the right direction in tackling the issue of accountability costs.[112] The annual meetings of AUT and NAFTHE took a strong line against the QAA. AUT delegates voted to boycott the review process and to withdraw from the review teams after John Randall had mocked what he called their previous and ineffective war-like noises. NAFTHE called for abolition of the agency and for a new regime that would "lead to a real rather than a fictitious improvement." Qaulity enhancement, it said, should be linked to proper resources. The hostility of the unions was a serious matter for the QAA because the union membership supplies the evaluators for the agency.

Even the retiring Permanent Secretary at the Department of Education and Employment, Sir Michael Bichard, admitted to a risk of government policies becoming overly prescriptive. On becoming Rector of the London Institute, he said he had discovered just how bureaucratic exercises such as the TQA actually were and that he wished to see red tape reduced. British academics could only marvel at how out of touch a Permanent Secretary could be.

Randall subsequently resigned as head of the QAA and began a campaign to defend regulation as a defence of consumers while at the same time casting doubt on the standards of the older universities. He found some support from the National Union of Students and from the Liberal Democrats. He particularly singled out Leeds for attack, no doubt remembering that devastating picture of a wall of files demanded by the QAA which the university had supplied to the media.

Re-election of the Labour government in the spring of 2001 brought a new minister, Margaret Hodge, who hinted she would go back on the promise to lighten the QAA load. She spoke of her dissatisfaction with the teaching she received at LSE as a student and announced that demonstrating quality teaching would be a high priority for the new government. She said students would take a keener interest in the QAA in the future and that it would become as accepted in the universities as Office for Standards in Education (Ofsted), the office responsible for standards in primary and secondary schools, was by parents of school children.

The Times Higher reported a deluge of abusive mail in response to the Minister. An editorial called the current arrangements unacceptable because "over-intrusive and bureaucratic and give rise to game playing." It suggested the QAA had too many different tasks—to inform students, to make the universities accountable to the taxpayers, to improve teaching in higher

---

[111]QAA, *Subject review in England—delivering lightness of touch. Statement on response of the Board to 'Future Strategy' paper*, 2001 April 18, QAA website.

[112]Universities UK, *Universities Welcome Blunkett Pledge on "lighter touch,"* press release, 2001 March 21.

education, to standardize degrees and to kite-mark institutions that are selling their services on the international market.[113]

As if to illustrate the problems with the QAA, the results of the subject review in thirteen philosophy departments resulted in ten with the maximum score of 24 out of 24, two at 23, and one at 22. There were charges of a philosophy cartel at work to defend a small-scale subject frequently under attack by budget cutters. One commentator said "I suspect the philosophers are poking fun at the entire methodology." The reviewers replied: "There is, of course, another possible explanation... namely that their provision is indeed excellent." Nor, they said, should this be surprising, since philosophy departments are small, well established, and have an ethos where faculty and students talk to each other.[114] But does anyone really know what the rankings mean?

The die had been cast against the QAA. Universities UK seized the moment and negotiated with the HEFC (England) on the basis of the previous Minister's commitment to reduce oversight of top-rated programmes. By the end of June 2001 a new blueprint had been agreed to commence in 2002. The new regime will emphasize audits of institution-wide quality assurance mechanisms, to establish risk and whether or not universities will be inspected at the subject level. This is expected to reduce inspections by more than the 40% promised by David Blunkett. It also looked more and more like a retreat to the regime run by the vice-chancellors in the early nineties. The government, after hearing bitter criticism at the Labour Party and TUC (Trades Union Council) annual conferences, also agreed to turn the Better Regulation Task Force on to the universities as recommended by the AUT. The Scots went further, ditched the subject review scheduled for 2002, and abandoned subject review entirely except in two new universities.[115]

In case British academics thought they had won the war against the bureaucracy, they were immediately faced with a new governmental initiative, namely performance pay. There had been hints of this before the attack on the QAA.

Academics had suspected for some time the government had plans to expand rather than reduce regulation. It had launched a £1 billion scheme for performance pay in the schools, and said it would require performance pay for further education colleges. The Minister was roundly booed when he announced the government action at a meeting of NAFTHE, the latter calling the scheme "obnoxious and demeaning, divisive, discriminatory and unfair." Can the universities be far behind, particularly when an HEFC document in December 2000 announced, as part of the "something for

[113]*THES*, 2001 June 22.
[114]*THES*, 2001 June 22, 29.
[115]*THES*, 2001 December 7.

something" approach, that extra funding would depend upon "annual performance reviews of all staff"?[116]

The government further decreed that quality will be maintained in the further education sector by employment of the school inspectorate, starting in 2001. This will involve inspection of all curriculum areas, not just a sample, through the use of school inspectors and specially recruited part-time inspectors.[117] In addition, the new Learning and Skills Council to oversee further education will require colleges to give up a large part of their autonomy in favour of local planning. Colin Flint, the Principal of Solihull College, noted the government had originally intended to put the universities under the Learning and Skills Council. "Universities might take a careful look at what has happened to further education because it still might happen to them."[118]

In the spring of 2001, outgoing president of Universities UK and incoming president of HEFCE Sir Howard Newby said university staff would have to accept performance pay as measured by appraisal if they want salary increases. *The Times Higher* said that "there can be no other industry in which output could have increased so much in recent years with so paltry an increase in staff numbers or pay." Academics should be paid for productivity increases before any performance system is set up. The AUT echoed this line. NAFTHE denounced performance pay as destructive of honest and reasonable appraisal. Roger Numas of Brighton University called it "a devious and dubious substitute for a decent basic salary.[119] Brian Towers, a professor of industrial relations at Nottingham Trent's school of business, said the issue was explosive and would leave the sector in turmoil:

> People agree with the principle that the harder you work, the more you get paid. The problem is that systems get corrupted and favouritism emerges. ... Success in working environments depends on teamwork. Performance-related pay is an individual exercise so that it has the potential to interrupt teamwork and destroy it.... There is enough evidence to make the government pause. Performance-related pay is often a mistake and to rush into it is quite wrong. Its introduction seems to be more about power and screwing down the universities rather than liberating them. In policy terms, [performance-related pay] would be a serious error.[120]

Since the British government has marched from folly to folly in higher education policy with little or no thought for the consequences, it would be romantic to assume it would engage in rational discussion about its latest enthusiasm.

---

[116]HEFCE, "HEFCE consults on extra funding to reward, retain and develop staff in higher education," press release, 2000 December 20.

[117]Speech of Chris Woodhead, chief inspector of Ofsted, *THES*, 2000 June 30. Woodhead resigned in late 2000.

[118]Colin Flint, "Come the Revolution," *THES*, 2000 November 17.

[119]*THES*, 2001 June 29.

[120]*THES*, 2001 June 22.

Rewarding Excellence in Teaching

Another and, some would say. better route to excellence is to spend money encouraging teaching excellence rather than on assessment, regulation and punishment. The central government did come to realize the importance of positive encouragement of good teaching but never put money into this enterprise on the scale of its inspection and punishment approach. Nor did it initially develop an effective working relationship with the AUT, indispensable for success.

The HEFCE created a Teaching Quality Enhancement Fund, with a current budget of £30 million. The Fund is to reward universities which adopted creative policies to enhance the quality of teaching, although the hand of the civil service could be seen in the requirement that funding be based on progress toward "measurable targets and outcomes."[121]

In 1998 the government encouraged creation of a university teachers' college called the Institute for Learning and Teaching, intended to welcome and to judge applications from individual teachers. The idea was to create a body independent of government, and controlled by its members. By July 2001 there were 5,400 members. The Institute awards small grants for teaching and learning projects, and forty national teaching fellowships of £50,000 each, the money allocated by the HEFCE.

Critics suggested teaching was not simply an individual matter but also a departmental one, and that departments should be able to apply, particularly those departments with a high level of approbation from the QAA. These difficulties soon drew the Institute into conflict with the AUT, which at one point decided to withdraw co-operation and consider setting up its own, modelled on that of the General Medical Council. The AUT saw the Institute as too bureaucratic and too costly and said it would take all possible steps to prevent any agency such as the QAA or the teaching inspectorate from claiming authority to regulate professional accreditation for university teachers. In April 2001 the AUT published a preliminary paper indicating how it would proceed to a fully functioning system by October 2002. The annual meeting, however, had reservations, and the AUT executive indicated it would negotiate with the new chair of the Institute, Sir Kenneth Calman, Vice-Chancellor of Durham University, and report back in December 2001.

There was considerable division as well, especially in NAFTHE, over a proposal for a £1,000 Institute for Learning and Teaching (ILT) incentive scheme. This was narrowly supported at the union's annual meeting, but the chair described it as a bribe that would discriminate against the vast majority of the membership who rejected the ILT.[122] Nevertheless the idea of such a university teachers' college has evident support in the pro-

---

[121]HEFCE, *Circular Letter 15/00*, 2000.
[122]*THES*, Letter of Tom Wilson, 8 June 2001; letter of Tom Hickey, 2001 June 15.

fession, provided the details of its function can be worked out with all interested parties.

The HEFCE also supported the Learning and Teaching Support Network, formed in 2000 to create 24 centres based on university subjects to develop networking and teaching in those subjects. The philosophy and religious studies centre was based at Leeds, psychology at York, law at Warwick, and history at Glasgow. Universities hosting such centres had to match the government's funds in cash or kind, which in the case of geography, earth and environmental sciences was £270,000. The work will be done through web sites, consultancies, commissioned research, and newsletters, with each centre pursuing its own preferred model.

Programme Director Cliff Alan noted that the Learning and Teaching Support Network (LTSN) provides "an antidote fo regulation.... [The] agendas are being influenced by practitioners—they are seen to be about 'caring and sharing' in contrast to the QAA's 'naming and shaming.'" Allan rejected a suggestion by the *Times Higher* and others that the LTSN might take on the regulatory work of the QAA, saying that "would be the kiss of death for any subject centre... trying to build support and development networks in subject communities."[123] This approach to better teaching could be quite useful—particularly since it is based on the dissemination of good practice—provided the centres maintain a pluralistic view of their subjects.

David Triesman, General Secretary of the AUT, suggested that the QAA be abolished altogether: "This Frankenstein's monster needs to be slain and its component parts returned to agencies better equipped to serve universities." The LTSN could take responsibility for quality based on dissemination of good practice. Degree standards could be assured by a properly funded external examiner system. The Higher Education Staff Development Agency could provide advice on peer review. A slimmed-down QAA could deal with institutional instead of subject audits.

By and large the British system of performance indicators and performance funding is a story of horror—a persuasive case that serves to warn other jurisdictions about what will happen if they set up similar structures.

Yet in the end it may be the market which destroys the United Kingdom's bureaucratic vision of the university, its world of highly-paid tenured administrators and more and more numerous non-permanent academics. Faculty projections in the United States and Canada suggest a decade of serious shortages of faculty that cannot be met by North American graduate schools, at least as matters stand. As a consequence the brain drain from the United Kingdom will accelerate—until politicians learn one of the most important performance indicators is how well they treat their academic staff.[124]

---

[123]Letter of Cliff Alan, THES, 2001 July 13.
[124]Sinclair Goodlad of the Imperial College of Science, Technology and Medicine has noted that in the Middle Ages: "If the universities felt restricted, they moved... in the Dispersion of 1229 the masters and scholars of the University of Paris, resenting

A CHRISTMAS PRESENT 2001

As we went to press, the *Times Higher* recorded three stories which beautifully illustrate our points about the British system of PIs and quality assessment.[125]

Bradford University was somewhat embarrassed to discover that one of the departments it is planning to close as part of its business plan—the Department of European Studies—was the *only* department in the university to receive the top 5* mark in the current RAE exercise. Nothing could more clearly show that business plans have nothing to do with quality and everything to do with bums on seats and total income earned.

In the Research Assessment Exercise results announced in December 2001, Oxford and Cambridge worked yet another interpretative fiddle which allowed them to artificially improve their standing (without of course investing an additional penny in research). The response from LSE: "The LSE is very surprised at the shocking interpretation of the rules. Cambridge may have won the 100 metres. We want to see if it fails the dope test."

The Department of Education and Skills set up a much-heralded scheme of Individual Learner Accounts (ILA) whereby students could purchase courses from the private sector or from further education colleges (with the intent of course of privatizing a section of higher education). The scheme collapsed before Christmas but not before overspending at least £60 million over and above the two-year budget of £202 million. 60 cases of fraud have emerged and the police are currently investigating 27 of them. Education Secretary Estelle Morris has said that "there was growing evidence that some training providers were abusing the system." Then 63 further education colleges told the Association of Colleges in a survey that they had lost more than £720,000 in course fees and wasted investment after the plug was pulled, even though they appeared to have only 28,000 of the 1.3 million active account holders. The colleges also warned that they could be out of pocket on a larger scale because of the bad publicity and loss of public confidence arising from the central government's mishandling of the ILA scheme.

---

injustices meted out to them by the ecclesiastical authorities, simply left Paris for nearly two years.... Oxford profited from this migration, and, similarly, Cambridge began as a university in 1209 when some disaffected scholars moved there from Oxford. No doubt they (or, rather, their faculty and students) will migrate again if they become threatened, but they should not be put in a situation that requires this." Goodlad in *Benchmarking*, 71–2.

[125]*THES*, 2001 December 21, 28.

4

New Zealand:
Neo-Conservative Laboratory

"Given New Zealand's aspiration to become a
knowledge society, it would be inconsistent for the
nation not to invest in its tertiary education system at
internationally competitive levels."
—*Shaping the Strategy*, August 2001

"Tertiary education is a complex area and it is often
impossible to predict which skills and fields of
knowledge will be most needed in the future."
—New Zealand Tertiary Education Advisory
Commission, *Shaping a Shared Vision: Strategy,
Quality Access*, Wellington, 2000.

New Zealand Glossary

AAU	Academic Audit Unit
ACT	Association of Consumers and Taxpayers
AUSNZ	Association of University Staff of New Zealand
CCMAU	Crown Companies Monitoring Advisory Unit
CUAP	Committee on University Academic Programmes
NZQA	New Zealand Qualifications Authority
NZVCC	New Zealand Vice-Chancellors' Committee
QAANZ	Quality Assurance Agency of New Zealand
TAMU	Tertiary Advisory Monitoring Unit
TEAC	Tertiary Education Advisory Committee
TOMU	Tertiary Ownership Monitoring Unit
UGC	University Grants Committee

Note: The AUS Tertiary Update is archived at http://www.aus.nz

THE NEW RIGHT BLITZKRIEG

For a small country of 3.5 million people, New Zealand has had a sustained impact on the world scene. For the first seven decades of the last century it was regarded as a model of moderate social democracy at work—Scandinavia in the South Pacific. The Labour Party became the vehicle for the creation of the welfare state as an "historic compromise" with capitalism. This compromise involved an active role for the state in terms of services and development, and a strong presence for trade unions —all protected by tariffs and access to the British market and financing. When Britain opted for the Common Market, it cut New Zealand adrift. This, combined with the oil shock, provided the backdrop for the country's abrupt turn to the right. New Zealand became the darling of the neo-conservatives, cheered on by the international business press.

Over the past fifteen years, New Zealand has seen the most extensive application of neo-conservative policies in the English-speaking world. It became a laboratory for the New Right. The revolution begun under Labour in the 1980s reached its peak under the National Party between 1990 and 1999. The Labour government elected in 1999 apparently intends some retreat from neo-conservative orthodoxy, but just how far remains to be seen.[1]

In higher education New Zealand followed the lead of the United Kingdom. Similar rhetoric about freedom, decentralization, and the end of government control combined in practice with greatly increased centralization and bureaucracy. Neo-conservatives justified this on the grounds that, until their goal of a wholly private system of higher education could be realized, the government perforce must continue some form of subsidy. This in turn implied detailed central government control in order to ensure funds were spent as government wished.

Use of performance indicators became an integral part of the New Right politics under the slogan of "accountability." But accountability for what, and to whom? The university sector was already struggling through drastic budgetary cuts. Were the new formulations designed merely to transfer blame for the inevitable resulting decline in quality from government to the universities?

The new system employed a style of government characterized by some in New Zealand as the *Blitzkrieg* or, in Brian Easton's phrase,

---

[1]Donald C. Savage, "Academic Freedom and Institutional Autonomy in New Zealand Universities," in Rob Crozier, ed., *Troubled Times: Academic Freedom in New Zealand* (Palmerston North, NZ: Dunmore Press, 2000) [hereafter *Troubled Times*]. See therein Chapter C.IV for a discussion of institutional performance indicators and personal appraisal systems and B.II for quality assurance mechanisms. See also Ruth Butterworth and Nicholas Tarling, *A Shakeup Anyway: Government and the Universities in New Zealand in a Decade of Reform* (Auckland: Auckland University Press, 1994).

directed by "the Bolsheviks of the Right."[2] This new managerial style was possible because, until the mid-1990s, New Zealand was a unicameral unitary state with first-past-the-post electoral arrangements, meaning there were no significant checks on the power of a majority government. When New Zealand moved to a proportional electoral system, more parties appeared in the legislature with diminished likelihood that any would achieve a significant majority. The new arrangement would have considerable impact on the politics of higher education.

The Labour governments of the 1980s emphasized deregulation, privatization, and commercialization to solve New Zealand's economic problems. The Treasury's views were set out in a 1987 *Brief to the Incoming Government*. Looking back in 1994 on his period as Prime Minister, David Lange said:

> The outcome was that, in the course of about three years, we changed from a country run like a Polish shipyard into one that could be internationally competitive.

The government sold off something like $NZ11.5 billion of state assets.[3] Sir James Fletcher, former chief executive officer of New Zealand's largest corporate empire, lamented that few people grew new businesses—most were interested only in asset-stripping.[4] Would that also be the fate of the universities?

Professor Gary Hawke of Victoria University thoroughly applied the Treasury vision to higher education in his report commissioned by the Ministry of Education.[5] Academic administrators were to be transformed into entrepreneurial businessmen and given the necessary powers to command and manage their institutions. Government control would be through mandated performance indicators and other monitoring systems (such as government audits) substituting for market pressures. Academic staff were viewed as a vested interest to be undermined.

---

[2] *Ideas: The Remaking of New Zealand*, broadcasts by the Canadian Broadcasting Corporation, 1994 October 12 and 19 [hereafter *Ideas*], at *http://www.cbc.ca*. Roger Douglas, Minister of Finance in the Labour government, told a Reform Party convention in Saskatoon in 1991 that consensus for quality decisions was best achieved *after* the decisions were made. He advised Reformers not to discuss their programme but, if elected, to implement it as quickly as possible in order to overwhelm the opposition. In 1989 he told the *Toronto Star* that if he had to do the New Zealand reforms again, "We would try to do it faster." (*Toronto Star*, 1989 October 11) Brian Easton has written several books about the neo-conservative revolution in New Zealand, including *The Commercialization of New Zealand* (Auckland: Auckland University Press, 1997) and *The Whimpering of the State* (Auckland: Auckland University Press, 1999).

[3] Roger Kerr, New Zealand Business Round Table, quoted in *Ideas*.

[4] Sir James Fletcher, quoted in *Ideas*.

[5] *Report of the Working Group on Post Compulsory Education and Training*, Ministry of Education, Wellington, 1988. The second part of the Treasury's *Brief to the Incoming Government* had dealt with education. For a full discussion, see Michael Peters, "Performance Indicators in New Zealand Higher Education," *Journal of Education Policy*, 7, 3 (1992): 270–98.

Labour's Performance Indicators Task Force reported in 1989, recommending as major goals student numbers, graduation rates, and employability. It recognized that the universities' record in these areas was likely to be seriously affected by circumstances beyond their control—the state of the economy, locations outside large urban centres, and so on—but no strategy was suggested to deal with this problem. The difficulties of measuring research output by counting research articles were acknowledged, again with no solution offered. Labour did realize that performance indicators could be used to stimulate change beyond providing the cheapest possible education. It required universities to report on implementation of equal employment opportunities programmes aimed at increasing the recruitment and success rate of disadvantaged groups. This aspect of performance was later de-emphasized, especially after the National Party came to power in 1990. A separate report on financial indicators was prepared by the Treasury. The two were integrated and circulated to higher education institutions in November 1989 under the title *Performance Indicators in Higher Education.*

Traditional forms of professional accountability took a back seat to managerial control through external forms of accounting, with the government as the major stakeholder keeping its agents in line through incentives and sanctions. The Association of University Staff of New Zealand (AUSNZ) branch at Auckland University predicted this would inevitably lead to a focus on *quantity* of activity rather than *quality* of outcome.[6] Labour notably omitted to make any rational cost/benefit analysis of its proposed measures—a failure continued through the next decade.[7] Because the government fell shortly thereafter, the Performance Indicators Report was never officially adopted as government policy. But it is remarkable how a bureaucratic report develops a life of its own once written and stored in the files.

Amongst a variety of higher education measures, in 1990 the Labour government abolished the University Grants Committee (UGC), the major buffer body lying between the universities and the central government. Labour considered it too much under the thumb of the vice-chancellors. One of the agencies for redirecting control was the New Zealand Qualifications Authority (NZQA), which reported directly to the Minister. At first the Labour government intended to give the NZQA sweeping authority over criteria and accreditation of courses, including power to validate university degrees and to prohibit students from enrolling in courses. Instead the vice-chancellors

---

[6]Peters, 278. The government included a section on performance indicators in the Education Amendment Act of 1990 where it required that they be developed by the councils of institutions for the purposes stated in the Public Finance Act. The indictors could therefore vary depending on the mission of the university.

[7]Michael C. Peters, John Freeman Moir, Education Department, University of Canterbury and Michael A. Peters, Education Department, University of Auckland, *Accountability and Performance in Tertiary Education*, AUSNZ, 1993 July.

created their own Committee on Academic Programs (CUAP) to continue the work of the Curriculum Committee of the UGC. They lobbied successfully to secure statutory powers for their own creation, rather than the new qualifications authority.[8] This was just as well, since the NZQA started life with a vigorous interventionist agenda whereby it would set performance goals for the system, ensuring uniformity across the sector by creating modular courses and requirements in all subjects.

NZQA did approve degree courses for polytechnics, provided they met the requirement of the Education Act that faculty in degree programmes be engaged in research. On the other hand, unlike the UK, they were not allowed to transform themselves into universities. The agency was also to regulate private providers, which could not call themselves universities as the Education Act required universities to have more than one faculty, be engaged in research, and show commitment to academic freedom. Bureaucratic schemes in the 1990s to remove these requirements as barriers to trade were never in the end carried out. Nevertheless by 1999 there were some 800 private providers of post-secondary education. Government subsidies to this sector ballooned from $NZ1.98 million in 1992 to a projected $NZ128.4 million in 2001.[9] Canadians, who hear rhetoric about how private for-profit universities will reduce the cost to the taxpayer, should take note.

CUAP then became a form of accrediting agency for new courses and programmes in New Zealand universities. It has had an increasing role in such academic matters as the definition of qualifications, criteria for joint degree programmes, and guidelines for the recognition of prior learning. It has moved from deciding between possibly competing programmes to pronouncing on the expected academic quality of proposed areas of study. This was very much in line with the competitive policy of the National government. The new Labour government has indicated that it will emphasize cooperation over competition, which may require some re-orientation by CUAP.

The vice-chancellors soon decided they required a more far-reaching system of quality assessment. New Zealand universities already used outside departmental reviews, as well as professional reviews in as law, accounting, and medicine. The vice-chancellors saw a need for a new structure to head off direct governmental control through the NZQA. They created the independent Academic Audit Unit, in which academics sit as a minority with representatives from the national employers' body, the national trade union body, the professions, the community, and students. The board includes a AUSNZ representative.

The AAU's mandate was two-fold. Its first role was to review university procedures for quality, PIs among them, in line with UK developments in

---

[8]NZVCC, *Committee on University Academic Programmes: Functions and Procedures 1998* (Wellington: VZVCC, 1998).
[9]*AUS Tertiary Update*, 4, 14 (2001 May 10).

the early 1990s. The second role was educational: to identify and commend to universities good practice in maintenance and enhancement of academic standards at the national level. The Unit did trial audits at Auckland and Lincoln in 1995, then reviewed all New Zealand universities between 1995 and 1998. These published audits cover a wide range of topics, including the state of academic freedom on local campuses (an approach suggested by the AUSNZ).

The AAU subjected itself to an audit (favourable) to demonstrate that the university audits were fair and perceptive, encouraging self-audit and international best practice rather than imposing bureaucratic and mechanistic models and the culture of punishment. It also welcomed suggestions about improving its own performance. Nevertheless, there were danger signs. Universities were encouraged to produce meaningless lists of pious intentions together with banal mission statements. The audit review of the AAU suggested the New Zealand Vice-Chancellors' Committee (NZVCC) and the NZQA work together to develop goals, objectives, standards, and PIs. Were this actually done, the defensive mechanism might well turn out to be worse than the disease, sacrificing autonomy and academic freedom to the centralizing drive of the NZQA.

Universities are required by law to produce an annual Statement of Service Performance on the achievement of stated objectives, using government PIs. These statements are reviewed by the Government Audit Office, which liaises with the AAU "to monitor what, if any, matters within the ambit of the Audit Office may properly be covered by the AAU, and in what ways, if any, double reporting may be avoided."[10] In addition the central government set up the Tertiary Ownership Monitoring Unit (TOMU) in the Ministry of Education to apply the new dispensation to the universities in detail. Given New Zealand's small size, it is remarkable how many agencies have a hand in monitoring the universities.

Academic critics of CUAP and the AAU fall into two categories. The first considers CUAP in particular as a barrier to the development of new programmes, since its procedures take so long that other universities organize competitive courses before the new idea can be launched. On the other hand, CUAP has failed to deal adequately with the reverse problem, closure of programmes. Competitive closure decisions in a small university system can easily mean the disappearance of important subjects with limited undergraduate bases—certain modern languages, theoretical physics, and aspects of chemistry and mathematics. The second category of critics considers the AAU's approach bureaucratic, centralizing, and ineffective. Charles Pigden of the Department of Philosophy of the University of Otago has written:

> In my experience, the Quality Programme has produced NOTHING BUT cynics, and the only shift has been to a culture of resentment.

---

[10]NZAAU, *About the AAU, www.aau.ac.nz/*, 1999.

Critics of CUAP have been much more vigorous than those of the AAU, but in neither case do they suggest what would happen were CUAP or the AAU abolished. The mostly likely scenario would be a takeover by the much more bureaucratic and centralising NZQA. As the external audit panel said:

> In the present political environment, with its increasing focus on accountability and value for money, it is essential that the university sector not only perform to a high standard but be able to demonstrate that it is doing so. Having taken the initiative in setting up the AAU, the universities must continue to show that they can manage the audit process without intervention.

Right-wing critics, such as the New Zealand Business Round Table, were quick to denounce what they saw as monopolistic regulatory arrangements and an infringement on the market. The Round Table opposed any compulsory accreditation system (but would tolerate a voluntary one), and insisted quality matters should be left to the institutions themselves. The interests of consumers would be protected by a more competitive market and, in the case of fraud or other criminal activities, by the courts. Agencies such as the AAU produced unwelcome homogeneity. Instead, the market should segment institutions according to quality and cost. Individuals would then be free to choose how much they wished to spend on quality in education just as they would purchase a car. This approach remains the view of the high and dry ideologues in parliament. For example, in April 2001 Stephen Franks, speaking for ACT, commended Victoria and Massey for setting up competing architecture programmes in Wellington, arguing this will create "a buzz of ideas." The President of the Victoria University Students' Association replied that this *demarche* would simply split the existing funds for architecture in half, with students in both institutions suffering as a result.[11]

The vice-chancellors never persuaded neo-conservatives that the universities could be exempted from the new order. But there can be little doubt that their new structures blunted the success of the 1990s right-wing campaign to take over detailed direction of higher education through the Ministry of Education.

From the beginning of the neo-conservative revolution, the bureaucracy saw PIs as *the* route to achieving their goals. When the National Party came to power in 1990, the State Services Commission advised the new government that accountability required the universities to specify the services they produced and "the precise relationship of these to the Government's desired outcomes." The Minister should purchase outputs from the universities whereby the Minister would contract for targeted education and training courses with the content being specified in the contract. This amounted to home rule for the *nomenklatura*. The government, it argued, could only enforce efficiency by breaking the power of all other interest groups, such as faculty and students.

---

[11]AUS *Tertiary Update*, 2001 April 4, April 10, and April 11.

Fortunately for the universities, the National government decided to do battle with the medical world first, then expended its energies on drastically curtailing social benefits for the poor and creating new labour legislation to undermine trade unions. Its policy in the universities became to cut budgets, increase student fees, and offer a student loan scheme. A decade-long discussion about the creation of a capital charge or tax on public universities to create "competitive neutrality" with private institutions came to nothing.

By the time government turned its attention to reforming the universities, the electoral system had changed and the National majority had dwindled to the narrowest of margins. Its major source of inspiration was the work of three international accounting firms—Ernst and Young, Price WaterhouseCoopers, and Deloitte Touche Tohmatsu—as well as the New Zealand Business Round Table. Ernst and Young produced suggestions in 1995–96, including a recommendation that some parts of their report should not be revealed to the university community.[12]

By 1994 the Ministry and the vice-chancellors were discussing new reporting and auditing mechanisms designed to entrench PIs.[13] Universities would be required to change their accounting systems, express their educational goals in business babble, and structure their accounts to a new reporting mechanism which focussed on "outputs."

> The distinction in accountability for outputs, rather than outcomes, is a major difference between the reforms in New Zealand and elsewhere. Organizations are not held accountable for outcomes (the impact on or consequences for society) because causality is difficult, if not impossible to establish.

Outcomes would be dictated by the Minister and by Parliament. Universities would relate their "outputs" to the ministerially-designated outcomes. The Minister would then purchase "outputs" from "providers" on the basis of comparative costs. "Outputs" turned out to be the number of courses divided into categories (arts, commerce and law, and so on), which meant assigning all administrative costs as overhead to the courses whose "outputs" were bought by the Minister. The unspoken purpose was to allow the Minister to purchase the cheapest "outputs." Library and computer facilities were, unsurprisingly, treated as overhead, just like cleaning services. Thus they should be ruthlessly cut, not treated as academic services that needed to be substantially improved in the face of international competition. Recognizing universities would have difficulty

---

[12]The U.S. Clinton administration accused international accounting firms of serious conflict of interest arising from confusion of their auditing function and their business as consultants. The consequence in the United States was divestiture of the consulting businesses into separate companies not directly controlled by the auditors.

[13]New Zealand, Ministry of Education, *Output Classes for Tertiary Education and Training*, draft memo, 1994 June 14. From the beginning in the late eighties there had been an emphasis on such "efficiency indicators" as staff/student ratios, operating costs per full-time student equivalent, and the net teaching area per full-time student equivalent. See Peters, *op. cit.*, 275.

relating this new structure to the outcomes set out in university charters, the Ministry advised amendment of the charters.

Standards in "outputs" purchased from the universities would be monitored by structures set up by the vice-chancellors. The Ministry recognized

> the strength of institutional self-evaluation and inter-institutional peer review derive, not from externally imposed standards, but from the pervading academic culture and the standards of education to which professional educators aspire

and that there were limits to quality review:

> There are aspects of quality service that are not usefully approached through a performance agreement. They are part of the fabric of the organization producing the service: how a service is designed and produced, even who it is produced by, the values of the organization and how it is managed. These factors are not easily contracted for. They are part of the orientation of the peoples themselves and the culture of the place they work.[14]

Still the Ministry had specific PIs in mind. One was to require institutions to record the number of calls for information about courses, and express them as a percentage of the number of individuals who actually enrolled. Another was the number of students by cost category. This latter was primordial, designed to allow the Ministry to argue that planning in regard to existing courses should be determined by the student market—that is, demand-driven—although it recognized the possibility of new programmes in priority areas determined by the Minister. Student enrolment, meanwhile, is much affected by the state of the economy, generosity (or lack of it) of loans and grants, and demographic changes.

Another significant PI was the number of students who completed their courses within the normal period, that is, three years for a three-year degree. This put enormous administrative pressure on academic staff to pass everyone, regardless of academic standards, since each repeated year meant a financial penalty. Nothing could be better guaranteed to dumb down the university curriculum.[15] Further, this particular PI assumed all university students were full-time students entering after secondary school—ignoring the cold reality that ever-increasing fees forced students to work part-time during the academic year, and failing to take into account mature students normally at work, single mothers, and the needs of Maori and Pacific Island students. In fact, the PI told universities they would do best to forget about such categories of people and concentrate on full-time middle class students who were immediate graduates of secondary schools. Universities could, if they wished, add other PIs, but these had to be measurable, i.e. quantifiable, and reportable, "focus on the needs of the purchaser," and "focus on key areas that affect purchaser decision-making." The Ministry hoped universities

---

[14]Ministry of Education, *Output Classes for Tertiary Education and Training* quoting G. Scott, "What's Wrong with Managerialism," *Public Sector* 16, 1, (1993).

[15]Robin Gwynn, *Massey Today—And Tomorrow*. Massey University, New Zealand, 1996.

would now concern themselves with effectiveness as shown by consumer satisfaction. Since some "purchasers" would naturally prefer high grades for minimal effort, the results for quality are not hard to guess.

The Ministry recognized there had been much debate about the usefulness of PIs. "Even measures of efficiency, for example, floor space per EFTS (that is, student), can be deceptive and misleading, particularly when considered in isolation." It realized also that PIs can be derived from potentially conflicting objectives: "[F]or example, social equity objectives may conflict with other objectives of efficiency and effectiveness." Efficiencies need to be considered "in the context of all costs, not just teaching costs."

The Ministry stated that in 1995 it would purchase "outputs" which contributed to a series of outcomes—which looked much like what the universities thought they were already supposed to do. These included "excellence in tertiary education, post-graduate study and research," attainment of qualifications, assisting in the creation of a highly skilled workforce, equality in educational opportunity, access for those with special needs, full participation of Maori, and improvements in effectiveness and efficiency. It was hard not to conclude that a vast amount of time and money had been squandered to produce a mouse.

Focus on "outputs" conveniently foreclosed discussion of "inputs" such as the level of investment in academic staff, libraries, and computer systems required for New Zealand universities to be internationally competitive.

THE HIGH TIDE OF ORTHODOXY

In 1998, by administrative fiat, the government created a new agency in the Ministry of Education: the Tertiary Ownership Monitoring Unit (TOMU). This monitored the finances of tertiary education institutions, but gradually became interested in academic developments as well. How can one separate the two? Its personnel were gung-ho for the new dispensation. Teaching and research were to be separated, and separately costed and organized. Detailed accounting to the central government would be the order of the day. The universities were deeply suspicious, fearing this was simply window-dressing for control by the Crown Company Monitoring Advisory Unit (CCMAU), which had a reputation for intervention and control designed to eliminate the so-called unprofitable and the inefficient. But what would be "unprofitable"?—the library? higher level mathematics and physics? music and fine arts?

TOMU became responsible for the monitoring of how equal opportunity legislation was applied in higher education, although, in the eyes of minorities, the legislative framework was weak.

TOMU's November 1999 *Briefing to the Incoming Minister of Education*:

• expressed an interest in seeing Tertiary Education Institutions taking a closer look at how to preserve and enhance their "intellectual capital"

- announced plans for a pilot project to provide an example for other institutions to follow in identifying exactly where their intellectual capability and capacity resides and how it can be protected, and

- expressed concern that university autonomy and ownership made effective monitoring difficult.

In 1996 the Ministry of Education had produced a document called "Drivers for Long Term Tertiary Funding," recommending PIs separate from CUAP and AAU. These ideas reappeared in discussions about monitoring throughout the decade. In 1999 TOMU wrote to the vice-chancellors demanding reports on the non-financial operations of the university with objectives that "need to be specific and measurable" and "quantifiable."[16]

Proposed policy was laid out in 1997 and 1998 in Green and White Papers,[17] which covered a lot of territory, including PIs. The Green Paper set out in surprising detail the banal and anti-intellectual vision of the neo-conservatives. Its overall assumption was that education is training for jobs; other objects of the traditional university, such as increasing knowledge and understanding, fostering culture, and encouraging tolerance for other views, became externalities that could not be costed and therefore should be downgraded or ignored. For instance, it proposed the universities be required to prepare annual statements of intent, including a statement of the nature and scope of their activities. The Minister would have unfettered power to require amendments, strike sections, and include new provisions. The Green Paper proposed significant increases in reporting that would require new and expensive databases, including a huge new database on individual students. Compliance costs were not identified. Even some right-wing commentators were hostile, arguing that if there was sufficient student demand for such information, private suppliers should take over the business from the bureaucracy. Others suggested the Ministry be privatized —an interesting thought—but unsurprisingly right-wing bureaucrats are just as entrenched as left-wing ones. The White Paper continued in much the same vein, retreating from some of the more extreme positions of the previous paper. One feature of both was a litany of abuse directed at universities, rarely with any justifying research, and an underlying disdain for academic staff.

The Green and White Papers exhibited a muddled view of quality assurance, suggesting a split between centralizers and de-centralizers. The Green Paper complained about different accreditation systems for different parts of the post-secondary world. It floated the notion that the government should establish a minimum quality requirement consistent for all qualifications, programmes, and providers, then went on to insist

---

[16]Tertiary Ownership Monitoring Unit, *Statement of Objectives 2000–2002* (Wellington: Queen's Printer, 1999).

[17]*A Future Education Policy for New Zealand: Tertiary Education Review,* (Green Paper), 1997 and *Tertiary Education in New Zealand: Policy Directions for the 21st Century* (White Paper), Wellington, NZ, November 1998.

it did not want a single standard. It specifically opposed self-regulation by the universities, and recommended external validation through the NZQA. It envisaged applying to all the NZQA standards for registration, accreditation and audit, developed specifically for the non-university sector. The NZQA would then be responsible for ensuring the quality threshold was consistently and fairly applied, and to do so it would accredit quality validation agencies to the job. The Green Paper finally tried to reassure universities by saying the current AAU audit procedure showed that universities already met the government's minimum standards. It seemed that the National government wanted to accredit CUAP and AAU through the NZQA.[18]

The subsequent White Paper continued the confusion. It claimed, without substantiation, that the mechanisms for auditing quality in higher education were weak—then went on to say that the system should recognize the wide variety of purposes in post-secondary education. and that new quality assurance arrangements should aim to strengthen the requirements for providers to manage their own quality assurance effectively. This seemed a retreat from the Green Paper. The new document announced the creation of a new agency, the Quality Assurance Agency of New Zealand (QAANZ) which, like its predecessor, would be directly under the Minster's control. It would not be itself a quality assurance validator but would accredit other agencies to conduct such audits (presumably including CUAP and the AAU). The agency would have the power to approve, monitor, or remove accreditation from an agency. It would also facilitate the creation of a new system for student complaints.

The White Paper then announced the government would require universities to list all their courses and programmes on the NZQA site. This seemed innocuous enough, except it then went on to require listing of the purpose and learning outcomes of each course, and to announce that the Ministry was preparing detailed subject classifications. This was justified on the grounds that only the Ministry could guarantee fitness for purpose, based on an outcomes analysis. "Each qualification will be examined on the basis of its fitness for purpose." This appeared to mean every course, an apparent return to the idea that the Ministry and NZQA as its agent would require standard courses to be taught in every department with the same curriculum.[19]

The universities vigorously opposed these ideas. They did not object to quality assurance mechanisms provided they were truly independent of

---

[18]They published a parallel paper with more details, *A Future Qualifications Policy for New Zealand: A Plan for the National Qualifications Framework.*

[19]The Hon. Wyatt Creech, Minister of Education, however, told the Association of Polytechnics of New Zealand that the government was abandoning the eighties view that one size fits all and henceforward it would favour recognising the different needs and roles of higher education institutions. Hon. Wyatt Creech, "Speech Notes," Association of New Zealand Polytechnics Annual Meeting, Auckland, 1998 November.

government, which NZQA and QAANZ manifestly were not, and focussed on quality, not the political enthusiasms of the moment. The legacy of mistrust from fifteen years of political assault on the universities and their academic staff meant few would trust any arrangement that gave arbitrary powers to the Minister. The vice-chancellors argued international and domestic university criteria were the essential component of any such system, and that the NZVCC should retain its statutory power to approve university qualifications. They were deeply suspicious of the idea of minimum standards, which might well become maximum standards for the purposes of funding. Nor were they pleased by the continuing assumption by the central bureaucracy that all post-secondary education was identical, and that all sectors and institutions should be treated the same. Professor Jane Kelsey, then President of AUSNZ, argued there was a real risk that new financial indicators would directly or indirectly include decisions on staffing and academic programmes. She argued the experience of the hospitals with CCMAU suggested a serious potential threat to institutional autonomy.[20]

The Ministry then set up a Pre-establishment team to implement the White Paper. The team issued a paper and invited comments, but later admitted it had no intention of making significant changes. The AUSNZ pointed out the inconsistency of focussing on quality in the context of ongoing cost-cutting, annually decreasing per student funding, a deteriorating university infrastructure, and increased workloads. Universities, it said, should be concerned about excellence, not minimum standards.

Luckily the government ran out of steam before it could implement this agenda. The last National Party Minister responsible for higher education did not share the zealots' faith that the curriculum should be decided by the student market of the moment. He had noted that the market was working so that fewer students took science and engineering. The Ministry, he argued, should be supporting excellence, increasing investment in science and engineering, and developing a more cooperative way of working with the universities.[21] Nevertheless the civil service believed it had a mandate to implement all parts of the Green and White Papers which did not require formal legislation. TOMU wrote to the vice-chancellors in July 1999, telling them to amend reporting arrangements to reflect the fact that "the move to fully demand-driven funding" was now in place, even though the White Paper had not been adopted and the

---

[20]Jane Kelsey, *Tertiary Education is* not *a Business,* speech to the Association of Polytechnics of New Zealand, 1998 November.

[21]Hon. Max Bradford, speech to the New Zealand Biotechnology Conference, Wellington, 1999 June 28. He also promoted a new research-focussed programme spelled out in *Bright Future: Five Steps Ahead,* Wellington, 1999. The Vice-Chancellor of Waikato, Bryan Gould, noted the similarity with the slogans of Maoist China with the focus on empty rhetoric devoid of any funding substance. See *THES*, 1999 November 12.

Minister was announcing policy in the opposite direction. It was fairly clear who was in charge.[22]

The general election of November 1999 brought an end to the era of the National Party. A decade of National rule had not addressed in any serious way the real problems of higher education in New Zealand—the burden of student debt, the lack of significant investment in research, the failure of the New Zealand business community to adequately support university research, the disdain in which the government and the business community held academics, the brain drain to Australia, the United Kingdom and North America, and the provision of higher education for Maori and Pacific Islanders. The percentage of university funding from the Ministry fell from 73% in 1991 to 50% in 1998, with the balance being made up by increased student fees and other revenues. Funding per FTE student was US$3,192 below that in Australia.[23] Twenty-three New Zealand academics living overseas wrote an open letter just before the 1999 election attacking New Zealand's political establishment for neglecting to nurture "a research culture with the right mix of funding incentives, and devotion to the spirit of intellectual inquiry."[24] A decade or more had been wasted on an ideological war against the universities and their academic traditions, with little to show for it other than more government bureaucracy and a drastic drop in morale in the universities.

The universities were left in a perilous funding position. Funding per FTE student fell in real terms from $NZ10,736 to $NZ6,915 between 1980 and 1999.[25] Student debt sky-rocketed. In September 2000 the Minister of Finance announced 10,344 former students no longer living in New Zealand owed $NZ135.9 million as of April 2000. This was up from 5,942 in the previous year owing $NZ71.2 million. Optimists said the former students were taking high salaried jobs elsewhere to pay off their debts;

---

[22]TOMU remained primarily interested in financial matters, but its scope extended into other areas. In September 2000 its web site indicated a draft document with detailed guidelines on higher education charters, other statements on the functions and responsibilities of higher education councils, and appointments to councils and their remuneration. TOMU also monitored the Statements of Objectives required of all higher education institutions. This included the performance measures necessary for the completion of the statement of service performance. It recommended that non-financial objectives and associated PIs be included. These statements are considered commercial confidences by TOMU and are not available. There is an annual round of discussions between TOMU and the institutions. See TOMU, *Statement of Objectives for 2001–2003.* The new Labour government changed its name to the Tertiary Advisory Monitoring Unit (TAMU).

[23]Guy Scott and Helen Scott, *New Zealand University Funding Over The Last Two Decades,* NZVCC and AUSNZ (Wellington: n.p., 2000).

[24]David Cohen, "Switching from Sheep to Computers: New Zealand Seeks a Knowledge Economy: A new government tries to place more of an emphasis on higher education," *Chronicle of Higher Education,* 2001 March 24.

[25]*THES,* 2001 February 9. Statement of President of AUSNZ.

pessimists assumed most would neither repay nor return The Government Auditor forecast that by 2024 students would owe $NZ19.4 billion.[26]

The annual report for 2000 of the New Zealand Vice-Chancellors' Committee admitted academic staff are "poorly paid and poorly supported in terms of research infrastructure and funding," resulting in "a steady drain of top researchers and difficulty in recruiting the best young talent."[27] Research funding by the private sector and by the government were below the OECD average.[28] The vice-chancellors argued the hiring of 590 extra academic staff would be necessary to meet the faculty/student ratios of equivalent institutions in Australia and the United Kingdom.[29] NZVCC and AUS jointly sponsored a study by Guy and Helen Scott on trends in state support for higher education since 1980. They concluded that funding per FTE student had declined steadily by an average annual rate of 2.3% per year while, at the same time, staff/student ratios increased from 12.5 to 18.4.[30]

The media began reporting departures of academics to other countries, particularly Australia and the United States. Noted economist Peter Earl, author of fourteen books on economic subjects, said he left Lincoln for Queensland because universities were becoming training centres rather than educational centres. He took a more junior post at Queensland with a higher salary, better pension arrangements, and other benefits. He also expressed concern about the standard of literacy of New Zealand students below the top 10%.[31]

THE NEW LABOUR GOVERNMENT—NEW VISION OR OLD IDEAS REMODELLED?

Tired of the fanaticism of the National Party, New Zealanders turned back to the Labour Party in hopes it had finally recovered some of its social democratic roots.[32] The results to date are somewhat mixed. Rhetoric has shifted significantly, from competition and free enterprise in higher education to co-operation, access for the excluded, and quality. The government's PIs were to create a co-operative and collaborative sector, excellence in teaching, scholarship and research, partnerships with

---

[26]THES, 2000 September 22; AUS *Tertiary Update* 4,22 (2001 July 5). Government figures suggest that nurses will take 23 years to pay off their loans, GPs just over 20 years, and secondary teachers around 16. This does not take into account that maternity leaves would extend the period for many women.

[27]NZVCC, *Annual Report 2000*; AUS *Tertiary Update*, 4, 13, [2001 May 3].

[28]THES, 2000 August 16.

[29]NZVCC, *Annual Report 2000*.

[30]Guy Scott and Helen Scott, *New Zealand University Funding Over The Last Two Decades*, NZVCC and AUS, Wellington, 2000 July.

[31]AUS *Tertiary Update* 4, 21 (2001 June 28).

[32]Jonathan Freedland, "Kiwis keep to the left," *Guardian Weekly*, 2000 May 11–17.

business and local communities, commitment to contributing to the nation's future direction, and accessibility (especially for Maori, within the context of the Treaty of Waitangi). Steve Maharey, the Associate Minister responsible for tertiary education, suggested the previous government had left the sector in a financially marginal position. These ideas were sufficiently vague that only time would tell whether they constituted a meaningful break with the recent past.[33]

The new government announced it would not proceed with the creation of QAANZ but instead create a new Tertiary Education Advisory Committee (TEAC) to advise the government. Its first head, Norman Kingsbury, fought a short, sharp, and successful battle with the Ministry to ensure the agency's independence. Not everyone in the Labour government or the Ministry favoured this development. Only vigorous lobbying by AUSNZ and other members of the university community enabled it to proceed.[34]

TEAC decided to issue four reports in 2000 and 2001. It then planned to self-destruct, having recommended the creation of a permanent Tertiary Education Commission (TEC) to cover all post-secondary education, an idea which the government accepted. The tertiary education responsibilities of the Ministry would cease and devolve onto the new body. TEAC thus temporarily became the think tank for the government's future higher education policies and its guide to the setting up of the new permanent commission. It was specifically instructed to deal with the system as a whole, not the operations of individual institutions, and to preserve "institutional autonomy and academic freedom." It assumed a differentiated higher education sector rather than a homogeneous one, and accepted the government's view that the new strategy should focus on co-operation rather than competition.

TEAC certainly produced a new rhetoric. It issued a preliminary report in July 2000 amplifying its terms of reference. The goals or PIs it set for post-secondary education reflect a broader view of higher education:

- inspiring and enabling individuals to develop their capabilities to the highest potential levels throughout life, so that they develop intellectually, are well-equipped to participate in the labour market, can contribute effectively to society and achieve personal fulfilment
- preserving, advancing and disseminating knowledge and understanding, both for their own sake and in order to benefit the economy and society
- serving the needs of an open, innovative, sustainable knowledge society and economy at the regional and national levels, including those of Maori, Pacific Island peoples, and the wider community

---

[33]*Terms of Reference Tertiary Education Advisory Commission,* Ministry of Education, Wellington, 2000 April.

[34]The AUSNZ had advocated the creation of a body such as TEAC when the previous Labour government abolished the UGC.

- helping to build and maintain a healthy, inclusive and democratic society and promoting the tolerance and debate which underpin it
- reducing social and ethnic inequalities, and
- displaying and nurturing a distinctive national identity, including greater understanding of the Treaty of Waitangi.[35]

Elsewhere the document recognized the importance of "building research capability and creating new knowledge," and the downside of the current higher education arrangements. It complained of "lack of good performance data." It noted the current "risk aversion, compliance mentality, change fatigue and low morale" as well as "credential inflation," "over-emphasis on procedural accountability" and the "lack of research on tertiary education itself." It commented on "the vulnerability of important research areas to volatile learner demand." "[M]indful of the dangers of over-planning from the centre," it noted: "Tertiary education is a complex area and it is often impossible to predict which skills and fields of knowledge will be most needed in the future."

The second and third reports focussed on structures to realize the new strategic vision.[36] The new Commission, appointed by the Minister, would steer the tertiary education system, including negotiating new charters for all those receiving governmental support and new profiles. Profiles would specify programmes and activities for each institution over a three-year period, and indicate which were to be funded by government. Charters would be for the medium-to-long-term, set out the special character of the provider, how the provider contributes to the nation's tertiary education strategy, and the scope of activities to be funded by the government. These would presumably replace the mission statement market babble favoured by the previous regime. TEC sub-committees would deal with specific elements of the sector and particular problems.

There would be a PI test for all new entrants into the higher education arena—a "desirability test" which TEAC argued should be embedded in legislation. The new Commission would assess all applicants, determining whether the proposal would

- give effect to the national strategic goals and/or tertiary education priorities
- enhance economic efficiency and effectiveness across the tertiary education system, and
- assist appropriate differentiation and specialisation across the system.

---

[35]Tertiary Education Advisory Commission, *Shaping a Shared Vision: Strategy, Quality, Access, the Initial Report of the Tertiary Education Advisory Commission,* Wellington, 2000, available on the TEAC web site at *www.teac.govt.nz.*

[36]Tertiary Education Advisory Commission, *Shaping the System,* Wellington, NZ, 2001, and *Towards a Strategy: The Future of New Zealand's Tertiary Education System,* Wellington, NZ, 2001. These can be found on the TEAC web site above.

This approach was clearly designed to limit the spread of private operators. Given the size of the private system in New Zealand and the dramatic increase in government subsidies, this was rather like locking the house after the robbery. TEAC did indicate that it would address the issue of private versus public funding in its final report, but announced itself seriously divided over this issue.

The government waffled on the subject. Universities, it said, should be "learning communities," not businesses.[37] Ultimately it placed some restrictions on the expansion of the private sector, which the Minister responsible for higher education called a "wild west" situation. He said the government would not support duplication of existing university and college courses by the private sector.[38] The government announced opposition to the transformation of polytechnics into universities, and introduced legislation to freeze the number of universities at eight. The public universities were extremely disappointed that more vigorous action was not actually taken by the government to limit the subsidizing of the private sector to compete with existing university courses.

The third report recommended strong emphasis in terms of performance at the bottom and at the top of post-secondary education. It stressed the importance of increased educational avenues for the disadvantaged, the Maori, and the Pacific Islanders, indicating that PIs could be re-directed to social purposes. It suggested a high priority for research, pointing out that university research in New Zealand was funded by student fees, unlike most other western countries where research councils or similar bodies funded research directly. It recommended the creation of centres of excellence, an idea picked up by the Labour government in its 2001 budget. It suggested one important PI for research should be the establishment of formal arrangements and training programmes for postgraduate students on the Australian model. It specifically recommended not only the creation of centres of excellence in areas of important economic development, but also centres in environmental sciences, the humanities, and the social sciences.

TEAC's ideas range from the sensible to the downright dangerous.[39] It wanted the demand-driven arrangements of the previous decade replaced by an emphasis on quality. To this end the Commission noted British assessment systems, without seeing their serious shortcomings or noticing that one major British player, the Quality Assurance Agency, was in a state of collapse. It downgraded the importance of traditional measures such as library holdings or staff/student ratios in favour of trendy but vague outcomes definitions. It talked about Taylorization or unbundling of

---

[37]Steve Maharey M.P., *Tertiary Education in the 21ˢᵗ Century*, Address to the APNZ Conference, Auckland, 1998 November. Then the Labour spokesperson for tertiary education, Mr. Maharey is now the associate minister responsible for that area.

[38]*AUS Tertiary Update*, 4,4 [2001 March 1].

[39]For a discussion of the new government's plans, see Bryan Gould, Vice-Chancellor, University of Waikato, *THES*, 2000 May 10.

services, so that each piece of the professorial work could be contracted out. It held this would allow faculty to focus on research, but it would more likely produce a piece-work culture, leading to ever more casualisation. It seemed interested as well in that other mirage of educational management, merit pay.[40] It hinted at a focus on completion rates without discussing the likely dumbing down effect. Most of its suggestions were nuanced, but would politicians and bureaucrats retain the fine-tuning?

On the other hand, the Commission recognized the limitations involved in employability PIs. It suggested a higher weighting be given to education outcomes likely to have a more lasting impact than a focus on short-term employment. It laid some stress on academic freedom, consistent with professional ethics, and on institutional autonomy within a framework of accountability. It distrusted strategic planning exercises. It recognized the importance of the humanities, social sciences, the performing and fine arts —areas usually scheduled for downgrading in such exercises. It pointed out that the strategic plan should ensure that certain subjects such as various foreign languages should be available somewhere in the country even if they cannot be sustained on every campus. It laid out a blueprint for a dramatic increase in university research and postgraduate education.

The Commission set out a seven-page tertiary education scorecard indicating a wide variety of national goals in higher education to be measured and improved. Many would require a substantial increase in financial contributions from both the central government and the business community. For example, it wished to increase the percentage of the workforce participating annually in structured training from 16% to 30%, and to increase the percentage of managers/enterprise owners with some form of management qualifications. The number of R&D personnel per 1000 of the population was to increase from 3.4 to 5.0, and New Zealand's R&Ds investment as a percentage of GDP increase from 21st in the OECD to a rank within the top ten. It recommended 10 centres of research excellence supporting economic development, at least one for each of the national strategic goals, two devoted to New Zealand history and culture, two on environmental sustainability, and one dedicated to Pacific peoples, with an increasing percentage of government social expenditure spent on social research. The percentage of the population with competence in the Maori language should rise from 4.25% to 8%, and New Zealand should achieve a rank in the top three OECDs countries for research on indigenous peoples' issues.

The new government was strongly in favour of maintaining and developing the NZQA "as having the key role to play as the guardian of the national qualifications network," and as "the registration body which enables tertiary providers to gain access to public funding."[41] It seemed,

---

[40]For a brief discussion of this idea, see the chapter on the United Kingdom.
[41]*NZQA's years of indecision over*, Press Release, New Zealand Government, 2000.

therefore, an odd time for the vice-chancellors to open a debate on the future of CUAP. During 2000 the Vice-Chancellors' Committee considered winding up CUAP and letting the universities self-regulate in terms of creating new programmes but subject to quality assurance mechanisms. By 2001 they appear to have backed away from this idea.[42] AUSNZ strongly supported the continuation of both CUAP and AAU, recognizing the important role they have played in restraining governmental attempts to take over the curriculum. It did suggest that the regime of quality assurance be applied to all institutions offering university level courses which would significantly increase the costs of private providers. Quality assessments should take into account the funding supplied by government. There should also be an exploration of the degree to which staff have input into the university's decision-making procedures.[43]

The appointment of Norman Kingsbury to head the NZQA encouraged the higher education sector and led to a less confrontational style. He was able to persuade the various higher education sectors to meet and discuss common problems in quality assurance without the threat of forcing a single regime on them.

As noted above, the government has begun to act on some of the ideas of TEAC, but it was unsettling that the government began talking about "efficiencies," a Thatcherite code word for budget cuts and casualisation of faculty. Much would depend, as the NZVCC commented, on how independent TEC proved to be and how much power it would have over individual institutions, and on whether the government would provide funds for competitive wages so New Zealand might actually compete in the OECD. The Council of Trade Unions welcomed the reports but warned that funding of the sector had to be sorted out, given the massive under-funding in the recent past.[44]

There were also signs that old Labour had not entirely vanished, especially the desire of Labour governments in the 1980s for detailed central government control and constant micro-managing. The government decided to allow the Education and Science Select Committee to announce it would review tertiary institutions on a cyclical basis even though this was not required under the Public Finance Act—despite the parallel work of TEAC. The AUS sourly observed that New Zealand now had "yet another review process with all the costs entailed, and no obvious benefits resulting from it," yet another demonstration the government does not comprehend university autonomy.[45]

---

[42]NZVCC, *Annual Report 2000; AUS Tertiary Update* 4,21 [2001 June 28].

[43]AUSNZ, *Submission on the Review of the New Zealand Universities Academic Audit Unit–July 2001,* Wellington, 2001, and *Submission to TEAC's Fourth Report: Implementation of the Strategy,* Section C: Quality Assurance, Wellington, July 2001.

[44]*AUS Tertiary Update,* 4,6 [2001 March 15].

[45]*Ibid.,*2001 March 4, 5, 8 4,5 [2001 March 8].

When four small polytechnics became financially troubled, the government chose to respond with a bill giving the Minister sweeping powers to dissolve a governing council, including a university council, if the Minister considered there was a financial crisis, and to replace it with a commissioner who would have total responsibility not only for finances but for all academic programmes. The *New Zealand Herald* called it an insidious centralization of power, and opposed another section which would allow the Minister to appoint his or her own delegate to a university council if the operation or long-term viability was considered at risk. There was no need for government spies, the *Herald* said. The NZVCC said the legislation was "premature, unnecessary and objectionable," contained no definition of "at risk," and should be retired until decisions are made about the proposals coming from TEAC. It pointed out that the government already had powers to deal with the financial situation at hand.[46] Any risk was caused by the drastic decline in government funding and the ill-considered policy encouraging maximum competition and thus over-capacity in some institutions.[47] The government made adjustments, but not to the central thrust of the legislation.

Overshadowing all discussion by the new government was the serious financial crisis in the universities, which seemed likely to drive most other issues to the periphery of the agenda. The new government promised during the election campaign to bring relief on student debt. It honoured that commitment by subsidizing the interest on student debt to the tune of $NZ420 million over four years. On the other hand, it forced universities to pay for a large part of that commitment by pressing them to freeze tuition fees in return for a 2.3% increase in tuition subsidies, which translated into an overall increase of 1.6%. Inflation in 2000 was almost 4% and other costs such as library and equipment purchases were seriously affected by the 28% depreciation of the New Zealand dollar. In consequence the universities overall lost $NZ17 million.

They had been led to believe this would be a one-shot deal. In 2001 the government continued the arrangement, telling the universities they could always refuse, receive no additional money from the government, lose their increase for the current year, raise their fees, and suffer the political consequences.[48] There was no discussion or negotiation with the vice-chancellors—just an announcement. It was much like the bad old days.

Universities choosing the latter route would be excluded from the $NZ40.6 million the government promised for new centres of excellence. The President of AUSNZ said there was "no principled basis" for such a

---

[46]*Ibid.*, 2001 March 4, 8, and 29; and April 9.

[47]NZVCC statement, 2001 April 3.

[48]The government said the offer was for 5.1% but was to be spread over two years, thus amounting to an increase in 2001 of 1.7%. Bryan Gould, "We don't want a fight but...," *THES*, 22 June 2001.

linkage, and the NZVCC called it "tantamount to blackmail."[49] The NZVCC recommended to its members that they refuse the government's offer, which was open until 31 August 2001. If the stand-off continued, the vice-chancellors threatened fees would rise dramatically, perhaps by more than $NZ500 per student.[50] The Minister of Finance insisted the offer was "take it or leave it."[51] Ultimately the government offered a sweetener of $34.7 million which it seemed would temporarily satisfy the vice-chancellors but left the AUS "underwhelmed" since it could not be applied to salaries.[52] The government seemed content to wait for the final report of TEAC dealing with funding.

That report came out late in 2001, recommending sweeping changes in the funding of the entire post-secondary system, particularly in the funding of research. The universities were likely to support in principle the recommendation to create a national research fund so that research would not remain mostly dependent for its financing on undergraduate enrolments and the consequent fees and governmental grants. It suggested significant limitations on the entry of private institutions into the post-secondary market. It favoured increasing standards for entry to universities and thus reducing the number of their undergraduate students, thereby shifting more of (perhaps ultimately all?) such teaching to the polytechnics. This would be achieved by removing the existing statutory requirement that those teaching university level courses be research active. A minority report noted that it was curious to demand increased standards for student entrance but lower standards for university teaching.

It discussed in detail various forms of performance and quality assurance for postgraduate research, and recommended a mix of PIs and quality assessment, based on extensive consultation with the vice-chancellors but not with staff representatives. This was inspired by the British Research Assessment Exercise and by a similar arrangement in Hong Kong. University scores would be based 50% on the quality rating of staff (self-assessment followed by random outside audits every five years of a 10% sample of staff), 25% based on external research income generated, and 25% on research degrees completed. This would determine access to a central research fund but one which would initially only be $20 million greater than existing arrangements. The Commission recognized the second of these criteria would likely steer most of the research money to universities with medical schools, but seemed incapable of suggesting any way out of this dilemma other than perhaps reducing that component. It also noted that this criterion would seriously compro-

---

[49]AUSS *Tertiary Update* 4, 18 [2001 June 7]; NZVCCs, *Electronic News Bulletin*1, 5 (2001 June 5).

[50] THES, 2001 June 8; AUSS *Tertiary Update*, 4, 24 (2001 July 19). If Massey chose not to raise its fees, it would face a deficit of $NZ11.5 million.

[51]NZVCC, *Electronic News Bulletin*, 1, 8 (2001 July 17).

[52]AUS *Tertiary Update,* 2001 August 9.

mise research in law, business, humanities and the social sciences even though other parts of the report recommended increased attention to these areas. Although the Commission is well aware of the perils of simply counting publications or citations, it seems likely that these forms of production will be the main test of whether academics are judged to do research at a national or international level. Nevertheless the proposal does avoid some of the key drawbacks to the British Research Assessment Exercise, notably the costs involved.

At the undergraduate level, the Commission copped out in a remarkable "on the one hand and on the other hand" chapter. It wants an elaborate scheme of PIs to measure access, retention, completion and destination of graduates although in other parts of the report it recognizes, for example, how a focus on completion can encourage dumbing down. It is also intrigued by American models of performance funding. While detailing their faults, it nevertheless recommends that their approach be adopted by the use of financial penalties for non-compliance with benchmarks. It attacked the AAU because its quality audit system did not include the power to impose penalties even though in an earlier report it had bemoaned the mentality of compliance created by such systems. Public reporting and public debate are a better way to go.

The Commission's approach appears to be mainly geared to increasing access for Maori, Pacific Islanders and the disabled. It is hard to see why the government should opt for such a bureaucratic structure to achieve this instead of simply funding programmes for students in those three categories. For example, in the case of disabled students, it would be much more useful to fund improved student services including more trained staff, increased technology making use of technical innovations for the blind and deaf (computer use, closed circuit captioning in classrooms and the like), architectural changes, how to provide for students with learning disabilities, and the like for all universities rather than creating more bureaucracy. It could also directly fund research on how to improve these services in co-operation with overseas universities working in this area. TEC could designate one university to lead this work, and New Zealand universities, as a matter of social l policy, could aim to become world leaders. However, the temptation for the government to instead require benchmarks for access for the disabled without putting up the money to make it a reality will be overwhelming judging by past performance—the perfect bureaucratic solution where nothing happens, bureaucracy grows, and blame is transferred elsewhere.

Finally the Commission threw up its hands and proposed a working party "...to establish consistent and appropriate benchmarks for, and definitions of performance indicators." It further suggested teacher certification be required of all new lecturers and, ultimately, everyone. This has all the possibilities of a bureaucratic horror story and will likely speed the transformation of undergraduate education into a type of secondary schooling, especially in light of the recommendation that university teaching need no longer be done by those involved in research.

On the other hand, if it is designed to encourage universities to develop their own individual professional development plans geared to their academic mission, including instruction in teaching, then the results may be useful. The report favoured creation of a Strategic Development Fund to promote improvements in the sector, which could be helpful if it became a truly independent agency dedicated to research about the post-secondary education system.

The unspoken deal is that if universities accept the regulatory regime, it will be progressive and respectful of intellectual attainment (unlike previous philistine versions) and apply to the private sector, most of whom, it is assumed, could not meet the requirements. There might also be a bit more money. The government said that it would consult through January 2002 before deciding what to do.[53] Nevertheless despite four reports, the universities, at the time of writing, still did not know the details of the proposed PI system at the undergraduate level, nor have any idea what it would cost. The devil, as always, is in the details.

New Zealand academics want to see the meat before making up their minds. They have seen a lot of commissions, reports, green and white papers over the past fifteen years, and know the new government has inherited a civil service dedicated to detailed state control of universities and contemptuous of academics. So, it seems, are some members of the new government.[54] The reports to date had remarkably little to say about the faculty members of the universities and other institutions, other than on how to measure and to evaluate them. University staff are not prepared to wait very long. Job actions provoked by the dismal economic situation of both academic and general staff spread across the sector through November 2001 and will likely escalate in the new year.[55]

■

Because the neo-conservative experiment of the eighties was launched by the Labour Party, there was no viable political structure for dissent. The opposition National Party simply said that it would go further and faster down the same street, and did just that during the '90s.

New Zealand has had almost twenty years to make the great experiment work, and the bloom has come off the rose. A central feature was application of the new market ideology to higher education—an almost complete fiasco—and an enthusiasm for PIs and performance funding that became a relentless tool of centralization. It all amounted to the exact opposite of the Thatcherite vision.

---

[53]Tertiary Education Advisory Commission (TEAC), *Shaping the Funding Framework,* Wellington, New Zealand, 2001November 7.

[54]Bryan Gould, Vice-Chancellor University of Waikato, "Not greedy, merely needy," *THES,* 2001 November 9.

[55] *AUS Tertiary Update,* 4, 40 [2001 November 15].

The new Labour government has the unenviable task of deciding what to do next and whether it wants to avoid being the prisoner of its inherited right-wing bureaucracy.[56]

---

[56]For a critical review of the neo-conservative experiment, see Jane Kelsey, *The New Zealand Experiment: A World Model for Structural Adjustment?* (Auckland: Auckland University Press, 1997, rev. ed.).

5

The United States or, Back to the Future with PIs

"Now I fear we may pass legislation that will do far more harm than good....The education bill requires our schools to make significant improvements in a short time—without providing the necessary resources."
—Senator Jim Jeffords of Vermont,
  New York Times, 2001 December 13

Performance indicators are merely the latest growth industry in the U.S. accountability market, following a line of business techniques and management fads that stretches back to the beginning of the century.[1] Demand for performance indicators arose from the quality assurance movement. Governments wanted to satisfy right-wing demands for tax cuts and reduced government spending simultaneously with parents' and others's insistence on greater accessibility to quality higher education. "Efficiency" was to resolve the contradiction—more bang for fewer bucks.

A 1996 report for the Ohio Board of Regents began with an unusually candid sentence: "In recent years, the relative funding priority of higher education in the state budgets has declined while financial demands for competitive salaries, integration of technology, and staffing have escalated."[2] Three years later a report for the American Association of Community Colleges began: "Increased costs along with decreased state resources have resulted in public demands that colleges and universities make efforts to ensure greater quality, productivity, and effectiveness of their institutions."[3]

But efficiency and excellence are not the same thing. It is efficient for one professor to teach 800 students in a lecture hall, but this seldom makes for excellent education. This distinction lies at the heart of the U.S. performance indicator movement, particularly when translated into performance *funding* (whereby state funding is tied to indicators). Unsurprisingly, many faculty believe the purpose of these exercises is simply to move blame for state under-funding onto the backs of the universities and the teaching staff.

These developments are one consequence of the enormous growth in American higher education since 1945 and the complex problems of managing such an expansion.[4] Ironically, most solutions offered under the guise of performance indicators, performance budgeting, and quality assurance involve massive centralization, bureaucratization, and homogenization of higher education in individual states. These solutions are curiously at odds with American rhetoric about the merits of uncontrolled and unregulated competition.

[1]See Chapters 1 & 2, and also Robert Birnbaum, *Management Fads in Higher Education: Where They Come From, What They Do, Why They Fail* (San Francisco: Jossey Bass, 2000). [Hereafter *Birnbaum*].

[2]Brenda N. Albright, *From Business as Usual to Funding for Results*, background paper, Higher Education Commission, Ohio Board of Regents, 1996 June.

[3]*Performance Based Funding: A Review of Five States*, American Association of Community Colleges, 1999 August 23.

[4]Student enrolments in universities in the United States rose from 2,338,226 in 1947 to 14,262,000 in 1995. National Center for Educational Statistics quoted in Sylvia Horton, "The United States: Self-Governed Profession or Managed Occupation," in David Farnham, *Managing Academic Staff in Changing University Systems: International Trends and Comparisons* (The Society for Research into Higher Education and Open University Press, UK, 1999).

ACCREDITATION

American universities have traditionally guaranteed quality through a dual system of private accrediting agencies. One oversees disciplines such as law and medicine, and allows substantive control by the relevant professions; the other is regional and deals with universities as institutions.

The six regional accrediting bodies employ a series of measurements —number of full-time faculty, amount of time students are in class, size of library, system of governance, and financial health. Their work relies on self-study, including comprehensive visitations every ten years and written reports with explicit findings and recommendations. Discipline is through probation: colleges are given a period of time to rectify reported short-comings,[5] with loss of accreditation as the last resort. There have always been criticisms that the agencies are not tough enough, and that only the smallest and most obscure institutions ever lose accreditation. Those in government see the reports of accrediting agencies as providing a minimum standard, while those in the agencies see themselves as a force for remedial work in higher education.[6]

Accrediting agencies provide a key barrier against the rising number of low-grade or dishonest institutions in the United States, especially those operating there from bases overseas. States use accrediting agencies to distinguish the crooks and the low-grade from the genuine article. When one state cracks down on diploma mills, which simply sell degrees, they move their address to a more accommodating state; the current favourite, Hawaii, now has more than one hundred such mills. These institutions prey particularly on foreign students desperate for a degree from the United States but unfamiliar with the niceties of the American university system. In a few cases such institutions try to reform; but, as one chief academic officer said ruefully, "When you go legitimate, the sad thing is that it is not a good thing for the money situation."[7] Problems created by such institutions mushroomed with the arrival of the Internet.

Critics argue the measurements used by regional accrediting agencies downplay student skill-acquisition over four undergraduate years. Students surrounded by the best libraries and faculty may still not learn very much. The "gentleman's C" at Yale University, now officially discouraged, epitomizes the problem. Anxious for a quick solution, some regional associations have embraced performance indicators as part of their remit, particularly to demonstrate student learning other than through marks in regular courses.

---

[5]For examples, see Beth McMurtrie, "Accrediting Agencies Place 3 Institutions on Probation," *Chronicle of Higher Education* [hereafter *Chronicle*], 2000 August 11.

[6]Beth McMurtrie, "Regional Accreditors Punish Colleges Rarely and Inconsistently," *Chronicle*, 2001 January 12. The toughest regional is the Southern Association, the only one to put a major institution, Georgia Institute of Technology, on probation.

[7]Sarah Carr and Andrea L. Foster, "States Struggle to Regulate Online Colleges That Lack Accreditation," *Chronicle*, 2001 March 23.

As the agencies move to change their rules, they are accused of eroding standards.[8] For example, the Western Association has removed requirements for a core of full-time faculty, 45 semester credits in general education, and a library (replaced by access to "information resources"). This demonstrates how, although nominally independent of government, such agencies are in fact closely attuned to the agenda of producing mass higher education on the cheap. Others object that the notion of the student as "consumer," with "student satisfaction" more important than traditional grades, guarantees the dumbing-down of institutions.

"I don't know how they're going to tell the difference between the good, the bad, and the ugly," says Jane V. Wellman, a senior associate with the Institute for Higher Education Policy. "Like it or not, the old standards helped accreditors reach judgements. When push came to shove, they had things which could stand up to litigation and politics."[9]

PERFORMANCE-BASED FUNDING/BUDGETING

Performance indicators may be defined as quantitative data on any aspect of a university's institutional or program performance. There are important distinctions between performance indicators giving "information or intelligence related to a program or institutional goal" and management statistics showing "activity or achievement in an area of management interest that is not directly related to a goal."[10] Performance indicators refer to measurable goals, such as retention and graduation rates, rather than to ongoing activities and processes hard to measure quantitatively, such as quality of teaching.[11]

Proponents of performance indicators argue they want to replace the older notion of "inputs"—library holdings, the number of full-time staff, faculty degrees, and the like—with measurement of "outputs" showing student outcomes. Despite insistence that output PIs are reliable and quantifiable, there are doubts on this score: outcome measures are frequently vague, especially compared with the now-derided "input" measures, and generally left to the institutions to implement. Some, such as honours essays, may well be valid but are also expensive and hard to compare.

Performance indicators appealed strongly to state governments who hoped to tie funding to performance. In some states they were applied to higher education as part of an attempt to impose 'performance funding'

---

[8]Letter of Stephen J. Nelson, Brown University, *Chronicle*, 2000 August 11; "Accrediting Agencies Place 3 Institutions on Probation," *loc. cit.*

[9]Beth McMurtrie, "Accreditors Revamp Policies to Stress Student Learning," *Chronicle*, 2000 July 7, 13.

[10]E. Grady Bogue, "Quality Assurance in Higher Education: The Evolution of Systems and Design Ideals," in Gerald M. Gaither, *Quality Assurance in Higher Education* (San Francisco: Jossey-Bass, 1998). [Hereafter *Bogue*].

[11]For an argument favouring implementation of PIs, see *Linking Higher Education Performance Indicators to Goals*, Educational Benchmark 2000 Series, Southern Regional Education Board, Atlanta, Georgia, 2000 February.

on *all* state agencies; in other states it was reserved exclusively for post-secondary education. This movement, which began in the southern states and remains strongest there, exhibits two main trends, not mutually exclusive. One is to create a range of performance indicators state institutions must meet, such as a fixed graduation rate. The second is to require testing of undergraduate learning in reasoning, writing, and the like, using the results to evaluate the quality of the programmes. Either way it was hoped an objective method could be devised to distinguish good from bad, and applied mechanically across the board to determine the budget of each university and college in the state, thereby eliminating the problems arising from individual quality judgements.

For example, the latest version of the Missouri strategic plan links funding to meeting certain objectives, such as raising graduation rates. This means public universities must submit plans for measurable results from any new investment of state funds. West Virginia will require public universities to enter compacts committing them to long-term improvements. In Virginia a Blue Ribbon Commission on Higher Education established by the Governor called for six-year performance agreements, tying state support to efficiency, better use of technology, and other improvements, especially closer ties with business in order to meet business needs. Universities, said the Commission, should assess how well students have mastered core competencies during their undergraduate careers. These would include reading, writing, and basic skills in mathematics, science, and computers—all of which might fit more reasonably within the ambit of secondary schools.

The *Chronicle of Higher Education* noted: "The views and needs of business are at the heart of nearly all the long-range higher-education plans that states have adopted or are considering."[12] States and their universities increasingly fear slipping behind in global competition. The Illinois Board of Higher Education has declared economic growth the first priority of its ten-year plan. Public universities will be accountable for their students' success in the work force, as measured by standardized tests, career placement, licensure examinations, and surveys of employer satisfaction.

Master plans can, of course, deal with matters other than the total number of computers purchased. Some American states include accessibility in their strategic plans: Colorado wants to do a better job of reaching rural students; Illinois, West Virginia, and Wisconsin want to provide more access for working adults; Missouri and Virginia are committed to limiting tuition increases. Some master plans, such as California's, actively invite public universities to assist the public school system, through improved teacher training and by direct linkages.[13] Still, most discussion of accessibility emphasizes technology rather than student finances.

---

[12]*Chronicle*, 2000 June 30.
[13]*Ibid.*

Performance indicators may be the newest craze, but they have been present in many and varied guises during previous decades. In the 1970s, for example, Massachusetts developed "Kelly Points" named after Senator James Kelly, who claimed professors were not working hard enough. The system mandated points for every professorial activity, which had to total a set figure each year. Kelly Points disappeared when Senator Kelly himself failed a basic political performance indicator by being jailed for extortion.[14]

Such events suggest indicators may be part of recurring North American bouts of anti-intellectualism, together with occasional waves of dislike for teachers and their unions. Teachers no longer conform to the image on the covers of the *Saturday Evening Post*; in their modern guise they are expensive, and prone to contrary views. Performance indicators could also be manipulated to penalize the humanities, the arts, and the social sciences in favour of such "practical subjects" as engineering.

Robert Birnbaum suggests it is wise for states to think about the future, but "silly" for them to believe that they can predict or control it, or solve their problems through new technology or unproven approaches such as performance-based budgeting.[15] "[T]hey offer no wisdom at all on whether the most effective response to poor performance is to cut one's losses or increase one's investment." He considers such indicators fundamentally false because (a) some key activities of the university are not statistically measurable and (b) large universities have multiple goals, difficult to correlate statistically. Institutions will continue to receive funding at historic levels because large-scale funding changes are politically unsustainable.

Others argue along somewhat the same lines: "[W]e tend to construct indicators that reflect the ease of capturing data rather than identify those criteria that will carry valid evidence of performance."[16] "What was available was collected and measured, what was measured—or measurable —was given value, and what was given value was reviewed for accountability and funding."[17] Roger Peters notes: "[E]ffective assessment requires a diligent search for bad news, which is more useful than good, but accountability encourages the opposite. Campus officials are understandably reluctant to bear bad tidings to those who fund them."[18]

Other critics suggest these criteria transform the universities into mere job training institutes at the expense of their traditional educational mission. Most of these schemes drastically devalue the liberal arts and pure sciences.

---

[14]Daniel Bernstein and Richard Edwards, "We Need Objective, Rigorous Peer Review of Teaching," *loc. cit.*, 5 January 2001 (hereafter *Bernstein and Edwards*).

[15]*Chronicle*, 2000 June 30.

[16]*Bogue*, 13.

[17]G. Gaither, B.P. Nedwek, J.E. Neal, *Measuring Up: The Promises and Pitfalls of Performance Indicators in Higher Education*, ASHE-ERIC Higher Education Reports, No. 5, Washington, 1994, quoted in *Birnbaum*, 82–3.

[18]Roger Peters, "Some Snarks Are Boojums: Accountability and the Ethos of Higher Education," *Change*, 1994, 26, (6), 16–23, quoted in *Bogue*, 13.

Ironically, some business leaders admit the articulate graduates they want —people who can think, write, and understand the global economy—are more likely to be produced through traditional liberal arts education.

Performance funding coupled with performance indicators push universities towards homogeneity. If there can be no classes with less than a fixed minimum of students, this eliminates specialties which may be vital to a full appreciation of the discipline or profession in question. This is especially marked in the more theoretical aspects of science and mathematics as well as the teaching of languages and culture. *The New York Times* has lamented the failure of American universities in the area of languages study. Only 8.2% of students take a second language and most elect Spanish, French, or German. In 1999–2000 American universities and colleges graduated only eight majors in Arabic. The consequences are readily at hand. Half the State Department's postings abroad are filled by persons who cannot speak the local language. The FBI possessed tapes on the bombing at the World Trade Center before the explosion, but could not translate them.[19] The events of 11 September 2001 dramatically escalated these concerns. "It is one thing to stage a teach-in on Islam, another to train experts in the languages and cultures of an enormously complex world," said the *New York Times*. "Are the universities up to the task?" it asked.[20] Not if the mindless number-crunchers have their way.

Other controversies centre on equity, particularly where institutional segregation formerly allowed unequal state universities for whites and blacks. Given the historic disparities in funding and public acceptance, it is unlikely that a former black university will do as well on the PIs as a former white one. In this scenario, PIs might become a "scientific" way to entrench racial prejudice. This is a particularly acute problem in the southern states.

In some states legislators enthusiastically vote for performance funding, but negative results—with the possibility of institutional closures in their home constituencies—quickly convince them to change their minds and instead to lobby on behalf of their local institutions.

Perhaps because of these difficulties, performance funding is gradually transforming itself into performance *budgeting*. Performance funding ties state funding directly to the achievements of public colleges and universities on specific performance indicators. Performance budgeting means state governments "[use] indirectly reports of individual achievements on performance indicators as a general context in shaping the total budgets for public colleges and universities."[21] In this much looser arrangement, current

---

[19]*The New York Times*, 2001 April 16.

[20]Eyal Press, "It's a Volatile, Complex World," *ibid.*, 2001 November 11.

[21]Joseph C. Burke and Andrea M. Serban, *Current Status and Future Prospects of Performance Funding and Performance Budgeting for Public Higher Education: The Second Survey* (Public Higher Education Program, The Nelson A. Rockefeller Institute of Government, State University of New York, Albany, New York, 1998), 3.

costs, student enrollments, and inflationary increases continue to dominate state budgets for higher education, but the government may include a small component of reward based on specific performance indicators.

Performance budgeting begins to disappear as the appropriations process grinds out the final budget. Only slightly more than half of executive budgets in states with performance budgeting refer to the performance indicators, and

> just above a quarter of the budget bills or related documents report on the performance of public colleges and universities. A legislative staff member, commenting on Florida's Performance Based Program Budgeting for all state agencies, quipped that the only obvious connection between funding and performance was that the indicators and the allocations often appeared on the same page in the budget bill.[22]

Furthermore, as the most recent of the annual reports of the Higher Education Program of the Rockefeller Institute of Government at SUNY indicates, the impact of the performance regime in any particular state rarely has a measurable effect below the level of the vice-presidents of the universities and colleges.[23] Dr. Joseph C. Burke, Director of the SUNY Higher Education Program, supports the principle of performance financing, but thinks it will have significant impact only if implemented at department and faculty level. His views are a strong reminder how supporters of PIs, who once claimed to have only system-wide statistics in mind, must finally accept that PIs acquire meaning only when they change the daily lives of professors and students. PIs are not just about system-wide efficiencies, but about the transformation of teaching and learning in post-secondary institutions.

Some states are recognizing that plans applied equally to all universities and colleges in the state do not make a great deal of sense. Some indicators should be unique to particular institutions, even generated by the institutions themselves. Some agencies envision longer planning periods for certain programmes.

All these developments suggest it is impossible to abolish politics, either in the legislature or in the state at large; that scepticism in academe about centralized quality agencies is not whimsical; and that there is no magic formula to abolish the need for hard work and perceptive judgement in allocation of funds to universities and colleges. Failure at the centre does not mean universities and colleges should escape public scrutiny. The political climate of the early 21st century demands transparency. But U.S. experience with performance funding suggests accountability and transparency are likely to succeed if they begin with some conviction at a local

---

[22]Joseph C. Burke, Jeff Rosen, Henrik Minassians, and Terri Lessard, *Performance Funding and Budgeting: An Emerging Merger?, The Fourth Annual Survey*, Higher Education Program, The Nelson A. Rockefeller Institute of Government, State University of New York, Albany, New York, 2000, 3.

[23]*Ibid.*, 12.

level. Universities and colleges must continue to make their case to state governments by indicating more clearly, to both politicians and the public, the merits of their spending decisions.

SOUTH CAROLINA

One of the best advertised state plans for a performance funding system was created by Act 359 of the South Carolina[24] Legislature in 1996. It is the most sweeping in the nation and has been regarded as a prototype by many of the devotees of PIs. The South Carolina Commission for Higher Education (the CHE)[25] was required to allocate all state appropriations for higher education based on performance in "critical success factors" in nine areas:

- mission focus
- quality of faculty
- classroom quality
- cooperation and collaboration
- administrative efficiency
- entrance requirements

---

[24]The South Carolina Commission for Higher Education divides the states' public universities into four categories—3 research universities, 9 teaching universities, 5 two-year regional campuses of the University of South Carolina, and 16 technical colleges. Two of the research universities (University of South Carolina at Columbia, and Clemson University) and one teaching university (College of Charleston) predominate in terms of student numbers. In 1999 there were 73,701 students in the 12 public senior institutions, an increase of 2.5% from 1995. There were 16 technical colleges with a total enrolment of 45,247, an increase of 10.8% since 1995. The technical colleges and the two-year campuses of the University of South Carolina subsumed the role of community colleges. USC at Columbia and Clemson University dominated graduate studies, although there were a high number of MA students at South Carolina State University. The State University remained predominantly black, with only 228 white students. In 2000/2001 public sector higher education universities and colleges received a state appropriation of $802,499,188, not including capital improvements and unique costs. There were 23 private senior institutions with a total of 31,311 FTE students, an increase of 16.4% since 1995. Bob Jones University is the largest private university. (*Ten Year Statistics*, South Carolina Commission for Higher Education, 2000.) In 1990 South Carolina had a total population of 3,486,703, of whom 31% were non-white (State of South Carolina, Population Statistics). See American Association of Community Colleges, *Performance Based Funding—A Review of Five States*, 1999 August 23, which includes a section on South Carolina, and South Carolina Legislative Audit Council, *A Review of the Higher Education Funding Process: Report to the General Assembly*, 2001 June (hereafter *Audit Council*), and special issue, *The State*, 2001 May 13.

[25]The Commission is responsible both for the implementation of accountability measures and for advocating funding levels to the legislature for higher education institutions in the state. When the budget process is complete in the legislature, the CHE allocates state funding to individual institutions. It also decides on new academic programmes. However, it has less power over the institutions than some other state higher education commissions although PIs have increased that control. See the CHE's web site for its *Strategic Plan*.

- graduates' achievements
- user-friendliness of institution
- research funding

The Legislature mandated the nine critical success factors as well as thirty-seven performance indicators. The CHE was required to develop and define how each indicator would be measured, told to use "objective, measurable criteria," and, over a three-year phase-in period, instructed to reach 100% of funding based on performance. After the CHE subdivided many indicators, their total number reached around seventy (since reduced). Funding based totally on PIs was to begin in 1999/2000.

Why would the legislature do this? Accountability systems for higher education were in vogue; some South Carolina legislators who dislike professors thought this new policy would stick it to them. Others, for political reasons, sought an excuse to depose the head of the Commission. More rational concerns included the lack of structures for students transferring between two-year and four-year institutions, class size (particularly in first year), competition for students by dumbing down, and the employability of graduates. But the overriding rationale was economic: there were too many universities and colleges in South Carolina. Performance funding formulae would magically decide closures and save a bundle of money, with no negative fall-out for legislators. Closures would in turn allow tax cuts. But the legislators forgot they had created many of the two-year institutions for political reasons. Their constituencies fought back when their colleges were threatened, and there have been no closures.[26]

South Carolina cannot boast a tradition of generous support to higher education. In 1998 the higher education consultant MGT of America found South Carolina institutions "were generally funded at a lower level than their peer institutions." Funding per FTE student was $7,862 in North Carolina and $7,562 in Georgia, with the average for sixteen southern states at $6,037 and South Carolina at $5,367.[27] Another statistic illustrates the results of historical under funding. Every year the Association of Research Libraries issues a ranking of university libraries. Currently the University of South Carolina ranks 50th, and Clemson does not make the list of the first 100. On the other hand, the University of North Carolina ranks 17th, Duke 25th, and North Carolina State University 35th—the latter making one of the largest increases in the country since 1995. The University of Georgia ranks 28th.

In 1999–2000 the Commission claimed it had reached its goal—appropriations were now based entirely on the performance of the higher education institutions. The Commission's approach had two major components: (a) determination of the financial needs of each institution,

---

[26]See "Focus on South Carolina Colleges," *The State*, Columbia, South Carolina, 2001 May 13.

[27]Five states were lower than South Carolina: Tennessee, Oklahoma, Kentucky, Alabama, West Virginia, and Louisiana.

and *(b)* "a process for rating the institutions based on performance across the indicators." The ratings involved setting a standard, sometimes for a particular institution, sometimes for a set of similar institutions. Ratings were then totalled and expressed as an average score.[28]

The Commission has tried hard to make its system more rational than originally conceived. Determination of financial needs, calculated on enrolment and other given factors, has become the crucial part of the formula. Despite all the pyrotechnics about performance indicators, assessment of needs for each institution is not greatly different from traditional incremental funding.

The Commission is circumscribed by the fact that the 37 performance indicators are set out in legislation. It accepted that performance could not be measured down to a percentage point, and now gives a leeway of 3% for error. It abandoned absolute benchmarks in favour of ranges when it discovered a slight variation downwards (for instance, in minority enrolments) could place an institution with overall high minority enrolments below one with fewer such students. It has accepted that continuous improvement is not always possible, and can discriminate against the very best. It has scaled down or abandoned indicators which cannot be measured effectively or which do not reveal information useful for making policy.

For example, early statistics showed over-large classes were not generally a problem in South Carolina, and thus statistics on class-size were not useful to planners. At first the Commission tried, with the assistance of other government agencies, to track every single graduate of the state's colleges and universities, recording what their employers thought about them and their education. Employability data were especially sought for technical colleges since they are tied more directly to specific local job markets. The Commission ultimately concluded that creating and storing this information was not only expensive but an invasion of privacy. On the other hand, it has been able to collect detailed data on race without backlash, presumably because South Carolina was for decades under court order to desegregate, and the courts required racial information to determine whether or not the state complied. The CHE has no indicator for needs-based assistance, as distinct from merit scholarships, and is not an advocate for such funds before the legislature.

Overall the Commission has created a state-wide data base through negotiated agreement on the definition of most categories and terms, which simply did not exist in any accurate form before. This is no mean achievement. In doing so it has encouraged universities and colleges to be more business-like in data collection. This, too, is useful (even if not on a par with excellence in teaching and research). All this tinkering of course

---

[28]*Performance Funding in South Carolina for Higher Education*, web site of the South Carolina Commission for Higher Education, 2001 February.

has a downside. Universities must rejig their databases, at considerable cost, making comparisons over time difficult.

■

South Carolina's involvement with performance indicators would be taken much more seriously if it abandoned rhetoric about 100-per-cent-performance-based funding. After an extensive 1999 survey of the South Carolina system, the *Chronicle of Higher Education* concluded only about 5% of institutional budgets were at risk under the system. It noted that the South Carolina Commission's use of financial needs as an indicator ensures funds for universities and colleges to cover the costs of increased enrolments and other requirements not specified in the original legislation.[29] The *Chronicle* noted that all institutions managed to pass, and 18 of 33 exceeded state standards. Perhaps the higher education sector has discovered the same solution industry found with Management by Objectives: set the objectives low and one will always pass. To forestall the use of such strategic devices, CHE recently mandated that some PI measurement be identical in similar institutions.

The South Carolina Legislative Audit Council came to much the same conclusions in its influential June 2001 report to the legislature. It found the CHE model similar to that which obtained before 1996; only about 3% of higher education budgets were affected by performance scores. It concluded the original legislation was flawed. Had it been carried out in full, extreme fluctuations of between 30% to 40% in individual institutions would have made planning impossible. For example, had true PIs been implemented, the University of South Carolina two-year college at Sumter would have received more funds than the main campus at Columbia, because Sumter had a higher performance score.[30] "The science of performance indicators has not advanced to the degree that the institutional scores have provided valid comprehensive assessments of institutional quality." In any event, the legislature's 1991/92 funding created a situation where, the report said, it would take $56 million to level the playing field for institutions. Some PIs could not be statistically measured, so questions about them could only be answered "yes" or "no." Moreover PIs have had "little effect on the elimination of waste and

---

[29]Peter Schmidt, "A State Transforms Colleges with 'Performance Funding'," *Chronicle*, 1999 July 2.

[30]CHE itself recognized the problem. As its Performance Funding Principles note, "The need for strong incentives and disincentives should be balanced with the need for a reasonable level of stability and predictability for planning purposes," and "a needs determination ... to ensure equity in funding." (Dr. Michael Smith, *Performance Funding in South Carolina: Fitting The Pieces Together,* Division of Planning, Assessment & Performance Funding, South Carolina Commission on Higher Education, revised 2001 April.)

duplication in higher education." However, CHE implemented data verification provided improved control over information about the public higher education system.

The Audit Council concluded that the legislature should amend the law to eliminate the requirement that all funding be based on PIs:

> Reasons that the performance measurement system should not be used as the sole determinant of institutional funding include: changes and volatility of the system, problems in measurement, the narrow focus of the indicators, and the use of some indicators that may be inappropriate for some institutions.[31]

Elsewhere in the country most states using PIs limited them to 1% or 3–4% of the budget. The Audit Council recommended the legislature continue to allocate a portion of the state funds based on PIs, but more in line with other states.

CHE agreed with much of the report, and reluctantly accepted that funding should be based only in part on performance indicators. But it argued that under the new system in South Carolina, the percentage of programmes accredited had grown dramatically in some sectors, SAT scores and other entrance data had shown increases, institutions had moved quickly to eliminate or to improve programmes found deficient in academic review, and the percentage of the budgets spent on academic rather than administrative expenses had increased.[32] It noted also that the cumulative effect of any cuts based on PIs would exceed 5%.

The CHE claims to have significantly encouraged accreditation in the non-research sector.[33] Most eligible programmes in the research universities were accredited before 1996, but this was not true elsewhere. The Commission notes a new clarity in transfer arrangements between institutions and new recruitment of minorities. It claims teacher education has greatly improved since 1996, and that higher education is paying more attention to licensure examinations in various professions,[34] thus increasing quality of instruction. It claims the performance indicator

---

[31]See also Peter Schmidt, "Performance-Based Aid Has Little Effect on Colleges in South Carolina," *Chronicle*, 2001 June 6.

[32]South Carolina Commission on Higher Education, *Response to South Carolina Legislative Audit Council Report: A Review of the Higher Education Performance Funding Process*, in *Audit Council*.

[33]Even such a straightforward indicator can produce difficulties. Some accreditations, particularly in business administration, are notoriously expensive, and the Commission is generally not prepared to pay the costs. Other accreditations may not prove relevant. For example, Clemson University has a master's program in fine arts and architecture. Even though this was never meant to produce professional accredited architects, the Commission nevertheless penalized Clemson for not seeking accreditation in architecture for the program. This would have cost a fortune and saddled Clemson with a full-scale architecture school it did not want.

[34]This too can create controversy. Is a law school concerned exclusively with training its students for the local bar better than a law school with an important research component, whose students may have out-of-state ambitions?

system pushed remedial education out of four-year institutions except where the universities were prepared to pay full costs themselves. (Others argue this was a separate and distinct decision having little or nothing to do with performance indicators.)

The Commission's peculiar structure may have contributed to its difficulties. It is chiefly responsible for gathering the statistical base on higher education and determining how the performance funding system will work. Because there is no minister or department of higher education in South Carolina, it also recommends the state higher education budget, defends it before the General Assembly, and distributes the results to individual institutions. This arrangement is bound to encourage suspicion amongst universities and colleges. Since the Commission has no independent appeals structure, its staff attempt to mediate disputes. If that does not work, the Commission acts as prosecutor and judge. To no one's surprise, almost all appeals fail.

The system, like many others, puts an excessive trust in anodyne mission statements promising excellence, commitment to learning, assistance to economic development, and respect for the local cultural heritage.[35] The performance indicators used in 2000–2001 were not only all over the map, but self-contradictory besides. Indicators which discourage recruitment of students from out of state, and encourage graduates to do their post-graduate education in the state, hardly promote excellence. Fixed graduation rates encourage dumbing-down of the curriculum because administrators pressure faculty to pass everyone. (The Commission says it finds no evidence of this in South Carolina.[36]) Incentives to increase faculty workloads contradict incentives to limit class sizes. Some colleges were actually penalized for small classes, despite evidence that smaller classes produce better learning and indeed are required in some disciplines, such as nursing. A perverse effect occurred at the University of South Carolina at Spartanburg: the University's effort to replace part-timers with full-time faculty hurt its "instructional quality" score because it reduced the number of hours taught by the full-time academic staff.[37]

Other PIs imply an interest in excellence. These rate institutions on the percentages of full-time employees who are faculty members, on faculty credentials as set by the Southern accrediting agency, on accreditation required in all programmes covered by recognized accrediting bodies, and on whether salaries meet or exceed national averages. Most academics

---

[35]See, for example, the Mission Statement of the University of South Carolina at Columbia adopted by the Trustees in 1998. See also Dlbert's mission statement generating machine at *www.dilbertzone.com/comics/dilbert/career*.

[36] In a recent survey by the Rockefeller Institute of the State University of New York, the data showed that the most opposed indicator was time to degree where 53% of administrators were opposed or strongly opposed with 29.6% in favour. *Performance Funding Opinion Survey of Campus Groups 1999–2000*, SUNY, 2000.

[37]*Chronicle*, 1999 July 2.

would no doubt applaud the negative judgement against the University of South Carolina's flagship campus at Columbia because it employed too many teaching assistants. (The university complained that this was how it managed enrolment increases in popular courses.)

Performance indicators encouraging higher admission standards make it difficult to satisfy other requirements for increasing the number of students from South Carolina, particularly minority students. PIs actively militate against a college like Francis Marion, whose explicit mission is to educate the especially poor residents of the surrounding region. The Commission has responded by using grade points and academic standing in the local school as well as SAT scores for admission. Homogenized standards are especially difficult to apply to specialized universities such as the Medical University of South Carolina and the Citadel, a military academy; this has led the Commission to consider a more customized arrangement.

There has been vigorous debate between those who argue the state should reward *quality* and those who say it should focus on *improvement*. Fascination with quality may ignore historical realities—for example, that a traditionally black university such as South Carolina State University was for decades under-financed—and could well set in stone inequality between institutions. On the other hand, to emphasize *only* improvement would inevitably penalize the best institutions. The Commission decided to create an improvement fund, deducting 0.25% from allocations to each institution to create pools in each of the four categories of public institutions recognized by the state. These funds are open to proposals for specific improvements from any institution. One such was the summer school created by the College of Charleston for high school students from low income areas; the College hoped this would encourage minority enrolment. The Commission would like to increase state funds for improvement, but does not expect this to happen.

The Legislative Audit noted that the original intent of performance funding was to take from the weak institutions and prompt their closure. The CHE has promulgated regulations for reduction, expansion, consolidation, or closure of an institution as a result of PIs, but, in the words of the Audit, the possibility of closure is remote. An official with the Education Commission of the States could identify only one closure of a public institution in the past fifty years.[38]

Unsurprisingly, research-based universities[39] are especially unhappy with a system based mainly on the functioning of undergraduate education. They claim their research activities, costs, and contributions to the state economy are weighted lightly in the Commission's scoring system. Nor, they say, does the Commission reward excellence already attained. The Legislative

---

[38]*Audit Council*, 24.

[39]The three research universities are the University of South Carolina in Columbia, Clemson University and the Medical University of South Carolina. They represent approximately one-half of the state's annual investment in higher education.

Audit agreed that performance indicators should be "appropriate to each institution based on the institution's unique mission and structure."[40] The Commission's activities have at least persuaded the three research universities to work together much more closely. They now present a united front to the Commission, and recently recommended a revised system of twelve indicators and weightings for their institutions. They insisted comparisons with universities of the same rank in other states are reasonable only if the state legislature produces comparable resources. "Simply stated, the Research Universities are willing to accept performance-based funding as long as the General Assembly and CHE are willing to accept funding-based performance."[41] They suggested the government provide funds in stages so research universities could compete fairly with out-of-state institutions; at each stage the Legislature could see whether universities were performing according to the indicators. The 1996 *Legislative Committee to Study the Governance and Operation of Higher Education in South Carolina* stated the research universities should attain Carnegie Research I status. This is not possible without considerably increased financing.

There is also debate about what actually prompts change in the system. For example, the strategic plan for the Department of Government and International Studies for 1999–2000 at the University of South Carolina outlines a good many changes. Most were suggested by a blue ribbon academic committee appointed by the dean in 1996–97, quite outside the framework required by the state, and in keeping with normal peer review evaluations of departments. This strategic plan illustrates the dilemmas inherent in the application of mechanistic formulae. The department has raised standards for the graduate school—a good result according to the state performance indicators; but this caused a decrease in enrolment—a bad result according to another indicator. The graduate programme is saved only by the creation of two new institutes expected to increase enrolments. The numbers actually enrolled in undergraduate courses appear to be heavily influenced by the decision to eliminate political science from the core curriculum of the College and of the College of Business Administration. The department laments that history secured a place in the core but they did not. Can a state performance indicator take such factors into account? The department's strategic plan indicates implementation will cost more, not less money. One might expect all departments to sooner or later discover this method for the leverage of funds.[42]

---

[40] *Audit Council*, 24.

[41] *A Joint Proposal To Modify South Carolina's Performance Funding System*, submitted by South Carolina's Research Universities to the Commission on Higher Education, South Carolina, 2001, 7.

[42] See, for example, *Linguistics Program Five-Year Strategic Plan 2001–2002*, University of South Carolina, Columbia, South Carolina.

One of the most important changes has hardly been discussed at all in South Carolina. Before 1996, the Commission reviewed each higher education programme or subject every eight years, choosing peer reviewers from those nominated by the universities. Proper subject reviews assess quality, and are not fixated on management fads. A subject review system continued after 1996 but was "suspended" for budgetary reasons in 2001. In fact, this suspension is permanent—the performance indicator bureaucracy has ousted program review. This is an academically perverse result. No doubt the three research universities will eventually do their own subject reviews, but few smaller institutions can afford to do so. For the three research universities the result may be a better system, locally-based and taking into account out-of-state comparisons in the subject area under examination. For the other thirty institutions, subject review will simply disappear. This illustrates the current orthodoxy among devotees of performance indicators: that subject reviews are too difficult to quantify scientifically, and should be replaced by numerical output indicators.

The new system also allows institutions to bring in controversial employment practices simply by transferring the decision to the legislature and the Commission on Higher Education. Lack of unionization made this relatively simple. "I think it was easier to implement post-tenure review when we could say our state funding was dependent on it," said Marcia G. Welsh, an associate provost at the University of South Carolina. When taken seriously, post-tenure review is hugely expensive in staff and administrative time, and, given rigorous tenure arrangements in most universities, unlikely to show more than one or two per cent of those reviewed to be "unsatisfactory." Instead these individuals could be encouraged to take employee development programmes, and dismissed if they showed no improvement, without using this expensive and contentious apparatus. South Carolina has yet to learn that, in a period of impending teaching shortages, treatment of faculty may prove the most important performance indicator of all.

In a speech lauding the system, South Carolina's Commissioner for Higher Education admitted it involved an immense amount of work.

> I am talking about hundreds of meetings (some rancorous) and thousands of hours of consultation with university representatives, business representatives, legislators and their staff, students, and other advocacy groups....

Nevertheless, he argued, the process had been healthy:

> It has prompted us to move beyond provincialism and to reassess not just how we teach and learn but why we teach and learn. Colleges and universities must take stock of what they want to be and then focus on spending money in the right ways to achieve those desires.

The new system came about because higher education institutions failed to convince the legislature, the public, and the business community that they were doing their job properly. In particular, the business community thought:

colleges and universities were not providing a well-prepared work force and were not, with some exceptions, sufficiently engaging the business community about its needs.[43]

No one has quantified the overall cost of all these hours and the Commission's ongoing activities and demands, although there are plenty of complaints about the bureaucracy involved. A dozen administrators told the *Chronicle* the system forces them to spend too much money and time gathering and reporting internal data, not all of it pertinent.[44] The Legislative Audit provided a telling example: the indicator measuring credit hours earned by graduates required staff to manually pull copies of all graduates' transcripts and assess whether they had more hours than required for their program. USC has three full-time employees who collect data for performance funding. Requiring institutions to collect data that has no specific use does not represent an efficient use of resources.[45] Said the President of Lander University:

> If you are not careful, I'm afraid you end up chasing performance scores rather than doing what you are supposed to be doing, which is educating students.

The Commission's Planning and Assessment Committee responded by recommending a number of changes:

- elimination of duplicate indicators
- easing reporting requirements
- reducing the total number of indicators scored annually
- tailoring of indicators to the mission of each sector and the strategic goals of each institution
- noting that where an indicator required compliance and the compliance had been met, the institution need not keep reporting

All this could be done, it was suggested, without violating the nine categories mandated by the legislature.[46]

Universities and colleges complained that the creation of this higher education machine has not been coupled with substantial increases in base funding, despite positive results in all 33 institutions. The pattern of funding in South Carolina has been that of many parts of North America—relatively flat in current dollars at the beginning of the decade, and rising gently towards the end following an upturn in the economy. In 1999 the

---

[43]"Explaining the 'Immense Amount of Work' in S.C.'s System," *Chronicle*, 1999 July 2.

[44]The survey by the Rockefeller Institute showed 80.9% of administrators wanted fewer indicators and 77.8% supported more institutional choice of relevant indicators by the institution. *Performance Funding Opinion Survey of Campus Groups 1999–2000*, Rockefeller Institute, State University of New York, 2000.

[45]*Audit Council*, 24.

[46]Minutes of the Planning and Assessment Committee, 2001 January 9, Division of Planning, Assessment and Performance Funding, South Carolina Commission on Higher Education.

Legislature increased the budget for public institutions by 2% and in 2000 by 4%, but in the latter case almost one-third of the increase went for enrolment growth, a reversion to traditional ways of state funding.

The performance funding system rewards institutions which exceed standards overall with a bonus equal to 3% of their appropriation for that year, and 1% to those which simply equal the standard. None received the 5% bonus for substantially exceeding the standard, and none were penalized with deductions.[47] The money that really counts, of course, is not bonuses but the state appropriation for base funding.

Like most American legislatures, South Carolina's pursues a vigorous tax-cutting ethos, whatever the impact on state services. In May 2001 the editors of a Columbia newspaper protested it would be unseemly to cut taxes at the same time as the legislature is cutting public services.[48] In 2001 the Governor proposed a 15% cut across the board in higher education, with no reference to performance. According to Scott Ludlow, the chief business officer of Clemson University, cuts to that university would be between $16 and $25 million, even though its performance rating had jumped a notch. "We could've surpassed the sun, the moon and the stars this year, and it wouldn't have made any difference."[49] "It is hard to see the value in working hard for a system that doesn't reward the effort," agreed Thornton Kirby, executive secretary to Clemson's board of trustees. Ultimately the Governor and Legislature compromised on an 5% cut. The funding crisis has been exacerbated by the Legislature's annual practice of approving *ad hoc* arrangements for particular programs rather than properly funding the base. Since the programs continued from year to year, these were *de facto* base funds, but when the revenues of the state declined, disaster struck.

The ultimate consequence was an increase in fees. Clemson decided to raise tuition for in-state students 41.8%, although it subsequently modified that figure somewhat. Charlie FitzSimon, legislative liaison for the CHE, said this increase "will certainly catch the legislature's attention," and expressed doubt that lawmakers "anticipated this type of increase from any institution." University President James F. Barker "would not go the route of deep cuts, larger classes, fewer course offerings and deteriorating facilities," preferring to maintain quality.[50]

There are two main cost-cutting thrusts in the legislature. The first demands the two-year regional colleges of the University of South Carolina be amalgamated with technical colleges. The difference between them was

---

[47]Until 1999 July each institution was guaranteed a state funding level at least equal to its 1996–97 funding.

[48]*The State*, 2001 May 13.

[49]"Colleges don't expect to see bonuses," *The Grenville News*, 2001 May 22.

[50] *Chronicle*, 2001 June 21. The fee for in-state students will be $5,090 and for out-of-state students $11,284, a 15% increase. Clemson can afford this increase because it has many more student applicants than places. The University of South Carolina decided to increase its fees by 10.4% to $4,160 for undergraduates.

well expressed by Jason Morris, a student who attended both and planned to transfer to a four-year institution:

> Over there [at the technical college], they would show you how to hook up electric circuits.... Here they kind of tell you the theory behind it.[51]

The other thrust is to eliminate one of the two medical schools, despite funding derived 75% or more from non-state sources. Such a proposal does not explain how the state could maintain its intake of physicians, since there is already a shortage, or where it might find sufficient teaching hospitals in one location in the state. Some suggest one medical university with two campuses, but this seems simply a device to increase the number of administrators, even if titles changed.

Ironically the Legislature allows universities and their local representatives to by-pass the CHE's annual amalgamated higher education budget and cut special deals. The Audit Council suggested this practice be brought to an end.[52] Such restraint seems no more likely in South Carolina than in Washington.

The Rockefeller Institute survey showed that 70.6% of administrators thought adoption of performance indicators had not improved funding; only 6.8% thought it had.[53] The universities and colleges are saying, as it were, we collected all this data, we met your standards, but we have not been justly rewarded.

THE TESTING SYNDROME

Standardized testing is a current favourite of many state governors. When the National Governors' Association met in 2001 to set up a policy academy on higher education, the single policy item on which initial agreement was reached was the need to increase student assessment.[54]

A decade earlier, the American Association of University Professors adopted a 1991 report from its Committee on College and University Teaching, Research and Publication on mandated assessments notably sceptical of the value of such tests:

> As a general rule it is safe to observe that undergraduates in American post-secondary education, and other academic programs, are more intensively and perhaps more frequently evaluated than are those in post-secondary education anywhere else in the world.[55]

---

[51] *The State*, 2001 May 13.

[52] *Audit Council*, 6.

[53] *Performance Funding Opinion Survey of Campus Groups 1999–2000* (Rockfeller Institute, State University of New York, 2000).

[54] Jeffrey Selingo, "Governors Seek Improvement and Innovation From Colleges," *Chronicle*, 2001 March 16.. See also Alan Ryan, "The Twisted Path to the Top," *New York Review of Books*, 1999 November 19 (review of Nicholas Lemann, *The Big Test: The Secret History of the American Meritocracy*).

[55] *Mandated Assessment of Educational Outcomes* (Washington, DC: American Association of University Professors, 1991). For a sceptical view of testging for innate qualities and ability, see Malcolm Gladwell, "The Examined Life: What Stanley H. Kaplan taught us about the S.A.T.," *The New Yorker*, 2001 December 17.

It pointed to the use of SAT and ACT tests for admission, GRE and LSAT for admission of post-baccalaureate programmes, frequent testing during the academic year, surveys of alumni satisfaction, and statistics on job placement. It noted that most universities are already reviewed by regional and professional accrediting bodies, and that comparisons are frequently more relevant across state lines.

The assessment movement went into high gear just as states were reducing their appropriations for higher education, yet demanding increased accessibility. The money involved in administering these systems could be better used, so the AAUP argued, to decrease class size, increase the percentage of full-time faculty, and create remediation courses for those who need them—all more likely to improve quality than a regime of standardized tests.

The AAUP suggested the real consequence of mandated testing was unwarranted external state intrusion into university autonomy, by-passing the roles of governing bodies, administrators, and faculty members. Standardized quantification applied system-wide diminished autonomy and discouraged uniqueness. Standardized testing encouraged faculty to teach to the test,[56] rather than dealing with broader conceptual issues and methods of reasoning. Emphasis on skill testing suggested universities were more remediating schools than true institutions of higher learning, and the likely result would not "do anything more than gauge the lowest common denominator." So-called value-added testing (giving the same test at different intervals in a student's undergraduate career) ignores the "increasingly migratory, part-time, and drop-in stop-out patterns of many American undergraduates." Such value-added testing encourages learning by rote "since the words themselves betray the assumption that one must add something measurable to something else in order to evaluate educational outcomes."

Mandated state testing makes universities vulnerable to ill-considered populism. State governors initially favoured such programmes, it was alleged, because research universities neglected undergraduate teaching. After the AAUP report was written, state governors have come to see graduate education and university research as a vital part of local economic development, and now want resources moved in *that* direction.

In the end, the AAUP suggests:

> It is likely that mandated assessment will force a change in curriculum, not in order to produce a better-educated student, but to enhance the 'measurability' of the outcomes.

Such systems will likely drive better teachers out of the university, just as they have done in many state school systems.

---

[56]Linda M. McNeil, *Contradictions of School Reform: Educational Costs of Standardized Testing* (New York: Routledge, 2000); *cf.* H. Goldstein and A. Heath, eds., *Educational Standards* (Oxford: The British Academy/Oxford University Press, 2000).

The American Federation of Teachers and the National Education Association share this scepticism. Speaking for the American Federation of Teachers, Perry Robinson argued degrees based on passing standardized tests reduced higher education to nothing more than job training.[57] Former U.S. Secretary of Labour Robert Reich has suggested:

> Paradoxically, we are embracing standardised tests just when the new economy is eliminating standardised jobs.... Training a generation of young people to become exquisitely competent at taking standardised tests and a generation of teachers to become exceedingly good at teaching how to take them, has little to do with preparing young people for what they will encounter when they leave school. And more disturbingly, the testing may have the opposite effect—dulling young people's interest in learning and dimming their creative sparks at just a time in history when learning and creativity are more important to the economy than ever.[58]

This debate has recently been rekindled by the President of the University of California, Richard C. Atkinson, who proposed elimination of the SAT as an undergraduate-admissions requirement.[59]

OTHER SOLUTIONS

The Pew Charitable Trusts have financed various experiments to see if universities and their faculty members can truly evaluate teaching in higher education.

The first examined the possibility of better organized peer evaluation. In 1994 the American Association for Higher Education created a consortium of twelve universities for in-depth, continuing peer evaluations. Inquiry into the substance of course work was to be combined with "a careful investigation of what students actually learned." Faculty members created teaching dossiers for their courses, including intellectual goals, sample assignments, examples of student work, and grade distribution. Peers would review this material, comment on it, and meet with the faculty members several times during the year. The result was better teaching, said the researchers. The main difficulty was the excessive amount of faculty time involved. Faculty doubted administrators would reward the time invested in such a project. Nor could faculty peers within the department be considered objective, since they were also involved in evaluation for promotion and tenure. Pew supported a different approach: to see if a sustainable multi-university system of peer evaluation could be created through examination of teaching portfolios among

---

[57]*Chronicle*, 2001 March 16.
[58]*THES*, 2001 May 11.
[59]Peter Sacks, "How Admission Tests Hinder Access to Graduate and Professional Schools," *Chronicle*, 8 June 2001. For a contrary position, see John H. McWhorter, *Chronicle*, 2001 March 9.

the universities of the consortium,[60] rather as research is peer-evaluated, but without site visits.[61]

The second approach was through the National Survey of Student Engagement.[62] This involved a survey of 63,000 freshmen and seniors in 276 institutions to determine five national benchmarks of effective educational practice:

- level of academic challenge
- the amount of active and collaborative learning, including how often students made class presentations, worked on group and community projects, or tutored others
- student interaction with faculty
- access to such enriching programmes as internships and study abroad
- level of campus support—for instance, how the university helps students cope with non-academic responsibilities and social life.

This approach was based on the assumption that impressive facilities do not necessarily produce excellent learning. Not surprisingly, small colleges did well, particularly those which mandate community service or equivalent experience. Despite their size, the University of Michigan at Ann Arbor and the University of Virginia were strong performers. However, a survey that tells us that Beloit College, Centre College, Elon College, and Sweet Briar College are the best teaching universities in the United States perhaps needs some further refinement. Nevertheless it has had an impact. Georgia Tech, for example, responded to its relatively poor showing on faculty/student interaction by appropriating $250,000 to help faculty involve under-graduates in faculty research.[63]

A third Pew initiative was to examine the dropout rate for four-year institutions—28.1% in public institutions and 24.9% in private institutions—as a basis for remedial action. Most dropouts happen in the first year. Pew funded a project called "Your First College Year," run by John Gardner of Brevard College in North Carolina and Linda J. Sax, Director of the of the Cooperative Institutional Research Program, UCLA, a before-and-after survey of 5,229 students at 19 institutions.[64] At the end of their first year 42.4% said they were overwhelmed (6% more than at the beginning of the year); 41.6% were bored (up 4.4%). Large lectures were the least favoured but the most common way of learning. Professor Gardner reports first-year

---

[60]The universities involved are Michigan, Indiana, Kansas State, Texas A&M, and Nebraska.

[61]Daniel Bernstein and Richard Edwards, "We Need Objective, Rigorous Peer Review of Teaching," *Chronicle*, 2001 January 5.

[62]Ben Gose, "A New Survey of 'Good Practices' Could Be an Alternative to Rankings," *Chronicle*, 1999 October 22.

[63]Leo Reisberg, "Are Students Actually Learning?," *Chronicle*, 2000 November 17.

[64]It intends to study more than 19,000 first-year students in 2001.

students are short-changed and first-year courses treated as "cash cows" —hardly revolutionary findings.[65]

All three initiatives share the advantage of having been developed in the university community, not imposed by politicians or state bureaucrats with suspect motives. All deserve study by Canadian universities, particularly in smaller institutions.

Perhaps report cards could be issued to state governments ranking their support of quality of higher education at the undergraduate level. In 2000 the National Center for Public Policy and Higher Education examined public and private universities, ranking the states in five categories. Universities generally performed worst in affordability and best in programme completion. Thirty-four states scored C-plus or worse in affordability. The Center did not give an overall grade for each state, but the *Chronicle of Higher Education* used the data to calculate that Illinois, Connecticut, New Jersey, Maryland, and Massachusetts were the best, and Louisiana, Arkansas, West Virginia, Georgia, and Nevada the worst. The report noted unevenness of opportunity resulting from so many students attending universities near their homes. "The unevenness of opportunity is the real surprise," said the President of the Center. "The benefits of higher education are still influenced by geography, income, wealth, and ethnicity." The responses by state officials were predictably defensive.[66] They did not like the idea that PIs could be applied to states as well as to the individual institutions in them.

■

American fondness for PIs in post-secondary education dates back at least to the early 1900s. Over the course of the twentieth century, it became evident that, like benchmarks and quality tests and management-by-objectives, PIs were likely to produce few of the desired effects. They provided governments with excuses to limit or cut public funding, but in themselves produced little or no savings. Nor did PIs substantially improve the quality of teaching or research, as the stories of accreditation and system-wide evaluation in South Carolina and elsewhere have shown. Decades of testing have shown that standardized measures of student learning do not reliably improve teaching. Rather, PIs and tests have the immediate effect of disenfranchising the very people who must do the urgently needed teaching and research. PIs no doubt make universities tidier and more efficient in gather data about themselves, but that is hardly their *raison d'être*. Costs, however, are the Achilles hell of centralized PIs—costs

---

[65]Andrew Brownstein, "With the Aim of Retaining Freshmen, a Survey Examines Their Experience," *Chronicle*, 2000 November 17.

[66]*Chronicle*, 2000 March 3 and December 31.

in dollars and especially costs in administrative and faculty time that are out of all proportion to any benefits gained.

Like the United Kingdom and New Zealand, the United States returned to PIs in the 1980s and 1990s as easy, mechanistic ways of dealing with complex problems. PIs certainly make it easier to end programmes unpopular with legislators or businesspeople while making such decisions look reasonable, business-like, and efficient. But almost without exception, the promises of PIs have not been realized. The American public likes to know things and to understand things, and their desire to do so is not limited by the standards of business or the requirements of accounting efficiency. Scholars and students are even more likely to want to study and to teach beyond the minimum.

The American example demonstrates a PIs regime is inconsistent with the practice, the content, and the politics of public service and public education. The American case illustrates how and why PIs have been so often reborn: not because they do any particular good, but because they are temporarily convenient for politicians.

The Canadian experience of PIs has been significantly different from that of our American cousins, limited by historical, cultural, and political forces. Even so, we have begun to make the same miscalculations that drew the citizens of South Carolina down the profitless path of PIs. Canadians have not yet profited from the bizarre experience of our British, Commonwealth, and American friends and colleagues. There is still plenty of time to turn away from PIs to a more fruitful path towards accountability and quality in post-secondary education. Before we describe that path, we turn to four Canadian examples of PIs in post-secondary education. They show that at the beginning of the 21st century, we have the potential to repeat the silliest mistakes of the century just ended—or not. We begin in British Columbia and end in Québec.

Part III: Reconstruction and Recovery

6

Canadian PIs from West to East

All statistics, all work that is merely descriptive or informative, imply the ambitious and perhaps groundless hope that in the incalculable future men like us, but with clearer minds, will infer from the data that we leave them some useful conclusion or some hidden truth.
—Jorge Luis Borges and Adolfo Bioy-Casares, *Chronicles of Bustos Domecq* (New York: E.P. Dutton, 1979), this citation from "An Evening with Ramón Bonavena," p. 25.

Canadian **Glossary**

AUCC   Association of Universities and Colleges of Canada

CAFA   Confederation of Alberta Faculty Associations

CAUT   Canadian Association of University Teachers

CEISS   Centre for Education Information Standards and Services
            (British Columbia)

CFI   Canada Foundation for Innovation

CIHR   Canadian Institutes for Health Research

CMEC   Council of Ministers of Education, Canada

CUFA-BC   Confederation of University Faculty Associations of British Columbia

CMEC   Council of Ministers of Education, Canada

KPI-BC(s)   Key Performance Indicator(s)

NSERC   Natural Sciences and Engineering Research Council of Canada

OCUFA   Ontario Confederation of University Faculty Associations

PEQA   Post-Secondary Education Quality Assessment

SSHRC   Social Sciences and Humanities Research Council

TIMSS   The International Mathematics and Science Study

UBC   University of British Columbia

UNESCO   United Nations Educational, Scientific, and Cultural Organization

PIs, DIVERSITY, AND SAMENESS IN
CANADIAN POST-SECONDARY EDUCATION

Canadians take almost perverse pride in their country's extreme geographical, cultural, and political diversity. It is a commonplace of national humour that the one factor common to Canada's regions is resentment of whatever federal government happens to be in power. Because Canadian post-secondary education is mainly a provincial responsibility, it has taken distinct and even disparate forms, adapting European and American models to linguistic and cultural differences and building specialized programmes and services. The overall structure and crucial features of post-secondary education remain familiar: well-rooted senate-style governance, guarantees of academic freedom, and assurance of due process in collective bargaining. Yet not only do Canadian universities and colleges look architecturally different, their students' and instructors' lives are qualitatively (and quantitatively) not the same.[1]

How could a management fad such as PIs cut through all these differences and particularities, pushing in the direction of market-driven uniformity, and putting in doubt the powers of senates, boards, students, professors... and even Ministers of Education?

Supporters argue PIs can do this because they solve a universal problem. From Memorial University in Newfoundland, to Laval in Québec, to Ontario's universities and colleges, to post-secondary education in the Prairies and British Columbia, Canadian higher education defies easy generalization, yet satisfies a pan-Canadian need. In one province student loans are seen as a depressing burden on students and their families; in the next, they are seen as equally depressing, yet one hears of bureaucrats who sneakingly admit the system is a back-door device for getting federal funds into provincial coffers. The common denominator? Student demand.

In the Ottawa area, for instance, demand for skilled labour makes Nortel extremely friendly to universities and colleges producing experts in electronics.[2] In another the demand is for civil engineers good at maintenance of wellheads in the oil patch. The PIs enthusiast will see demand for higher education as the common denominator, a demand expressed through markets. It is the university's job to respond quickly to that demand. PIs in fact guarantee universities and colleges will give in to that demand, no matter what.

In large universities the business of research funding and publishing has acquired unstoppable momentum. Mid-sized and smaller universities and

---

[1]For these matters, see Christine Storm, ed., *Liberal Education and the Small University in Canada* (Montreal and Kingston: McGill-Queen's University Press, 1996); and Cynthia Hardy, *The Politics of Collegiality: Retrenchment Strategies in Canadian Universities* (Montreal and Kingston: McGill-Queen's University Press, 1996).

[2]Northern Telecom [Nortel], *The Supply of High-Technology Professionals: An Issue for Ontario's and Canada's Future* (Ottawa: Nortel, 1998), 51 pp.

colleges are disadvantaged by history and policy, unable to collect their fair share of the Natural Sciences and Engineering Research Council of Canada (NSERC), the Social Sciences and Humanities Research Council (SSHRC), Canada Foundation for Innovation (CFI), Canadian Institutes for Health Research (CIHR),[3] and other funds. Pan-Canadian institutions which could remedy the negative effects of regionality and difference, and restrain the erratic and educationally unsound demands of the market, do not fulfil that function. Why? Often these national bodies have adopted, in the name of a perverse "fairness," a system of policy and resource allocation driven by numbers and PIs. Thus we get PIs coming and going... from demand to supply. Nowhere in Canada have performance indicators become as detailed and as carefully policed as in the United Kingdom or South Carolina, but in at least two provinces they are well on the way to that unhappy condition.

Canadian educational history is replete with psychological and management fads that passed through political boundaries, cultural frontiers, and historic limits with the greatest of ease. In his widely-read study of curricular history in Canadian public education, George Tomkins wrote that Canada is covered by a singular view of public and private interest, however different Canada's regions are in language, cultural, social and demographic arrangement, and political attitude. He was struck by the successful implantation of an Upper Canadian/Ontarian view, even in colonial Newfoundland, which also managed to become influential (if never entirely adopted) in Québec.[4] Whether it be 19th century Québec or Alberta, the elementary school readers of the Irish National Board were in evidence. The advantages of a centralized inspectorate and detailed statistical reports were agreed on by nearly everybody, including the boosters of post-secondary education. This Ryersonian view of education was a kind of distilled 19th-century fad which had no trouble penetrating the Interior of British Columbia and the northern reaches of the Canadian Shield. The fad's popularity held up until the 1960s.[5]

Canada has passed through all phases of PIs development, albeit on its own special terms, and with the traditional healthy scepticism Canadians bring to most innovations. We already offered (Chs. 1–2) examples illustrating Canada's phase of socially-responsible statistics, its decades of fascination with testing, the rising interest in TQM and MBO in the 1950s and

---

[3]National Science and Engineering Research Council of Canada; Social Sciences and Humanities Research Council of Canada; Canada Foundation for Innovation; and Canadian Institutes for Health Research. All are Canadian federal government granting agencies, primarily concerned with the promotion of research and publication in their several fields.

[4]George Tomkins, *A Common Countenance: Stability and Change in the Canadian Curriculum* (Scarborough: Prentice-Hall, 1986).

[5]J.D. Wilson, R. Stamp, and L.-P. Audet, eds., *Canadian Education: A History* (Scarborough, Ontario: Prentice-Hall, 1970), esp. Chs. 3–6; and J.D. Wilson, "The Ryerson Years in Canada West," in Brian E. Titley and Peter J. Miller, eds., *Education in Canada: An Interpretation* (Calgary: Detselig, 1982), 61–92.

1960s, and the peculiarly Canadian version of neo-conservative government in the 1980s and 1990s. Although we don't want to attach too much weight to our Five-Phase schema, it helps to show the roots of PIs, and to suggest why they have been so readily agreed in corporate board rooms and cabinet offices across the land.

In the pages to come, we shall add detail in several provincial case studies to illustrate that PIs are still under the influence of the Canadian rule, and thus not at the same stage of operation in each and every university and college. Yet we can confirm Professor Tomkins's view, this time in post-secondary education. There is indeed a common, unwritten programme at work in the policy and practice of higher education funding and control at the turn of the 21st century and it is about numbers, cuts, and control.

The bad news is that PIs have begun to undermine the carefully-wrought Canadian balance between market demand and larger social objectives. In Ontario, a whole new "quality assurance agency," presumably complete with PIs, began work in spring 2001with the appointment of a Chair.[6] In Québec, a compulsory pattern of *contrats de performance* has been adopted in 2000–1. Although Québec plans modest increases to funding for higher education, even those will be available to universities and colleges only if they sign performance contracts. In both cases, standards of performance and quality are drawn from PIs like those we met in the United Kingdom, New Zealand, and South Carolina. The balancing acts and variety which make Ontario and Québec post-secondary education so vibrant and so excellent are of no particular interest to a PEQAB or a Québec bureaucrat with the power to accept or to reject a performance contract.

When the Ontario government decided to allow public accreditation of private and/or foreign post-secondary providers, it simultaneously announced a new system of quantitative and qualitative tests of excellence. Minister Dianne Cunningham assured the public that tests will guarantee newcomer universities are as good as the public old-timers already in place. The government assured everyone it aimed merely to provide more choice, more institutions, more opportunities for students... more everything except more funds for public colleges and universities

---

[6]The new Postsecondary Education Quality Assessment Board "will assess and advise the Minister of Training, Colleges and Universities on proposals for new degree programmes to be offered by Ontario colleges and new institutions wishing to offer degrees in Ontario." That is, established universities will not face accreditation by the Board, only "institutions." Behind this phrasing lurks a remarkable innovation, the Ontario government's decision to allow "new degree programs including those proposed by privately funded institutions in Ontario." Once the government had decided to allow Canadian and foreign institutions to set up shop in Ontario, and to offer degrees, the government was compelled to find some way of judging the quality of new institutions' programmes—thus the PEQAB.

that reliably offer first-rate teaching, research, and development services to the province.

The Ontario scheme evaded any questions of principle for instance, whether private institutions of post-secondary education should enjoy the fiscal benefits that go along with charitable-educational status in Canada. We put aside these important questions to underline the point that PIs were necessary in the first place, if any Quality Testing Agency were to be brought in. That is, PIs have a tendency to bring with them a whole range of unexpected and possibly unpleasant consequences.

Ontario, like all Canadian provinces, worked long and hard to find a balance between secular and religious educational providers, to decide how much private funding it would permit/demand in support of educational institutions, and to build an arrangement of professional and industrial education driven by the public interest.[7] PIs put this balance in doubt. They invite the creation of new, private programmes and institutions that need only meet a "performance standard."

We contend PIs are not friendly to difference/s in post-secondary education, nor do they respect the historic balancing act in Canadian post-secondary education. They encourage managerialism and discourage participatory, open-minded governance. It is so much easier to consult a table of statistics than to debate matters of educational importance in senates and in public.

Worse, PIs grow bigger and stronger in periods of fiscal "restraint," and acquire force under regimes which do not live up to their promises of non-interventionist government (Harris in Ontario, Klein in Alberta). PIs are *inevitably* accompanied by two things: *(i)* budget cuts and *(ii)* intensified centralized control.

HOW PIs GAINED A NATIONAL PRESENCE: THE ROLE OF CMEC, OECD, AND OTHER ALPHABETICAL ODDITIES

Despite its peculiarities and particulars, Canada after 1980 came to resemble closely its sister countries in development of PIs. Every OECD nation created, or gave new funding to, bodies charged with thinking up new statistical descriptions of higher education, and new ways of tying it to "the economy." In Germany, every *Landesministerium* reported on university-industry employment/development linkages, sometimes monthly. France, a late bloomer in the field of normative post-secondary education statistics, nevertheless boasted a whole panoply of the centralized structures needed to build up an instant database. By 1990, every OECD member had carried out a formal policy study of its education system, using questions and procedures common to the whole Organization. Canada's long provincial tradition of statistical reporting on post-secondary education had not necessarily been tied

---

[7]On these themes, see esp. R.D. Gidney, *From Hope to Harris: The Reshaping of Ontario's Schools* (Toronto: University of Toronto Press, 1999).

primarily to the worlds of work, industry, and economic development. The impact of the OECD was to encourage precisely these kinds of ties.[8]

While the OECD conducted quantitative and qualitative studies in each country, it did comparative and multi-national studies as well. The International Labour Organization was also busily doing quantitative studies for its own purposes, and so was the United Nations Educational, Scientific, and Cultural Organization (UNESCO). To the list of test-oriented and PIs-minded international bodies, we would add The International Mathematics and Science Study. Based in Canada, and aimed mainly at elementary and secondary teaching in mathematics and science, this study, in several iterations, has influenced the outlook of government and business in Europe, North America, and Asia. Without The International Mathematics and Science Study (TIMSS), a favourite in Canada and the United States, the PIs movement would have had much less of a purchase on policy and practice in the world.[9]

In Canada, the Council of Ministers of Education (CMEC) took up the work of *(i)* defining educational performance in terms of outside market conditions, and *(ii)* linking public education funding and overall direction to client satisfaction, or "public expectations."[10] The Council has done

---

[8]See OECD, *Education at a Glance 2001* (Paris: OECD, 2001), Chapter E, "Individual, Social and Labour Market Outcomes of Education."

[9]Compare the discussion of PISA, another OECD/CMEC testing scheme, described below, Ch. 6.

[10]Council of Ministers of Education, Canada [CMEC], *A Report on Public Expecations of Postsecondary Education in Canada* (Toronto: CMEC, 1999 February). This Report embodied the views of provincial bureaucrats and politicians. It started (pp. 4–5) from the UK's Dearing Report's list of central functions for post-secondary education, but quickly branched off into a list of "Key Areas of Expectations" that will by now look familiar: quality, defined as "high quality educational outcomes and intellectual environments"; accessibility; mobility and portability (a demand that helps to strengthen the creation of nationally-recognizable performance indicators, rather than locally-rooted indicators, and that strongly favours such "innovations" as Prior Learning Assessment); relevance and responsiveness (to whom?); research and scholarship (defined in a way we think entirely apt and encouraging); and accountability (defined as open accountability for achievement of mandates and outcomes, and means of "reassuring citizens, and students in particular, that resources are allocated to active maximum value and sustainability of postsecondary education" [p. 7]). Governments have a regulatory duty in all this, but not necessarily a financial one.

Government escapes its full fiscal duty by asserting (p. 14) that universities and colleges are not yet sufficiently accountable. But even when full accountability finally does arrive, markets and the private sector will play a crucial role in finance, since only through financial devices can "demand" properly be described and asserted.

Thus, in the name of accountability, universities and colleges must accept output and outcomes assessment, benchmarking, "efficiency and effectiveness" measures, and a willingness to rationalize their offerings, that is, to close programmes that are "inconsistent with their missions."

useful work on the distribution of educational opportunity in Canada, even tackling the thorny question of social class and accessibility in post-secondary education. Some might say that the Council's studies of funding levels, attendance patterns, student and teacher demography, and graduates' careers are a little old-fashioned in an age of PIs. We shall be content merely to note that this work has been most recently done with the help of an Education Statistics Council, created in partnership with Statistics Canada. As so often in the history of PIs, educational statistics in Canada have been a mix of socially responsible research with statistics that almost *invite* intervention, fiscal restraint, and outside intervention and control. According to Statistics Canada, in 1998 48.8 % of 18- to 21-year-olds from low income families had attended college or university compared to 71% among the highest income group.[11] Of course such statistics merely tell us what we already know. Instead of persuading governments to fund needs-based student grants, experience suggests they will prompt them to create yet another PI universities cannot afford to meet.

To the roster of national and international organizations interested in or curious about PIs, and sometimes overtly committed to them, one should add a long list of local and regional Canadian bodies that were supposed to help co-ordinate the governance of higher education, thus reducing duplication and assuring fair distribution of public funds but in the end helped to impose PIs. In Canada, these include the Maritime Provinces Higher Education Commission, the Council of Ontario Universities, the Universities Council of British Columbia, and their like in most provinces.[12] Some of these organizations grew up in the 1970s, then died under the stress of continuous fiscal crisis during the 1980s, a period John Macdonald calls the "long dark age of the world's universities." In the forms these bodies had in the 1990s, the old objectives of co-ordination and fair funding were no longer terribly noticeable, as the wave of excitement about indicators and PIs swept over them.

Canada Takes the Ideological Turn

A story from Ontario in the mid-1990s will help to explain why these various bodies changed. On 1994 October 25, Bob Rae, then the NDP (social democratic) Premier of Ontario, proclaimed:

> [O]ur standards and our achievements should be truly international in scope. We should draw comparisons in our testing and assessment of how we're

---

On these matters, see also D.A. Wolfe, "Quality and Accountability in PSE Research: The Measurement Challenge," background paper prepared for the Council of Ministers of Education, Canada, 1998 November (Toronto: CMEC, 1998), 20 pp.

[11]*Montreal Gazette*, 2001 December 8.

[12]John Macdonald provides a wry and mildly self-deprecating view of life in the COU, the Council of Ontario Universities, of which he was Executive Director at its foundation in 1971, in his *Chances and Choices: A Memoir* (Vancouver: University of British Columbia/Alumni Association of UBC, 2000), pp. 156–71.

doing and we should use these comparisons to improve how we do things. In most businesses, it's called benchmarking. And it's something the public sector had better get used to.

Mr. Rae's frustration with public education was palpable. He wanted performance benchmarks, and thought schools and universities "must be held accountable" if they do not meet or surpass those benchmarks. By accountability, he meant control through funding mechanisms and control by clients. Mr Rae only hinted at the final form of a system based on accountability as he understood it:

> If you were to come from Mars and watch TV, your assumption would be that lawyers and doctors and those involved in the criminal world are the three occupations. It's very important to realize the culture we are up against is a culture that doesn't recognize enough the importance of science and mathematics... we have to create wealth before we can share it.[13]

The way forward according to Mr Rae (and also the Ontario Council on University Affairs and a number of Ontario university presidents) was through benchmarks and inter-university rankings on PIs.

By 2000 Mr Rae's successor as Premier, Conservative Mike Harris, much further. Where the PIs of the 1980s and early 1990s had been mildly interventionist, and possibly even helpful in the cause of broader access to liberal, post-secondary education, the PIs of the *fin de siècle* became wildly interventionist. One reason for the change in direction is not hard to find. The PIs of the early- to mid-1990s had a controlling and sometimes punitive tone, but rarely referred to the private sector. It is a crucial and revealing fact of educational politics in 2000 that PIs have made the move from public to private. Now they don't simply mention the private sector: they tie the universities, as the Lilliputians tied Gulliver, to a world and a way of life that have little to do with education and everything to do with the private interests of companies and investors.

The tone began to shift in Alberta, where the provincial government set aside an "envelope" of "performance funding" available to institutions that do well in the PIs sweepstakes but may not otherwise merit additional funds. Ontario in 2000 announced its intention to do likewise, acting on advice received as early as 1994.

Across the country governments and business argued, energetically, that the usual forms of academic governance must be set aside or profoundly reformed. No longer need university Senates decide whether Italian or Physics should be taught, nor university administrations negotiate the funding of courses. PIs would be rapidly decisive, making due process an unnecessary side-show. Statistics on costs of instruction, student through-put, student (read "customer') satisfaction, and employability would bring in a new system capable of nimble and resilient action in response to the

---

[13]"How to upgrade education: Ontario needs higher standards, more focus and more challenges for kids," *Ottawa Citizen*, 1994 November 01, pp. 58–9.

latest news from the NASDAQ (National Association of Securities Dealers Automated Quotation).[14]

Provincial governments have only now begun to act on these extremist ideas, but our study of the several phases of PIs history suggests it is entirely possible to move far and fast. Since cuts to public funding of education began in earnest, in 1983, the commercialization of post-secondary education has encouraged the performance indicator movement on one hand, and continued declines in public funding on the other.

More than any other cultural, political, or intellectual force, the rise of neo-conservatism accounts for the willingness of politicians (social democrat and private-enterprise-minded alike) and corporate leaders to imagine a world run on PIs.

Some would argue the commercialization and privatization of university research and teaching is a consequence of policies adopted by the Mulroney and Chrétien governments. But this is too short-sighted. The several phases of the history of PIs, by whatever name one chooses to call them, show no single government's policy really accounts for the rapidity of the movement.

In Canada's Natural Sciences and Engineering Research Council, it was government preferences and policies that pressed the Council to agree by 1992 to a policy requiring the private-sector matching of substantial public research funds. By spring 1995, the president of the Social Sciences and Humanities Research Council of Canada was asking social scientists and humanists to start looking for corporate partners.

In 1996, Finance Minister Martin announced a new programme of funding for advanced "mission-oriented" research, the Canadian Foundation for Innovation. Legislated in the 1997 spring session of Parliament,

> The Canada Foundation for Innovation (CFI) is an independent corporation established in 1997 by the federal government to strengthen Canadian capability for research. The CFI will achieve this objective by investing in the development of research infrastructure in Canada. The CFI's mandate is to increase the capability of Canadian universities, colleges, hospitals, and other not-for-profit institutions to carry out important world-class scientific research and technology development. [T]he Foundation, in co-operation with funding partners, provides infrastructure for research and development that will:
>
> • support economic growth and job creation;
> • lead to improvements in health, the environment, and quality of life.[15]

---

[14]See Mary Burgan, "The Corporate University and Its New Ways," unpublished manuscript, Spring Council, Canadian Association of University Teachers, Ottawa, 1997, for a survey of contemporary business management theories of university governance, and their requirements that academics and universities become nimble and responsive to economic change and rapidly changing market demands.

[15]From the Canada Foundation for Innovation Web site, at *http://www.innovation. ca/english/about/index.html*.

The funding for CFI, nearly a billion dollars across five years, was the first infusion of new money for public post-secondary education in some time. Like the funding for many NSERC and SSHRCC programmes, it required "cooperation with funding partners" (generally, 50% funding), and would support investment in "infrastructure," not basic or "core" operating funds.

Without quite saying so, the federal government's requirement that universities acquire matching funds from the private sector, in general equalling what they get from CFI, amounts to a performance indicator. In a sense, it is a perfect "performance indicator." Those universities most able to find matching funds in private industry will do better than those that cannot or will not. The result is "automatic" expenditure of public funds for post-secondary education based on "performance" in the private sector, without the bother of having to gather statistics, or to take explicit and public decisions on funding! And the redefinition of the public interest to mean the private interest, achieves one of the great objectives of Thatcherite and Reaganite neo-conservative theory: the "automatic" reduction of government in size and pretension.

In March 1999, the federal government's Expert Panel on the Commercialization of University Research produced a first version of "Public Investment in University Research Reaping the Benefits." The CAUT responded

> that the report's recommendations would facilitate the expansion of corporate control over university research. This would happen because the report's recommendations encourage the steering of research toward the commercial interests of private corporations, undermine the tradition of open communication between scholars, and provide for the expropriation of the results of university research to the corporate sector.[16]

The Expert Panel advised universities to take commercialization as a core function of higher education in Canada, recommending they incorporate professors' commercialization track records in decisions on promotion and tenure. The Panel announced it was not aiming "primarily to produce new revenue streams for universities [since] the revenues from commercializing research constitute a small addition to university budgets, generally below 1 percent."

In recommending the hiring of administrators and new industrial liaison offices, at public expense, the Panel followed well-developed international practice. In New Zealand, Australia, and the United Kingdom, the tremendous cost of developing and publishing and using PIs is ignored. It is as if PIs cost nothing, either in time or in money.

---

[16]From the CAUT Web site: *http://www.caut.ca/English/PublicPolicy/Comercialization/comment commercialization.htm.*

THE CANADIAN PATCH-WORK:
INTRODUCING OUR FOUR PROVINCIAL CASES

Some provinces are keener on PIs and the New Accountability than others. But it is a little too easy to say that Ralph Klein's Alberta went down the Thatcherite path faster than anybody else until the election of Ontario's Mike Harris; or that these two provinces have historical reasons for being so enthusiastic about New Government, the Exiguous State, and so on and on. In the mid-1990s, the Government of Newfoundland was happily producing annual PIs whose form and content would be familiar and acceptable in Edmonton and Toronto.

Recent developments in British Columbia and Québec show how closely in step those provinces are with the rest of the country. From Nunavut to Manitoba, the themes of Alberta's and Ontario's educational policy are strongly present, albeit in confusingly different mechanisms.

At the moment, the forces that support PIs are winning the day. All provincial and territorial education ministers attend meetings of the Council of Ministers of Education, Canada [CMEC], which includes representatives from the silent but essential 14th Minister of Education, the federal government minister or ministers responsible for indirectly funding higher education. There is always more agreement than disagreement. In Edmonton, Charlottetown, Ottawa, or wherever CMEC happens to be meeting, the question is always how to make public education more instantly responsive to labour force requirements, more pliant in meeting new demands for usable research and development, and more global in outlook.

It remains true that provincial and regional differences give each new application of PIs a different appearance. As Richelieu once opined, appearance is reality in politics, at least some of the time. So it is essential in understanding PIs in Canada that we accept a double truth: PIs will share fundamental characteristics, but their political expression and practice will differ significantly from region to region.

These differences matter a great deal. The overall weaknesses of PIs are so great, we argue, that they should be limited radically in use, or simply discarded, as an idea whose history and practice left a trail of mediocrity and disaster. Yet at the regional level, in country after country, local political and business leaders have been misled into thinking their particular region is sufficiently unique that maybe PIs will work, just this once. Canadians have the time and the opportunity to call a halt, at the local and regional level, to a policy found bankrupt in nation after nation.

Alberta's grand plan was called "Measuring Up," in direct imitation of at least a half-dozen similar schemes in the United States, the United Kingdom, Australia and New Zealand. In Ontario, the new funding regime and the new approach to quality control used wording and institutional structures straight out of Canberra. In both cases, the reasoning and the goals had become terribly familiar by the mid-1990s: reduce government, just because it's necessarily and always a good thing to do that; tighten the reins of control over post-secondary education, using budget cuts to make that happen quickly; link what goes on inside post-secondary education to the latest demands for skilled labour in industry; and, finally, accept all reforms and innovations as they come along, provided they tie Canada's colleges and universities to the global economy, the information age, and the necessity to compete against all comers in the universe. The ideal university would be one whose graduates were instantly employed in the industry *du jour*; whose research was helpful to companies in Canada or abroad wanting to push up exports; whose management teams talk the way managers talk in Nortel and the Bank of Montreal; whose accountants can list the main products of the university, the unit costs of each product, and the relative efficiency of each part of the university's contribution to making those products.

Even here, there are differences. Alberta tried after 1996 to assign an envelope of funding to universities and colleges that performed better or worse on PIs. Ontario talked about funding corridors, and listened (for some while) to advice that PIs might work for one corridor (say, undergraduate education) but not another (say professional training, as in medicine). It is an unfortunate fact that much of the debate over PIs has taken place in bureaucratic backrooms, where highly-trained and experienced civil servants argue the benefits of different kinds of PIs-driven funding. This one example, the different views on how and if PIs could drive funding (envelope versus corridor) provides a way into the politics of PIs; if we can find a way to clarify and simply such arguments over funding, and understand how these arguments are the result of local political factors, we have the beginning of a political strategy for the undoing of PIs, at least in their silliest and most destructive forms.

We start with British Columbia, which has yet not made a commitment to a full PIs regime, but whose policies (like those of every other province) show signs of the five phases of PIs development. We will make frequent comparisons with other provinces, using the B.C. example as a jumping-off point. Having shown the commonalities in policies on funding and control in Canada, we will turn to Alberta and Ontario, whose two schemes continue to be influential. Finally, we deal with the recent development of Performance Contracts in Québec. This may have struck Canadians as a surprising development in a region with a known commitment to social-democratic policy in education, from the Quiet Revolution onward.

In order to provide a national background, we offer a table showing the history of provincial funding in post-secondary education from 1992–2000, including our four cases, but also the other provinces. Ontario's 30.6% cut and Quebec's 27.8% cut, in both cases between 1992 and 2000, give an unmistakable colouration to the rationales for PIs in these two provinces. To say that PIs are about quality, efficiency, accountability, responsiveness, resilience, or anything else in that long and inane list is, we think, entirely misleading. The figures and the facts show that they are about cuts, and destructive ones at that and about control.

Provincial Operating Grants to Universities, 1992/93 to 1999/00 ($1992 per capita)

	92/93	94/95	96/97	98/99	99/00	% change 98/99– 99/00	% change 92/93– 99/00	99/00 rank
Canada	203	188	163	153	152	-0.7%	-25.1%	–
Newfoundland	233	222	200	189	201	6.3%	-13.7%	1
Prince Edward Island	210	184	178	161	158	-1.95	-24.85	6
Nova Scotia	216	199	177	178	182	2.25	-15.7%	4
New Brunswick	196	197	194	186	186	0.0%	-5.1%	2
Québec	255	253	216	186	184	-1.15	-27.8%	3
Ontario	180	159	129	126	125	-0.8%	-30.65	9
Manitoba	195	178	177	176	175	-0.6%	-10.3%	5
Saskatchewan	177	158	154	153	158	3.3%	-10.7%	6
Alberta	204	176	155	150	147	-2.05	-27.95	8
British Columbia	167	161	149	148	149	0.7%	-10.85	7

Source: Calculations based on Council of Ontario Universities, 1999 Resource Document

British Columbia

The University of British Columbia opened to undergraduates in 1915. A year later, the provincial budget and the Annual Report of the Department of Education contained, respectively, a two-page discussion of the new institution, and three lines detailing the amounts of money spent on the place.

A curious inquirer might telephone or write for a copy of the University Calendar, where she would discover a good deal about the "present progress" of UBC, but little information on finance. Apart from gross statistics of enrolment, there were few signs of even the first stirrings of PIs. Indeed, there wasn't much of anything in the way of systematic information on UBC finances, physical plant, or the demography of UBC. By 1925, most documents on university finance and governance came from the same two sources, the University and the government.

On this basis one might think PIs would never develop in British Columbia. But there was a clear basis for PIs in BC by the 1920s, and it has strengthened in every subsequent decade. British Columbia was, it turns out, a participant in the international PIs movement. Although it resisted the extremism of provinces to the east, and its huge neighbour to the south, BC developed home-grown PIs.

Throughout the PIs story in British Columbia, the picture is of many levels of authority and accountability, and multiple strands of reporting and control. With time, the effects have been to create a system which is subjected to more closely-detailed control from the centre with a rush to detailed bureaucratic control in the last decade. In this sense British Columbia is typical of all the Canadian provinces.

There is, as we shall see, in no Canadian province or region a single, easily-detected centre for PIs administration of the UK variety; rather, the sources are found in at least a half-dozen routinized streams of reporting and statistics. Working together, these streams produce the effects of the centralized PIs to be found in other jurisdictions.

Even KPI-BCs, the Key Performance Indicators that infest the college and university college sector in British Columbia, Alberta, Ontario, and elsewhere, are but one of several strands of reporting-and-control which have slowly transformed management and teaching in those institutions. In British Columbia (as in nearly all provinces), PIs are legally required of the colleges, but not yet of the universities. But the legal basis of PIs is a topic of surprisingly little practical import, for the effects of multiple streams of reporting and statistics have an effect at least as complete as most legally-mandated systems have done. Once again the Lilliputians are at work.

We've compressed a populous group of PIs into just three main streams, for ease of description and discussion. They show how far government and business has already succeeded in circumscribing the work of post-secondary education in this, and as we shall see, all the provinces.

Stream 1

To begin, it is worth recalling how from 1915 to the 21st century, a constant stream of detailed financial and planning data passed from the UBC President's office to the Office of the Premier of British Columbia, and to various federal ministers. This first, quasi-formal stream of reporting-and-control became a permanent feature of post-secondary education governance in the province from the day the first President (Wesbrook) was appointed. Much of it was in letters that aimed to procure new funding for buildings, instructional programmes, or research, and always those letters included numbers to prove that UBC was spending public funds very wisely indeed.

That stream of documentation is as strong and as substantial in the early 2000s as ever, and perhaps wider and deeper. Exactly analogous streams of reporting-and-control are integral to the histories of universities and colleges in every province.[17]

In the early 1920s, UBC worked hard to get the necessary funds for its move from temporary to permanent accommodation. Towards that goal, its President and Deans offered details on student numbers; ratios of floor space to anticipated academic use, including laboratories, a library, and professorial offices; and evidence of early UBC successes in industrial and agricultural development.[18] At times, this correspondence became intense and not especially friendly to the University.[19] Under the long presidency of Larry Mackenzie, the Premier W.A.C. Bennett through the 1950s and 1960s took an erratic interest in the detailed costs and benefits of post-secondary education.[20] Bennett himself retained the Finance portfolio, and wielded strong influence over education funding at the

---

[17]A convenient way to see how these practices grew up and took permanent root, is to listen to the accounts of past-presidents of universities Johns in Alberta, Murray and Spinks in Alberta, Falconer in Toronto, and so on and to historians who have dealt with the endless problems of university presidents coping with interventionist premiers. A helpful bibliographical source is at: *http://www.umanitoba.ca/libraries/ units/education/ univbib.html*. See also the extensive and well-considered bibliographical apparatus in Paul Axelrod and John G. Reid, eds., *Youth, University and Canadian Society: Essays in the Social History of Higher Education* (Kingston: McGill-Queen's University Press, 1989).

[18]Harry T. Logan, *Tuum Est: A History of the University of British Columbia* (Vancouver: University of British Columbia, 1958), pp. 86–90.

[18]See also the President's Papers, 1920–1944, Archives of the University of British Columbia, Vancouver, Canada.

[19]Michiel Horn, "Under the Gaze of George Vancouver: The University of British Columbia and the Provincial Government, 1913–1939," *BC Studies* 83 (1989), 29–67.

[20]P.B. Waite, *Lord of Point Grey: Larry Mackenzie of UBC* (Vancouver: UBC Press, 1987), 158–94.

Treasury Board. When Bennett became distracted or bored, his Ministers of Education were only too happy to take up the slack.

In the crisis days of fiscal restraint after 1975, especially between 1983 and 1985, the stream of documentation between BC universities and colleges and the Victoria bureaucracy became a torrent.[21] By 2001, no college or university could hope for provincial funding of its programmes without submitting detailed programme profiles (that is, information on course content, admissions rates, and instructional costs) to the government's many supervisory branches. British Columbia may not have a Commission like that of South Carolina, or an RAE like that of the United Kingdom but the regime of detailed supervision and control is almost as complete and effective.

Stream 2: Audited budgets

From the start an annual audit of UBC budgets provided a more official source of data for the curious. This became especially interesting after the late 1950s when the earliest form of the British Columbia Public Financial Information Act was passed. By the 1960s all public sector bodies controlled under the University Act (and, later, the various university and college acts) were required to report all salaries and payments. This made it possible to connect audited statements and annual budgets to detailed expenditures, department by department. Academics at the BC universities quickly became accustomed to annual publication of their salaries. We mention the matter as an example of transparent and appropriate public information on the work of the post-secondary system.

This stream of data was rarely used to test the efficiency of individuals or academic units until the 1980s. Nobody looked at CVs in the medical faculty to see if relatively high salaries were matched by similarly high performance in research and grant acquisition. All this changed in the 1980s, 1990s, and early 2000s.

The trouble began when audited statements were first presented in the provincial legislature, and the trouble has never quite abated. The words "efficiency" and "effectiveness" became common currency in Hansarded budget debates about post-secondary education funding from 1915 on. As both levels of government did their best to resettle World War I veterans and to recover from the economic dislocations of the first decades of the century, efficiency acquired extremely practical meanings: whatever would house and educate veterans, and encourage reinvestment in the local and national economies, was good. The same held for post World War II veterans and professional education in the late 1940s.

---

[21]In W. Magnusson, *et al.*, eds., *The New Reality: The Politics of Restraint in British Columbia* (Vancouver: New Star Books, 1984), see essays by Patricia Marchak, "The New Economic Reality: Substance and Rhetoric," 22–40, and G. Shrimpton, "A Decade of Restraint: The Economics of B.C. Universities," 258–68, on the provincial government's increasingly invasive demands for reports, statistics, and documentation after 1983.

Already the idea was that audits could demonstrate much more than the mere fiscal rectitude of institutions of public higher education. Audits began to have a new function: to ensure that higher education would accomplish a range of non-academic goals, and to respond to market forces.

Hansard for 2000, along with minuted reports from Standing Committees of the British Columbia House and debates on the annual estimates, included much discussion on the economic impact of post-secondary education in every region of the province. The question of PIs, as we have defined them, is, obviously, no longer moot; they are legally required of the colleges, and practically speaking the universities must produce them too.

Stream 3: From Testing to Full-Blown PIs

As noted earlier, British Columbia stepped on to the North American and European bandwagon early, accepting IQ and other standardized tests as devices for testing the efficiency and efficacy of education. But as in the United States, post-secondary education in British Columbia was never subject in a detailed way to these tests, instead becoming their sponsors and organizers.

The brand-new Professor of Education at UBC, George M. Weir (subsequently a long-term Minister of Education and much else in the Liberal government of T.D. Pattullo), was asked in 1924 to co-author an extensive Survey of education in British Columbia.[22] Some eighty densely-constructed pages (pp. 436–509), provided under commission by Sir Peter Sandiford, dealt with tests of intelligence and school achievement. We have at p. 455 a fabulous (no other word will do) table showing IQ scores of children and adults in school and university, according to their fathers' occupations, and further on (pp. 461, 508) even more striking surveys of intelligence by European origins (Scots, English, Irish, and so on) and by Asian origins (*vis-à-vis* Caucasians). At p. 505, we have one of several conclusions of the following kind: only intellectually mediocre kids attend Junior Secondary Schools (Grades 8 to 10, roughly) rather than regular high schools.

If the overall objective was that students would rapidly and effectively move into their "right" occupations—in some cases an "occupation" as a university student—then some schools were better than others. It has the sound of statistics in the 1990s on university and college graduates, and their rapid "and effective insertion into job markets." The move from testing of the kind we saw in Phase II (see Chapter 1) to PIs was gradual but unstoppable.

For a few years (1945–52) UBC's annual Calendar reported on the geographical, professional, ethnic, and religious origins of students in a series of pie-charts. But the kind of reporting that began with the Putman-

---

[22]J.H. Putman and G.M. Weir, *Survey of the School System* (Victoria: King's Printer, 1925).

Weir Report also became the task of quite various agencies: the Dominion Bureau of Statistics (later Statistics Canada), federal departments of state (especially agriculture, defence, and economic development), and the provincial department of education. The university (after the early 1960s, universities and colleges, plural) did not have to bear the statistical burden entirely by itself.[23]

By the early 2000s, the stream of data that began with standardized statistics in the 1920s had evolved to become much more diverse, and much more economistic. From the reportorial mode of the 1940s, it had moved to the mode of social engineering—or should we say "process re-engineering"?

British Columbia PIs and Their Effects

At the web site of the Office of Analytical Studies, Simon Fraser University (*http://www.sfu.ca/analytical-studies/gfs/g98s00/index.html*), a sequence of indicators gives course enrolment and grade reports, undergraduate and graduate student job destinations, and systematic data on customer satisfaction. Convenient links give access to "fact books" at all universities in British Columbia. If one visits those sources, the pattern is repeated: post-secondary education costs, physical space ratios, faculty-technical-library resource "loading," throughputs and retention rates all are given in exquisite detail. Many of these data are undoubtedly necessary background for budget-making, or institutional planning, whether for classroom organization, acquisition of library books, purchase of laboratory equipment, or staffing. But they also have a political purpose.

At the University of British Columbia, the Budget Planning and Accountability Document for 1996–7,[24] now supplemented and partly replaced by web-based data offered by UBC Planning and Institutional Research,[25] provides a sequence of indicators which matches precisely those in South Carolina and the United Kingdom. By 2000–1, UBC, like SFU, had surpassed the college system in offering an extremely detailed picture, department by department, of faculty work-loads, costs of instruction, graduation and throughput rates, sources of student by region, gender, visa, and so on. It remained only to factor in the satisfaction indices available elsewhere, and the employment patterns of students after graduation, to produce a system capable of detailed policing and control. This has not yet happened, at any rate, not in an explicit and punitive way. The use of bibliometrics, patent counts, research grant acquisition rates all are possible, given the plethora

---

[23]There is an instructive parallel with American PIs. See particularly National Center for Education Statistics, The Condition of Education, 2001 (Washington, DC: NCES, 2001), and from the 59 main performance indicators applied in the document, nos. 46–51 for post-secondary education, pp. 76– 87.

[24]Vancouver: University of British Columbia, 1997, ca. 480 pp.

[25]*http://www.pair.ub.ca.*

of data available, but there are few signs that detailed curricular and staffing decisions are being generated automatically by the numbers.

The fascination of these numbers for managers and bureaucrats is undeniable. (We, too, admit to being fascinated by by the numbers, though ours is the fascination of the cobra for the fakir.) How reminiscent it all is of the 1920s and 1930s, and the grand discoveries of testing and statistics of those not-so-distant days!

We note that the funding history of post-secondary education in the province has no integral part in the PI reports of SFU, UBC, UVIC, UNBC, Royal Roads, TechBC, colleges, or university colleges. SFU and UBC do report their financial conditions in pages not very distant from those that portray their instructional and research work.

Yet the connections are not made, even though between 22% and 27% of public funding disappeared from public post-secondary education in British Columbia after 1975, in real or adjusted dollars. It would be hard to tell this from reports on Key Performance Indicators in British Columbia. That is, British Columbia PIs are being developed by universities, colleges, and provincial bureaucracies, but under the pretense that they have nothing to do with the financial and political climate in which these entities exist.

There are numerous reminders, in the SFU and analogous sites elsewhere, of the statistics of 1925. The Presidents' Council of the provincial universities and the Centre for Education Information Standards and Services (CEISS) are especially interesting in this sense.

The University Presidents' Council of British Columbia is to BC what the Association of Universities and Colleges of Canada (AUCC) is to Canada—a managerial organization concerned with presenting data and information in plausible and attractive forms to government and business.[26] The Council's Survey of Graduates tells what jobs university graduates have, whether those jobs are in the fields for which they trained, how much they earn, whether they stay in British Columbia, and whether they would take the same

---

[26]The AUCC Research File, 1, 2 (1995 June): 1–7, offers "A Primer on Performance Indicators." [*http://www.aucc.ca/bilingue/research/rf12e.pdf*] AUCC accepts that PIs are "goal or result-oriented," allow comparisons across institutions (benchmarks), provide "strategic information about the condition, health or functioning of the institution/ system," and are evaluative. The author suggests PIs should have internal university uses "to enhance the quality of education, research, community service and other functions." By 2001, it was obvious in all the developed world that PIs had gone far beyond "internal" uses, and were devices that had only marginal utility in improving quality of education, research, and so on. We mention the AUCC position partly because we find it a pleasant, but completely unrealistic one. We could support internal measures that help to improve "quality of education, research, community service." Alas, there are painfully few measures that are reliably and validly tied to these things. We are left with old-fashioned intelligence, informed judgement (including judgements that make use of quantitative data, of course), and public debate in universities, colleges, and the community: these are the best, and indeed the only reliable and non-marginal ways of improving quality in post-secondary education.

programme of studies again and/or pursue further studies. Lurking in the background, of course, is the further calculation whether post-secondary education adds value to students' economic lives.[27]

The CEISS[28]

BC College and Institute Student Outcomes project collects, analyzes and publishes information relating to the education experiences of former students at 21 public colleges, university colleges, institutes and agencies. Each year, about 30,000 former students are contacted nine to 20 months after they complete all, or a significant portion, of their program. They are surveyed on what they have done since leaving their program, and if they were satisfied with their education and skill development.

The fifty-five pages of the CEISS 2000 Key Student Outcomes Indicators for BC Colleges and Institutes surveys 21 colleges or college-like institutions. For our purposes, the indicators for Kwantlen University College will do (at pp. B-18–19).

The Kwantlen PIs are divided into three main sections: Programme of Studies, Attributes of Survey Respondents, and Skill Development. It should be remembered that this report is the mirror image of the similar report on graduates' life chances and employment. We have then the main elements of a comprehensive indicator system:

- We know the attributes of students (sex, age, kind and extent of "prior skill-set," previous certificates and degrees, and whether employed while studying.
- We know exactly what programmes of study, and with what vocational objectives, the students are taking or have taken.
- We are told the beginning and ending skill-levels of students, a true KPI-BC, even if it is uncertain what "skills" are on the testers' minds.
- We are told on a scale of 1 4 the average satisfaction level of students by programme and by skill (for example, mathematical reasoning, written communication, and so on) for Kwantlen.

Every non-university institution in the province is thus described.

As before, we hear little about the funding consequences of KPI-BCs, nor how much it costs to collect the KPI-BCs in the first place. Further, we are not told how far programme decisions at the institution and at provincial level are based on KPI-BCs but of course, they are, in some so-far-undefined degree. For a well-rationalized discussion of KPI-BCs, used as an integral (but not the only) element in decision-making, consider the University College of the Fraser Valley, eastward from Vancouver. Its strategic plan for 1994–

---

[27]See for example F.T. Evers and Sid Gilbert, "Outcomes Assessment: How Much Value Does University Education Add?" *Canadian Journal of Higher Education*, 21, 2 (1991): 53–69; also, Mireille Laroche and Marcel Mérette, "Measuring Human Capital in Canada," unpublished paper, Statistics Canada [Economic Conference 2000], 34 pp.

[28]For this and all CEISS material, see *http://www.ceiss.org*, or more exactly on outcomes, *http://outcomes.ceiss.org/*.

1999[29] provides a 17-page list of outcomes and objectives, most (but not all) susceptible to statistics. The College report ends with a section on financial objectives, without financial notes, indicating (p. 14) that it is arguing vigorously for "additional funding and programmes to Ministry officials."

The British Columbia example demonstrates widespread agreement in government, in the private sector, and in university management circles that the principles of performance indication are... just fine. It remains to put those principles into full practice, and to drive university and college funding on that basis. The British Columbia government's Performance Plan 2000–01[30] gives a clear warning it is not willing to wait much longer ("A Well-Educated Citizenry and Labour Force: Strategic Objectives"), and lists twenty pages of "Key Initiative, Performance Measures, Target and Accountability" (pp. 17–37). All are accompanied by lists of programme outcomes, performance measures, targets, and accountability. At page 22, we learn that "High tech will have greater weight in new programs review process" the plan mentions TechBC (the Technical University of British Columbia) by name and says the Universities and Institutes Branch will "make it happen."

Any doubt about this was removed in 1993, when the provincial auditor general and the Canadian Comprehensive Auditing Foundation collaborated with a number of college managers to produce a little-known but crucial book titled *Reporting on Effectiveness in Colleges and Institutes*.[31] This book called (pp. 47–8) for radically precise and extensive mandate statements, linking all university and college programmes to precisely described market "needs," direct measures of outcomes (including tests of knowledge before and after), benchmarking for nearly everything, long-range physical-plant planning, and on point communication of data to "the public." The book was a good-humoured one, but given the experience of such auditing schemes everywhere else in the world, its influential and pioneering status is extremely worrisome. Nowhere in *Reporting on Effectiveness* is there any discussion of the need for independent evidence-based research, academic freedom in teaching and research, or of the value of reason and dialogue in such places as Senates and Faculty meetings.

British Columbians who care about quality, accountability, and academic freedom in post-secondary education do indeed have something to worry about. And they have less time to act than they may realize. It was this urgency that led the College and Institute Educators Association

---

[29]At *http://www.ucfv.bc.ca/strat-plan/Background/plan98.htm*.

[30]British Columbia, Performance Plan 2000–01 9 (Victoria: Ministry of Advanced Education, Training and Technology, 2000), 37 pp. [at *http://www.aved.gov.bc.ca/annualreports/2000-01business_plan.pdf*].

[31]Ottawa: CCAF, 1993, 67 pp.

of British Columbia to enter into an agreement[32] with the British Columbia Ministry of Education, Skills and Training (as it was in 1996), setting up a revitalized partnership in post-secondary education rejecting a client-driven, market-driven policy for advanced education, but accepting a list of closely-circumscribed, outcomes-based devices for assessing the system's "progress." With the election across Canada of governments that explicitly accept client-driven and market-driven models for education, the several streams of PIs in British Columbia are set to join as one great river, and to become a flood of centralization and mediocrity in teaching and learning.

The speed with which these things can happen was well illustrated in the Province of Alberta, where the performance indicators regime went quickly onward to its logically final step: control of public finances under automatic formulae driven by... KPI-BCs.

Alberta

Aadvanced education funding in Alberta fell by 16.8% in the five years between 1992 and 1997. At the same time, the Klein government began to re-engineer government under the general banner "Measuring Up." The 1993 provincial budget called for development of three-year business plans, straightforward emphasis on "results, not complaints and whining from the universities" (as Minister Jack Ady was supposed to have said in 1994), and PIs borrowed from successful organizations in the private sector. Target audiences, clients and customers satisfaction, bang-for-buck: discussion of education in Alberta moved away from history and politics and humane economics, and it moved fast. After a couple of years of province-wide consultation, the government did indeed require all universities and colleges to bring in business plans. And they began to move ($15 million promised in 1999) to tie at least some funding to institutional PIs.

At the end of the millennium, Alberta planned to have a system that was accessible, responsive, affordable, and accountable. Most Albertans would have been surprised that the system was not already accessible, responsive, affordable, and accountable. Polls consistently showed a huge majority of graduates to be quite happy with the education they received in Alberta's universities and colleges. Albertans as a whole were equally persuaded their post-secondary education system was excellent, accessible, and appropriate to a large and complicated province. But the Klein government took little interest in these polls. Indeed, when it heard messages like these during its consultations, and was confronted by hundreds of ordinary Albertans who rather liked the province's education system, it was made clear that the

---

[32]Ministry of Education, Skills and Training, *Charting a New Course: A Strategic Plan for the Future of British Columbia's College, Institute and Agency System* (Victoria: Ministry of Education, Skills and Training, 1996). The agreement also involved college presidents, and members of boards of governors.

objectives of "Measuring Up" were not about quality and accountability. The new directive was all about cuts, efficiency, and new forms of control over public post-secondary education.

The government aimed to increase enrolments and decrease staffing, to find new sources of funding in the private sector, and to raise its standing in the national and international hunt for research grants, top-flight scientists, and fine graduate students all with the least possible investment of new public funds. The University of Alberta did not reach the required level in new enrollment in 1997, and received a 1.75% base increase, whereas other universities found ways to attract 4% or more new students, and therefore got 2.5% from the "enrollment envelope" of the provincial budget. The University of Alberta found itself having to do more, a lot more, with less. It is all too reminiscent of F.W. Taylor and his halcyon days in the New Jersey chemical industry, ca. 1911.

On a long-term perspective, it is hard to tell if the use of PIs to decide enrollment levels is worse or better than the use of PIs to encourage/ discourage programmes of study in the sciences, the professions, the humanities, and the social sciences. Both empower bureaucrats and make politicians less accountable (at any rate, to their victims in the universities and colleges). Both neglect the knowledge that has been acquired in universities and colleges, and undermine the faculties, senates, departments, and public institutions which made knowledge-acquisition possible in the first place. Both of these uses place the burden of running the system according to market-oriented goals on the university or the college, not the government that sets and enforces the goals.

We think the policy on Research PIs is at least as dangerous as the others. Here is the May 1999 Business Plan of Alberta Learning[33] (the Ministry of Education)'s announcement of its intentions for the universities:

Goal: Research Excellence

The system, through its universities, will pursue research excellence to increase access to and development of new knowledge.

Actions: Provide leadership in setting goals and in advocacy; develop performance measures and establish benchmarks; publish research excellence performance indicators. Continue implementation of the action plan based on Fostering Excellence.

Expected results: enhanced institutional, learner and public awareness of research; improved university research.

The crucial portion of Fostering Excellence[34] is as follows:

---

[33]*http://www.aecd.gov.ab.ca/learning/publications/business_plan/business/plan.htm.*
[34]*Fostering Excellence: A Policy Framework for Alberta's University Research System.* See *http://www.aecd.gov.ab.ca/is/programsServices/UniversityResearch/REE/ fe_pol_frame_dept_strat.htm#Set standards and measure performance.*

2. Set standards and measure performance

2.1 Establish and monitor measures of quality through key performance indicators

The department and universities have developed an initial set of key performance indicators to measure research excellence. They have been chosen to provide indications of quality and relevance. The indicators will generate reliable information to Albertans on the performance and status of the university research system. Some of the research indicators will be used in providing input to the performance component of the new funding mechanism. (see Strategy 3.1)

The key performance indicators for research include:

1. research intensity the ratio of external grants, contracts and other sponsored income for research to the operating budget of an institution;

2. the total number of graduate students, the number of research-based graduate students and the number of graduate student awards (from the federal granting councils) as a ratio of total full-time faculty;

3. the number of publications, which reflects the outputs of research, and the impact of those publications (citation rate) as measured by the Institute for Scientific Information ;

4. council success rates the number of dollars received from the federal granting councils (as awarded by national peer review);

5. industry and community revenues for research, which indicate a measure of technology transfer;

6. licensing revenues and invention disclosures, which indicates a measure of technology transfer;

7. distance education research and development (unique to Athabasca University) focuses on multi-media materials, technologies, systems and other works related to distance education;

8. undergraduate publications the number of works published by undergraduate authors, which indicates a measure of undergraduate involvement in research. (This measure is unique to The University of Lethbridge.)

Working with the universities, the department will monitor and evaluate the key performance indicators to ensure they provide meaningful information. This commitment to evaluate the indicators and the data they generate means that there will be a solid performance baseline by which the department and Albertans can gauge the "health" and performance of the research system.

It is tempting to say *Maclean's* magazine guidelines are preferable to these. After all, *Maclean's* does worry about the kind of library a university has, and how many professors are on staff, and how those professors are encouraged to combine teaching and research, creatively and consistently. The Alberta research PIs show little evidence of caring about these things, and certainly provide no strong support for them.

These PIs, individually and collectively, constitute a guarantee that the real world of research its governance, its ethical and social values, its internal life, its financial support and long-term well-being, and its connection to the rest of the university will no longer be a primary or even a secondary concern to the Alberta government and its bureaucrats. Narrowly defined outputs will be everything.

Meanwhile, as the Confederation of Alberta Faculty Associations noted in a 1997 brief, *(i)* salaries continue to stagnate in Alberta post-secondary education; *(ii)* structural inequities persist in a system where urban institutions have a permanent head-start; *(iii)* these problems are made worse by federal funding of big science in big universities, further exacerbated by continued federal unwillingness to pay for costs of infrastructure; and *(iv)* the government persists in offering funding for ever narrower targets ($100 million for science and engineering recently), yet uses poorly-funded research in the humanities and social sciences to justify that narrowness! This is a striking indictment, since there is no conceivable way PIs could by themselves, directly or indirectly, do anything to remedy these difficulties.

The effects of the Albertan PIs regime are numerous and depressing. In the field of teacher education, for instance, the combined pressures of fiscal exigency and applied PIs have caused whole departments to disappear, whatever their future contribution to public education might have been, to be swallowed whole by ever-larger administrative units (at, for example, the University of Alberta). At many regional colleges, reductions of staff by 30%, while keeping enrolment steady or rising, has meant massive workload increases. It all looked good from an efficiency standpoint; but these developments hardly give new and higher quality to post-secondary education in Alberta. PIs were the cosmetic under which a the body of post-secondary education developed a new set of very deep wrinkles and worry lines.

In mentioning Faculty Associations, we point to a key group of actors in the universities, nearly all of whom face a future where their salaries, working conditions, teaching responsibilities, and ultimate retention on staff might be determined however indirectly by PIs. Collective bargaining, the usual means of negotiating and deciding these thing, risks becoming an empty shell.

A striking portrait of a world yet to come appears in a 1998 document on "Key Performance Indicators at Mount Royal College," produced by local consultant Patricia Harvey.[35] Her report begins with the question "Which Key Performance Indicators best reflect the strategic change proposed in Mount Royal College's Technology Integration Plan?" Harvey quotes Bogue and Saunders (p. 1) that "quality is conformance to mission specifications and goal achievement within publicly accepted standards of

---

[35]P. Harvie, "Technology-Based Key Performance Indicators; Technology Integration at Mount Royal College: Key Performance Indicators at Mount Royal College," at *http://www.mtroyal.ab.ca/olt/results1b.htm.*

accountability and integrity."[36] Harvey goes on to say that "conformance to mission and goals is the substance of assessment" and requires measurement of "the presence or absence of expected educational results." Institutional accountability means "building a body of evidence."

On this view, the structure, the procedures, the form of governance, the way of life, the culture, the values, the history, and the moral commitments of the university or the college become simply irrelevant. "Conformance" means the death of creativity and the triumph of the safe and mediocre.

Lastly, Ms. Harvey quotes G. Hanson to the effect that "institutional effectiveness" is a matter of knowing "whether or not our educational programs contribute to the attainment of important educational goals over and above the 'input' characteristics students bring to college."[37] We are then offered eight pages of PIs, line by line, a list reminiscent of the Boston Latin School case in the early 1920s (see Ch. 1). These are to supplement the relatively short list of Alberta government PIs (on completion rates, throughput rates, research indicators, and so on), and were apparently to help the Mount Royal College to surpass, not merely satisfy the new requirements of accountability in Alberta. A sample:

Success levels of alternative delivery populations [undefined]

Student satisfaction with accuracy of course content, technical interventions represented, and equipment need communiqués regarding technology courses enhanced/offered by traditional vs. alternative deliveries

student satisfaction with accuracy of advertisement, recruiting and admissions materials regarding student skills and expectations in technology-enhanced courses

student satisfaction with help desk service delivery

student satisfaction with computer lab support service delivery

...and a list of 28 plans and investments that should be measured for impact on the four "satisfaction indices" above.

This document expands and intensifies the usual PIs on employment its form, relevance to previous education and training, and so on and ventures far into territory usually inhabited by the senate ("satisfaction of students with testing methods; relevance of tests to content"). By page 17, we are in the present of a method whose madness has left method behind. Poor Mount Royal College, had it adopted this report holus-bolus (there is no evidence that it did, only that the report was "influential") would have been free to ignore its historic and social connections to Calgary and to Alberta, to jettison programmes in the arts and sciences whose PIs could not be made to match the structure in the Harvey report.

---

[36]Her reference is to E.G. Bogue and R.L. Saunders, *The Evidence for Quality* (San Francisco: Jossey-Bass, 1992), p. 20.

[37]The quotation is from G. Hanson, "Using Multiple Program Impact Analysis to Document Institutional Effectiveness," unpublished paper, Association of Institutional Research, Atlanta, Georgia, USA, 1992.

Across town, at the University of Calgary, the administration has jumped on the PIs bandwagon. Here is President Harvey Weingarten's official press release on the new Calgary PIs:

> According to U of C President Dr. Harvey Weingarten, the indicators help the university benchmark its performance and chart the progress the university has made in its 35 years of existence.

> "I was surprised by this benchmarking exercise because the data tell a story of a university that has made incredible progress," says Dr. Weingarten. "We are comparing our performance against universities that are 100 years old or older. It's quite a positive story."

> Dr. Weingarten points to charts showing that U of C students this year were the most successful in competition for postgraduate scholarships from the Natural Sciences and Engineering Research Council; that the U of C has done more than any other university or college in Alberta to accommodate the increased demand for post-secondary education; and the U of C is in the top 10 universities in Canada in terms of sponsored research revenue.

> He also highlights the fact that the U of C ranked third in a recent Wilfrid Laurier University survey of Canadian universities that measured the degree to which universities are prepared to hold themselves accountable.

> The indicators will serve as benchmarks for the university to gauge the institution's progress over time. "The only way you can know whether you are making progress, whether you need to shift strategies to increase your rate of progress, or whether you've met your goals is to measure those things in the first place," says Dr. Weingarten.[38]

President Weingarten's enthusiasm makes sense in light of Alberta's ten-year long dalliance with officially imposed, budget-based PIs. He would not want to be odd-man-out, one presumes.

But in the detail, the Calgary PIs are pale cousins to the Mount Royal variety. Calgary's charts and tables[39] compare its age since the University's foundation to the ages of older universities in Canada, its research grant income, enrolment levels and rapidity of enrolment increase, and its economic impact (measured by amount of contribution to the Calgary United Way!).

We doubt the mavens of PIs, tucked away in their Edmonton aeries, will be satisfied with the Calgary PIs. Indeed, the Calgary strategy seems to be to publicize PIs that make Calgary look rather good, in the background meanwhile accepting compulsory provincial PIs, and hoping for the best. The difficulty with this strategy is that is places so little attention on the due process of university governance, puts undue emphasis on research as opposed to teaching (just because research can be safely measured), and accepts by implication that PIs move the university toward accountability, quality, responsiveness, and so on. By this time, it should be painfully clear that PIs do none of the above.

---

[38]*http://www.fp.ucalgary.ca/unicomm/news/Nov_01/kpi-bc.htm.*
[39]*http://www.fp.ucalgary.ca/unicomm/KPI/.*

Tom Pocklington, in an essay on the marketing of the university,[40] makes what he calls "two modest proposals" to fight the marketization of the university:

> The rear-guard action is to stop reproducing the obsession with research, and the devaluation of teaching, that is characteristic of the most commercialized parts of the university.... The offensive step is for universities to promote incisive criticism as a social good every bit as important as the creation of saleable technology....What about, as a very modest start, a university requirement that, for every hundred dollars used to purchase the university's 'intellectual property,' businesses contribute ten dollars to a fund for basic research, the liberal arts, and student financing in these areas?

These are attractive ideas, but unlikely to give pause to PIs mavens.

David Strangway, former president of the University of British Columbia, asserted in 1992 that universities and colleges in Canada are already massively accountable. Strangway gave a long list of the outreach work his university then did, the innumerable public reports it issued every year, and then got to his underlying point:

> It seems to me that many people are pushing universities to make them do what they themselves want the universities to do. That, to me, is not accountability, that is an attempt to intervene in decision making. They want us to do the research which they judge to be important. They want us to move the universities to produce more of the kinds of people who they believe they are going to need. They want us to cut back enrolment in the humanities because they don't believe these subjects are as important as other fields of study. In my view, in such a case accountability and intervention have become confused. This suggests to me that what some people want is something remarkably close to a centrally planned economy.[41]

Another strategy for Albertans is the creation and publication of alternative statistics on post-secondary education, closely tied to the real world of teaching, research, and learning in that province. First steps in that strategy have already been taken. In spring 2001 the Confederation of Alberta Faculty Associations and the Alberta Colleges and Institutes Faculties Association published Post-Secondary Education in Alberta (at *http://www. higher.ca*). Their emphasis is on public financial support, shown in easily-understood maps of increases in the American and Canadian states and provinces from 1995 on, then a survey of education and employment levels of graduates (all of them high and rising), the depressing picture of tuition fee increases and net student debt in this relatively wealthy province,

---

[40]Thomas Pocklington, "The Marketing of the University," in T.W. Harrison and J.L. Kachur, *Education, Globalization, and Democracy in Alberta* (Edmonton: University of Alberta Press/Parkland Institute, 1999), 45–55, this reference to p. 53.

[41]David Strangway, "The Scope of University Accountability," in J. Cutt and R. Dobell, eds., *Public Purse, Public Purpose: Autonomy and Accountability in the Groves of Academe* (Halifax: Institute for Research on Public Policy/Canadian Comprehensive Auditing Foundation, 1992), 251–2.

faculty-to-student ratios, faculty renewal and faculty salaries, and the condition of the "intellectual infrastructure" (library resources, and the general state of the buildings in Alberta's colleges and universities). These well-founded, tidily-presented data tell a story of a system that wants to give highest priority to students and to education, to access and to sustained quality, and not to reducing the taxes of the wealthy, nor to labour market demands for training *ne plus ultra.*

It remains to be seen when the costs and the complications of Alberta PIs will finally outweigh their demoralizing and mediocritizing effects.[42] One can only hope that day is not too far distant.

Ontario

Bob Rae and Mike Harris have guided Ontario's political culture as successive premiers through the 1990s and early 2000s. The first was a "social democrat" by some description, the second a "neo-conservative" by any description. From end to end, the decade witnessed the rise of PIs in colleges and universities across the province. The period began with an economic downturn, as the government of the day liked to say, followed by a period of unprecedented prosperity which in turn ended abruptly in 2001. These economic factors, and the ideological differences between Mssrs. Rae and Harris, have made not one whit of difference to the people who flog PIs. Onward they have marched.

Even before the end of the Rae regime and the Common Sense Revolution of the Harris Tories, some universities and colleges were far down the PIs road. Queen's developed its own set, knowing they soon would have no choice since PIs would inevitably become compulsory. By 2000, seven iterations later, the Queen's PIs still retain their ingenuity, emphasizing the features of Queen's "output" that make that University's quality visible to all. Their twenty PIs describe the elite quality of the University's intake of students; the faculty's Killam, Steacie, and other awards, not to mention its gender composition; the kind of library at Queen's and the university's student-faculty ratios; and the excellent student satisfaction ratings Queen's continues to enjoy.[43] Now, though, the Queen's web site offers the following note:

> The province of Ontario (through the Ministry of Training, Colleges and Universities' OSAP policy) requires all post-secondary institutions to provide access for students and prospective students to three provincially determined

---

[42]On this general question, see Bob Barnetson and Marc Cutright, "Performance Indicators as Conceptual Technologies," *Higher Education*, 40 (2000): 277–92, with its argument that the effects of PIs are even worse, as they "shape what issues acdemics think about and how academics think about these issues."

[43]*http://www.queensu.ca/irp/pdfiles/fallheadcounts/pi2001.pdf.* We have yet to find a student-satisfaction rating that is anything but "good" or "excellent." This has been so for as long as the surveys have been done. One wonders why the surveyors have not got the message.

measures regarding graduation, employment, and Ontario loan default rates. The following presents Queen's University's "OSAP Indicators." These indicators support Queen's own established efforts to document our progress toward institutional goals, and further demonstrate Queen's position as a quality leader.

Compulsion has come to Queen's,[44] as it has to fifteen other universities whose PIs web sites appear on the Queen's page.[45] And because it won't do any harm whatsoever, the Queen's site publishes an article from the *Maclean's* university rankings of November 2001.

The Queen's strategy is a revealing one, since their administration has from the beginning acted rather than reacted to the coming deluge. Alas, it has not prevented the flood. As the *Maclean's* article on the Queen's site indicates, Queen's faces a 4% cut in public finance in coming months (as of late 2000). The question might be, "Would the cut have been worse if the university had resisted PIs massively and from the start?" This would be the wrong question; for it is next to certain that neo-conservative governments will cut budgets for public services. The question surely is, will the combination of cuts and accountability PIs undermine quality, autonomy, and sense of purpose?

We think the Queen's approach was a good one for the time, and continues to be necessary as a defensive mechanism, provided the university does not talk itself into thinking or acting on the view that if you cannot measure it, it isn't significant. But Queen's ought to move on to a range of new ideas. Working with sister institutions, Queen's might well take the lead in Ontario in attacking province-wide, centralized PIs just as the London School of Economics did in the UK in March 2001. Acting locally as they already do, and provincially as they could do, Queen's and other like-minded universities and colleges have an opportunity to put an end to a wasteful and damaging policy. With the addition of our suggestions in chapter 7, they can demonstrate that all the data any reasonably student or other citizen wants is already publicly available, most of it on the university web site, and that, therefore, the provincial bureaucracy is irrelevant and expensive. But the British experience shows that reason must be joined to political will and effective action if there is to be a favourable result.

In working up its own PIs, Queen's was not alone. Trent University, a few kilometres inland, did exactly the same in 1994, providing its own carefully-hewn PIs. Because the devil is in the detail, and because this general strategy of is so important, we turn to describe the way the Trent PIs were created.

Trent University President L.W. Connolly struck a committee on PIs in 1994 June. The Committee's proposals appeared in the 1994 September

---

[44]*http://www.queensu.ca/irp/accountability/.*
[45]*http://www.edu.gov.on.ca/eng/general/postsec/uindicator.html.*

issue of the *University Gazette*.[46] By 1995 June, the Trent administration had decided to implement the new system. Trent's Faculty Association and Senate discussed these PIs, but were bystanders in the decision to apply them. This point is a crucial one. If the strategy of creating one's own PIs is to work in a college or university, and if the purpose is to strengthen the usual organs of critical, public academic discussion then you don't want your administration making and communicating your PIs on its own. This is what happened not only at Trent, but nearly everywhere else perhaps because PIs are seen as a management device, and therefore should be dealt with inside the administration and Board of Governors. At all events, this has turned out to be a wrong-headed approach, as disputes over PIs in universities as different and distant as York, Windsor, Carleton, and Toronto have shown.

Like the Queen's University PIs, Trent's came out before the Council of Ontario Universities Indicators did.

> [W]hether we like it or not, others will take measurements of us so we had better take whatever control we can of the process. The market success of the *Maclean's* survey illustrates that students and parents demand some quantitative description of universities, and understandably so. The provincial government is clearly moving in the direction of quantitative assessment.... (p. 1, 1994 September *Gazette*)

Like most university-developed PIs, Trent's system is based on that university's "Statement of Goals" and its "Institutional Goals." Each goal is interpreted to produce one or more quantitative indicators. Significantly, the Task Force refused to interpret Institutional Goal No. 7:

> Create and sustain an environment (intellectual, physical, fiscal, and social) that advances learning through quality teaching and research while encouraging respect, tolerance and sensitivity. (p. 4)

The Task Force wrote that

> properly developed performance indicators will assist Trent in achieving its stated mission of excellence by presenting all of its constituents with clear, evaluative evidence of our degree of success. (p. 1)

The Task Force makes no argument to show *how* PIs would lead to "excellence." Chairperson Drewes (Economics, Trent) merely wrote that a weak performance would help Trent "recognize problems that prevent us from achieving that mission."

Drewes says the case against PIs "turns entirely on the inability to quantify the important dimensions of the university."

> It is not possible even in principle to approach the degree of commitment to "promotion of free inquiry and expression" statistically or to measure success in instilling a sense of "ethical conscience." ...[W]here proxy measures are proposed they will be... subject to a high degree of interpretation. (p. 1)

---

[46]The Trent PIs appeared in the Fortnightly Supplement to the *University Gazette* (1994 September), pp. 1–4.

PIs invite "facile but incorrect comparisons between universities" and would tend to "replace the mission statement as the operational guide to Trent." The Committee's Final Report[47] came down with an indicator of research output that requires "a simple tally of the number of scholarly publications" (Deans' offices to decide what counts as a publication), meanwhile collapsing reports of NSERC and SSHRC grant totals.

Nevertheless Trent went on to create a series of twenty-five performance indicators dealing with research, teaching, students, supporting environment, and the like. In many cases, these PIs came back to haunt Trent since, of course, endless improvement on quantitative measures is impossible and finally undesirable, but demanded year by year by provincial bureaucrats. As at Queen's, Trent's system was designed to keep the province at bay. This remains an illusion until the data become part of an effective provincial campaign to demolish the centralized PI system.

Again we have to ask how it all happened, and so fast. A recent report to the HSSFC[48] includes an informative and helpful discussion of the Ontario background. It reminds the reader that the Ontario Provincial Auditor was worried by 1990 that university accountability for expenditure of public funds was not good enough. The Ministry's answer was a twelve-member task force under William Broadhurst.[49] A Progress Report ended with an appeal to meet the rising and strident demand for tight control, and tight accountability, by

- re-describing and re-defining the rôle of the Board of Governors, and by implication of the Senate, accepting that the world has become a more complicated place since these bodies were last "reformed"in the mid-1960s;

- becoming explicit about the dividing line between the budget-making responsibilities of Board and of Senate, so that everyone can see who has which budget tasks, which budget obligations, and why;

- revising and "improving" management budget/administration practice, some of which came from the Dark Ages (to quote one member of the Force);

- making Boards meet openly and often, and ensuring Boards are representative of a changing Ontario society; and most important of all,

- creating "an independent monitoring body," with auditing powers roughly like those of the Ontario Council on University Affairs in its

---

[47]Drewes Committee, "Measuring up to Our Standards: Final Report on Performance Indicators for Trent University," Trent University, Peterborough, Ontario, 1994 November. Typescript, 11 pages.

[48]G. Grosjean, J. Atkinson-Grosjean, K. Rubenson, and D. Fisher, Measuring the Unmeasurable: Paradoxes of Accountability and the Impacts of Performance Indicators on Liberal Education in Canada, unpublished research report, Humanities and Social Science Federation of Canada, 2000 May 3. See also the Federation web site for a complete text: *http://www.hssfc.ca/english/policyandadvocacy/researchprojects/performanceindicators.cfm*.

[49]W. Broadhurst, *et al.*, *Task Force on University Accountability: Progress Report and Issues Paper* (Toronto: The Task Force, 1992), pp. ii+62.

review of Graduate Studies (resulting in the approval, removal, or melding of various programmes in the late 1980s). Indeed, Broadhurst thought the Ontario Council could perhaps do the job again, taking that position in the Final Report of 1993.[50]

By that time, the political winds were shifting with the election of Mike Harris in 1995. Universities and colleges were not keen for yet another external watch-dog. Rather than do anything right away, the Minister in 1996 therefore appointed David Smith, a former Principal of Queen's University, to advise on new techniques for detecting quality and efficiency in the university sector. His reports ("How shall we recognize quality?" and "How shall we find enough professors?") were balanced accounts of the control and finance of post-secondary education, and were well received. But the underlying force of the PIs movement was far, far greater than these various reports suggested or allowed. Smith underestimated the power and force of neo-conservatism in the Harris government. In a way, it was all over many years before; the new audit and control culture we described in the 1940s and 1950s simply took a little longer to manifest in Ontario. When it did, it arrived *con forza*.

There were clues a PIs explosion was on the way. In 1993, at the height of the Rae government's work in post-secondary education, the Premier's Council on Economic Renewal and its Task Force on Lifelong Learning had commissioned Edward DesRosiers and Associates of West Hill, Ontario to write a document entitled *An Information Framework Linking Educational Outcomes to Economic Renewal*.[51] Despite its amazingly turgid prose, the Framework manages to be crystal-clear on some points. It recommends a unified and detailed PIs system that crosses all institutional boundaries in the public and private sectors. It notes (p. 4) that it has little interest (!) in performance, but rather "with relationships between the component parts of the educational system and the way in which they interact... to meet the human resource requirements of the province's economy."

That is, PIs are about outputs. Inputs and processes don't matter much. The report sees universities and colleges as "delivery agents" (p. 7), so a "process" PI would be, for example, "Volume of teaching activity," (p. 9), a measure self-evidently linked to a product. At p. 16 we have the Outcomes that DesRosiers *et al.* consider worthwhile: transitions to post-educational activity, labour-force participation, unemployment, distribution of employment by sector, and so on, ending with average income, and

---

[50]Broadhurst, 36–44.

[51]E. DesRosiers, *et al.*, *An Information Framework Linking Educational Outcomes to Economic Renewal* (West Hill, Ontario: Edward DesRosiers and Associates, 1993 October 15). The same business group wrote *An Information Framework for Higher Education in the Maritimes* (1995 October 18). These documents are of the greatest interest, and the authors of this present book, have therefore lodged copies of the Des-Rosiers materials with the Libraries of the University of Toronto and of British Columbia, and at the Canadian Association of University Teachers, in order to facilitate research and study on the roots of neo-conservative PIs in their rawest, clearest forms.

social assistance costs per recipient (since inadequate performance in a university may mean unemployment...and time on the bread lines).

In subsequent reports, DesRosiers and other consultants dealt with such technical matters as the "corridor" funding system in Ontario. Finally, by 1997–8, there was a cluster of documents recommending that detailed PIs on courses and enrolments and costs should be tied to eventual graduation rates, and then to the successful placement of graduates in jobs. But not just any jobs: they would have to be jobs in the fields for which they had been trained (90% or more). And not just in those fields: but in the tertiary economy for all university graduates, and in a varying proportion, also for college graduates.

And thus we have a programme of complete PIs, detailing the quantitative manipulation of post-secondary education to fit precisely the vocational and the capital requirements of Ontario (and world) marketplaces.

Ontario universities and colleges have found it increasingly hard to get degree and programme approvals based on merely academic arguments. They have been encouraged, by implication and by explicit policy, to accept that the road to freedom from bureaucratic centralism lies through privatization. They have been told that competition for ever-higher PIs is a natural and desirable feature of the new World of E-Knowledge. The Ontario example is one that offers encouraging cases of resistance, but also a model case of a political system that has (temporarily one would like to think) lost faith in the quality, accountability, and clarity-of-goals of its own public institutions. The Ontario case shows, as few can, how utterly useless PIs are if one wants quality, accountability, and clarity-of-goals. And it hints at a way forward. But that we leave to our final chapter. In the meantime, we have a final and revealing Canadian case to examine, and once again, it reveals the worst silliness of PIs-gone-mad, and yet the possibility of a way forward, to the re-acquisition of "l'université comme service publique."

Québec

By the mid-1960s, every Canadian province was building colleges and universities at a remarkable pace, reconstructing university governance as it went. Québec in many ways exceeded other regions and provinces. By 1980, in not quite two decades, the older francophone universities in Québec and Montréal had been transformed into vibrant secular institutions, open to new worlds of research in the humanities, social sciences, and natural sciences. Québec's creaky systems of training in education, law, pharmacy, and other fields were energetically modernized.

A large multi-campus provincial university, the Université du Québec, grew to serve whole new populations of students across the province, and its foundation symbolized and embodied the innovative forces at work in the period. Accessibility acquired powerful, new meanings in the Québec system: women became more numerous than men in many programmes of study, and people from all ethnic groups found they had homes in the system, whether on its anglophone or francophone side. Provincial commitment to research funding, in tandem with rising federal support, helped institutions from Sherbrooke to Laval to work as rough equals in advanced studies in most fields.

The sharp contrast with the 1940s and 1950s alone makes Québec's achievement especially noteworthy. But the adjustment of instructors and students to this new world was not without incident. The renaissance of the Québec system was part of a larger resurgence of a sense of historic community, and in the construction of new modern identity. The long hallways of the new campuses in Trois-Rivières, the many buildings tucked away at the Université du Québec à Montréal, the laboratories at McGill, the downtown presence of Concordia, the outreach of Rimouski were all signs and symbols of a huge political and fiscal commitment to making a new Québec. A culture of collaborative teaching and research, supported by sustained public finance, made Québec universities unique in Canada, possibly in the world. Funding from Québec joined finance from the federal capital to make research and publication an integral feature of post-secondary educational life. Creation of a new province-wide system of Collèges d'enseignement général et professionel [CEGEP], offering the final year of secondary education and the opening years of post-secondary education and training in large centres and small meant significant capital outlays in the service of social, cultural, and industrial development, all as a matter of public policy.

Until the late 1980s and the 1990s, community-building and cultural construction—work with a mainly francophone and Québécoise expression, and without analogue anywhere else in the world—was achieved mainly through the contributions of the arts and the sciences, and largely in universities and colleges. But after the late 1980s, a new language and new politics took over with remarkable speed, completeness, and a certain brutality.[52] Now it was Québec's turn to hear the language of performance, job readiness, private sector linkages, and targeted funding, and to experience the shock of massive, damaging, and incessant budget cuts. The great public experiment of the 1960s and 1970s became an exercise in declining public financial commitment.

So complete was the turn in Québec government policy and practice that by 1997 the Fédération québécoise des professeures et professeurs

---

[52]Cf. Claude Hamel, "Les universités québécoises rendent aussi des comptes," *Le Devoir*, 1995 juillet 12, with a strong claim that the Université du Québec was well advanced in the adoption of detailed indicateurs d'acitivité universitaire, and was happy to be a pioneer in this respect. Compare this with Roch Denis, "La thèse de la diversification des sources de financement fait figure de nouveau dogme," *Le Devoir*, 1998 novembre 6, whose discontent with market-based indicators was, if anything, underlined by a broader review of public opinion in B. Breton, "Seuls les recteurs sont contents," *Le Soleil*, 1999 octobre 27.

d'université found it necessary to publish a strong and eloquent plea for the reconstruction of post-secondary education in Québec as a public service.[53] The Fédération held that the very idea of autonomous and accountable higher education was at risk.[54] Between 1995 and 2000, nearly 25 per cent of public funding for post-secondary education was lost.

Nowhere else in Canada was the PIs revolution so unexpected and negative in its psychological impact. Here is the official Québec government position on university finance as of early 2000, based on a policy enunciated in 1999 October (all translations by the authors from documents in the original French):[55]

> The main objectives of Québec government policy in university funding are as follows:
>
> • to maintain a balanced budget, all the while satisfying government expectations of transparency, equity, predictability, and consistency
>
> • to respect university autonomy and therefore to arrive at agreed performance indicators with each institution
>
> • to decide on the universities' share of public budgets using a dynamic approach
>
> • to leave room for appropriate and selected actions.

We forebear from commenting on the oxymoronic quality of the second point, and simply indicate that it foretold the current regime of contrats de performance.

The government said in early 2000 that it would devote 85% of its budgets to "general financing" of the system, but would henceforward use a system of "targeted funding" for teaching, research, maintenance, reserving the remaining 15% for special projects. Its most recent list of targeted budgets is twenty-five items long. It is difficult, if not impossible, to see how local institutions would have much room to decide anything "in an autonomous manner" in such a budgetary structure. This feature of Québec policy is closely reminiscent of the Ontario approach to "corridor funding," and equally open to the application of detailed, centralized, performance-oriented controls.

To ensure that financing of the system would produce equally precise results everywhere in Québec, the government announced in February of 2000 a system of Performance Contracts. Here the Québec government was again opening new ground in Canada, proposing to remedy financial harm

---

[53]Fédération québécoise des professeures et professeurs d'université, *L'université comme service publique* (Montréal: FQPPU, 1997).

[54]An unaffiliated group of Québec university teachers made the same point in a tidily-argued letter-article of 2000 avril 3, once again in *Le Devoir*: M. Beaulne, *et al.*, "L'étalon de la formation universitaire n'est pas le marché du travail."

[55]Ministère de l'éducation du Québec, Fiche synthèse de la politique québécoise de financement des universités (Québec: Ministère de l'éducation, 2001): at *http:// www.-meq.gouv.qc.ca/reforme/pol_financ/fiche_synthese.thm*.

done to universities and colleges by restoring just some but not all of the essential public funding previously cut but it was to be restoration only on the basis of the new Contracts.

Under this scheme, the government proposed to reinvest, over a three-year period, additional "new" funds equal to 25% of the 2000 budget (itself a much-reduced cousin of the budget of, say, 1988). University and college teachers were to get a 25% increase of poverty-level funding over three years. Janyne Hodder of Bishop's University in Lennoxville noted that the reinvestment would "bring us only to the level we enjoyed in 1994–95." As Guy Demers, a Ministry official put it in May 2001,

> [T]he Minister of Education called upon university-level institutions to participate in an accountability exercise that is, to say the least, demanding, that they accept publicly to achieve explicit objectives, to explain how they will move toward the results they claim to want to get, and to sign a formal contract between the two parties that seals the deal.[56]

M. Demers added another rather manipulative note: "Each performance contract is unique, thus reflecting the autonomy of each higher education establishment."[57] To qualify for supplementary funds, and to have any hope of recovery from a half-decade of budgetary disaster, one had to sign a Performance Contract pleasing to the Ministry. What did this really mean?

Minister of Education François Legault signed four performance contracts at the turn of year 2000/1, then got into budgetary difficulty. After a few weeks of political cliff-hanging, the sums required for the remaining 14 Contracts suddenly appeared. If this looks manipulative... it was. After five years of savage cuts, cliff-hanging would keep the universities in an appropriately desperate frame of mind, willing to bow to the unacceptable. M. Legault maintained throughout, in a splendid *non sequitur*, that the Québec government's historic commitment to students (the lowest tuition in Canada) proved the government would never bring in any policy that was bad for learners. In a final manipulation, as one Performance Contract after another was signed with hungry university administrations, the government reminded everyone that this was an utterly transparent and equitable arrangement.

Oddly, the latter claim may be correct. The method was indeed transparently intended to impose uniformity on a diverse post-secondary system, to compel a new responsiveness ("réceptivité") to markets, and to force administrations across the system to adopt industrial techniques reminiscent of F.W. Taylor. At Concordia, since 1994, 151 programmes of study have been eliminated or fused, and 15 others temporarily suspended —figures that satisfy the mentality of cuts-for-cuts' sake, but have little to

---

[56]Guy Demers, "Autonomie, imputabilité et évaluation," unpublished paper, Canadian Society for the Study of Higher Education, Annual Meeting, 2001 May 25, Université Laval.
[57]Demers, "Autonomie," *loc. cit.*

do with quality or accountability.[58] At Concordia as elsewhere, the idea now is to expand student enrolment, no matter the early damage done to base budgets and services after years of savage cuts, and to ensure faculty pass virtually all students each year.

Under the new regime, universities must balance their budgets by 2003–4 by clarifying objectives (MBO), increasing professorial and staff productivity, accepting benchmarking ("production de données d'étalonnage") across the board and building toward new levels of research subvention (20% increases at Montréal and Rimouski in three years; 17% at Laval; 100% at Hull). In yet another manipulative twist, the Minister throughout 2000–2001 reminded everyone that it is traditionally and legally required for any entity receiving 50% or more of its funds from the Québec government to be audited by the Auditor General. Since 1995 June, a committee of the legislature conducts a parallel review of university financial statements and budgets. The auditing required to show that the books are balanced would not stop there, of course; at one point in early 2000, there was talk (later retracted) that professorial work-loads would be also regulated by the province.

The general thrust of the new regime is clearly in line with the historic development of PIs, and depressingly similar to arrangements bedevilling public post-secondary education in the United Kingdom, South Carolina, and so on. The hard lessons learned in those places have neither been or heard nor applied in Québec or anywhere else in Canada.

Lysiane Gagnon wrote in a *La Presse* editorial (2001 March 6) that

> in tying the funding that universities so desperately need to performance contracts approved by bureaucrats in his own ministry, M. Legault puts universities under the direct control of bureaucrats without competence in the area, and works toward goals that have absolutely nothing to do with the basic mission of universities, that is, the advancement of knowledge.

If only university administrators had been as consistent as Ms. Gagnon in responding to the new Contract system! On the whole the Council of Québec University Rectors and Principals (CREPUQ) has been disposed to accept their new managerial tasks, whatever the drawbacks. By contrast, students and professors have been energetic in their determination to call the Contracts what they truly are: an engine of sustained and continuing underfunding and control.[59]

There are not many novelties in the Québec Performance Contracts scheme, modelled as it is on United Kingdom and American forerunners,

---

[58]Jean Bernatchez, "Contextualisation et analyse comparée (du point de vue des enjeux) des contrats de performance des universités québécoises," unpublished paper, Canadian Society for the Study of Higher Education, Annual Meeting, 2001 May 25, Université Laval.

[59]Fédération québécoise des professeures et professeurs d'université, *Pour l'Etat, malgré lui: Mémoire présenté au Conseil supérieur de l'éducation* (Montreal: FQPPU, 2001), esp. pp. 8–11.

and owing much to Alberta schemes since 1995. Two features deserve attention for the help they give in making an estimate of the social effects of such a bluntly instrumental approach to PIs, and for the light they throw on the language of PIs anywhere at any time.

The first is the uniformity of government demands expressed in the new Québec Performance Contracts and the uniformity of universities' responses to those demands.

The Bishop's Performance Contract required the following:[60]

• a balanced budget

• benchmarking of all programmes (see sec. 3 of the Contract, comparing teaching, library, computing, and other programme budgets [note: no comparisons of programme content] with 12 sister universities of approximately the same size or ambition, a scheme apparently borrowed from CAUBO and *Maclean's* magazine)

• improved research performance (to fill a Canada Research Chair slot, to get more funds from national research funding councils, and to release more professorial time for research, all the while maintaining the university's strong commitment to teaching. How Bishop's would achieve the miracle of releasing professors for research while at the same time maintaining its commitment to teaching was unexplained.)

• increase the graduate rate by 5% (all Québec universities are required under the new regime to graduate at least 80% of entering students in a fixed time; Bishop's rate was, until 2001, just over 80%).

An Appendix lists a group of programmes eliminated after years of cuts. Perhaps this list is given to persuade the Ministry that Bishop's is operating in good faith, or that Bishop's truly wants to accept a regime of tighter administrative control at all levels in return for more cash; perhaps it is offered to demonstrate that Bishop's has already experienced more than its share of pain. Programmes dropped include a Joint Major Programme called CPR: Classics, Philosophy and Religion; at the behest of the Ministry of Education, graduate level educations programmes were replaced by a Bachelor of Education degree.

Compare this with the McGill Performance Contract. In return for $100 million in new funding between 2000 and 2003, McGill will (we italicize items that are in common between the Bishop's and the McGill contracts):[61]

- increase McGill's "market share" of Québec students from 9.3% to 9.8%, and international students from 21.3% of the McGill contingent to 25%
- hire 100 *new professors*
- build *new strengths* in bioinformatics, language acquisition, e-commerce, and others

---

[60]*http://www.ubishops.ca/administration/principal/cont_eng.htm.*
[61]For a summary, see the *McGill Reporter*, 33, 8 (2001 January 11): 1 2. For the complete text, *http://www.mcgill.ca/administration/g/performance_e_long.pdf.*

- raise *research grant revenues*, and sustain the present high rates of publications-per-professor at McGill (pp. 16–20 gives a complete sequence of *benchmarks*)
- increase student services, especially for francophone Québec students
- raise graduate rates in music and religious studies so they approach *the mystical 80%*
- increase the percentage of courses taught by tenure-track professors
- undertake cyclical *review of teaching units*, and intensify teaching evaluation procedures (with an eye to making public reports on client satisfaction—indeed, all of these last four are closely linked to likely improvements in student satisfaction PIs).

Despite differences in size and mission between Bishop's and McGill, their treatment is the same, and, one might safely argue, "market-driven."[62]

We turn next to a mid-sized francophone university, Sherbrooke.[63] Its main listing of contracted promises exactly matches those of Bishop's and McGill, an unsurprising fact in light of criteria and standards laid out in the prior Québec government policy, especially the announcements of October-December 2000. But at pages 48 to 64, the Sherbrooke document moves on to a list of no fewer than 28 indicators it considers more exact, and more revealing of its work, than anything the Ministry has envisaged. It asks what have been the effects at the "margins" of long-term cuts and indebtedness, and what it would mean to continue balancing its budgets. The answer is: a continued dependency on external research funding, an enforced reliance on Sherbrooke's traditionally strong and successful "co-op" programmes (which it makes a centre-piece of the entire 108-page document), and so on. That is, the impact of financial stress is made out to be not entirely negative, especially as Sherbrooke was already a market-oriented school.

The completeness and factual depth of the Sherbrook contract is exceptional but risky. Why does one want the Ministry to know that some undergraduate and graduate programmes (never identified) will never reach the mystical 80%, whereas others (identified) will? (pp. 15 ff.) Elsewhere the same spirit of completeness and detail leads the writers to submit Sherbrooke, by formal contractual obligation, to detailed plans for

---

[62]One market-driven element in performance contract, the manipulation of graduation rates, would (one imagines) have attracted substantial and sustained criticism in Québec. One Rector (Bishop's) and one professor came out against this particular PI (Ian Irvine, "Performance contracts aren't the answer [to making graduation rates rise]," *Montreal Gazette*, 2001 February 7) at the height of the performance contracts controversy. There were no others during the quarter-year following the contract announcements. We think this may have to do with the sheer number of PIs imposed on the universities at one time, but for the first time, in some instances, in so public a forum.

[63]The complete text is at *http://www.usherb.ca/npp/general/contrat-performance.pdf*.

computerization, e-learning, and e-commerce which could only the gladden the hearts of PIs proponents everywhere.

Québec's rectors and principals have been consistent in claiming university autonomy to be no less strong now than before. The facts say otherwise, and it is regrettable that political opportunism requires the rectors to deny the truth.

Throughout these documents, mechanisms of regulation and reporting are centralized and complete. But the existence of these mechanisms does not mean that provincial bureaucrats take decisions. Instead, they leave in place an underfinanced structure; and they require universities and colleges to pay close and mathematically precise attention to various markets and client groups. So close is this attention that, by definition, universities and colleges will find their margin of manoeuvre reduced bit by bit in each year of the contract. Annual reports under such a system draw ever tighter the net of demands and controls linking markets and clients on one hand, to post-secondary teaching and research practices on the other. The provincial Auditor-General is there to make sure that it all happens.

■

In Hindu-Buddhist cosmology, Indra is the Warrior King of the Heavens, the god of war and storm. Indra's Net is inescapable, except to those who are fully aware of its existence and its purpose. Will Canadian universities use their intelligence to detect and to understand the net, to move through the net, and thus at last escape it? For the sake of public post-secondary education in Canada, we believe they can and will.

7

Toward a New Accountability

"The function of the university is not simply to teach bread-winning, or to furnish teachers for the public schools or to be a center of polite society; it is, above all, to be the organ of that fine adjustment between real life and the growing knowledge of life, an adjustment which forms the secret of civilization."
— W.E.B.Du Bois, *The Souls of Black Folk*, 1903

"The college was not founded to give society what it wants. Quite the contrary."
— May Sarton, *The Small Room*, 1961

Earlier chapters examined management fads and follies in higher education, and the price the university has had to pay for them in misapplication of its resources, loss of autonomy, and prostitution of ideals.

PIs are the most enduring of these fads. As in most interventionist ideologies, PIs have next to nothing to do with liberal education, but everything to do with market discipline and control. Unlike many interventionist strategies, this one claimed to be anti-interventionist. A good many neo-conservative supporters of PIs talked as if they were proponents of hands-off reform schemes. But PIs instead lead to dramatic increases in the size and the scope of centralized bureaucracy—the polar opposite of the Thatcherite vision.

Margaret Thatcher herself apparently had second thoughts, much too late. According to one of her disciples, she confessed that her "unintended centralisation" had led many distinguished academics to see Thatcherism as a mere philistine subordination of scholarship to the Treasury. This had threatened the future autonomy and academic integrity of universities. She insisted she had never intended such a result.[1] Alas, her acolytes have generally ignored this recantation.

An optimist might argue we need only wait a year or two longer for PIs to fade away. The latest university rankings in the United States and Canada show how and why the problem of PIs can't be left to solve itself. Dr Leon Botstein is president of Bard College in Annandale-on-Hudson, New York. An article in an August 2001 number of the *New York Times* noted that Dr Botstein, ordinarily calm and analytical about most things, was anything but calm at the end of summer 2001. For toward the beginning of September, *U.S. News and World Report*'s annual ranking of American colleges and universities was to be published. Where, President Botstein wondered, would Bard place in the rankings? How many parents would be influenced by the numbers? How many research grants and private donations would go away, just because the ranking might go down, even if the difference between one institution and the next on the list was statistically insignificant?

Professor Botstein told the *Times* he considered the ranking criteria "ludicrous," calling the whole exercise "the most successful journalistic scam I have seen in my entire adult lifetime. A catastrophic fraud. Corrupt, intellectually bankrupt and revolting."[2] A *New York Times* editorial came to much the same conclusions, albeit in less colourful language, noting "the rankings make up in visibility what they lack in precision."[3]

President Botstein's view of the *U.S. News and World Report*'s totemic rankings parallelled that of most Canadian academics and administrators towards the *Maclean's* rankings from the early 1990s on. For example, in

---

[1]Simon Jenkins, "A bewildered tribe," THES, 2001 October 19.
[2]A. Kuczynski, " 'Best' list for colleges by *U.S. News* is under fire," *New York Times*, 2001 August 20.
[3]*New York Times*, 2001 August 27.

autumn 2000 Lakehead University learned its position in the *Maclean's* survey had fallen. In spring 2001, Lakehead and its surrounding city were surprised to learn they might not after all be chosen as the site of a west-Ontario teaching hospital and medical school. It was widely suspected the shifting policy of the Ontario government had something to do with the *Maclean's* ranking. It would be difficult if not impossible to prove a direct causal connection; but the fondness of Ontario's government for competition among universities, rather than co-operation, suggests it would be inclined to listen to such rankings, and to pay attention to them, whatever their weaknesses.

Similar national rankings and formal PI systems are in place in every Canadian province, most American states, and most of Europe, Australia, and New Zealand. One defence strategy is to criticize and to attack PIs, in all their forms and fashions. President Botstein was doing just that. His criticism was sensible and fair, but not quite on the button: his fundamental objection is that the rankings measure the wrong thing.

Judith Shapiro, president of Barnard College (No. 29 on last year's list of the best liberal arts colleges in the USA), said: "It's the old story about the drunk looking for his car keys under the lamp post because the light is good there." Like most administrator-critics, Professor Shapiro says she is happy to see the widespread publication of information about post-secondary education, but insists that the factors crucial in making a good university simply cannot be measured statistically.

What the rankings do measure, Botstein, Shapiro, and other administrators will agree, are the wealth (that is, the endowment and regular operating budget) of a college or university; its reputation, as judged by certain corporation presidents; student satisfaction, as judged by the level of alumni donations; percentage of faculty with doctorates; and student quality, as measured by results on standardized Scholastic Assessment Tests.

We argue that these measures are mostly wrong-headed. It is interesting in a sociological sense to know the views and prejudices of corporation presidents about the quality of universities across the country, but the likelihood that these are based on comparative scientific study of the actual quality of each university is very small. No one is surprised that rich institutions get richer. But democratic communities might also be interested in other questions, such as accessibility and the independence of the teaching and research on offer.

We would go on to ask a further question: where do such measures lead? What kind of world would they produce, were they to survive triumphant? The answers indicate the urgency of the problem. Recall that many critics of popular rankings are unhappy because such rankings do not go far enough, because they are weak, and because they do not rely on measured outcomes of learning, using standardized tests.[4] Remember, too, that the world of intensified and standardized ranking systems would necessarily include devices to measure the outcomes of courses on Shakespeare, logic, applied physics, and social work even when all of these wholly disparate subjects were presented as part of a single student's BA course work.

Thus the effects of popular rankings must not be downplayed. They encourage the belief that markets—the job market, corporate markets, the student satisfaction market, the family-demand market—should fundamentally determine the curriculum, the teaching, the research, and the services of colleges and universities. They support people who criticize *Maclean's* and *U.S. News* because those rankings do not go far enough, and they provide popular political support for the hard-core proponents of PIs. Purists would argue that if the result is a rash of business and media courses and a significant drop in enrolments in science and engineering —as is happening in the UK and as happened in New Zealand—then so be it. However, some of the disciples are now worried about this, particularly after 11 September 2001, and talk about a new *dirigisme* to promote science, engineering, and—breathe it not among the philistines—the study of modern languages, foreign cultures, and international politics.

It is true that popular rankings do not measure learning, and certainly not through standardized tests. We mentioned earlier the Pew Foundation in the United States, whose studies of student life and learning hold the promise of describing teaching/learning in colleges and universities in ways that may not arbitrarily put at risk their ability to govern themselves accountably. But even Pew Foundation results are reported as standardized statistics. However helpful, those statistics could be used to build detailed rankings and league tables. Government officials, think-tank consultants, and media pundits will as always be tempted to construct such tables and to use the rankings improperly that is, for purposes of mechanically applied budget cuts, the imposition of ever-more-bureaucratized systems of control, and the creation of standardized course content, purged of innovation and controversy, which is easier to measure statistically. These aims have nothing to do with improvement and support of post-secondary education, and everything to do with cuts and external control.

In short, popular ranking systems give aid and comfort to those in the PIs movement, encouraging governments, companies, and ordinary citizens to accept cuts in funding, and to agree to lower standards of openness and accountability especially on academic questions.

---

[4] Amy Graham and Nicholas Thompson, "Broken Ranks: U.S. News' college rankings measure everything but what matters," *The Washington Monthly*, 2001 September: *http://www.washingtonmonthly.com/features/2001/0109.graham.thompson.html.* Graham once worked for *U.S. News* but considers that its rankings do not offer direct measures of learning, and thus an "objective" way of comparing colleges and universities to one another.

An effective criticism of PIs or of popular ranking system must begin and end with questions about motivation and effect. Too often the motive behind PIs is to make teaching and learning into commodities for sale; to take post-secondary education out of the public sector; and to say that standards of due process and critical thinking are no more necessary in higher education than they are in the management of an ice cream factory. The proponents of PIs are too often concerned to privatize and to mediocritize. *The Times Higher* reported in October 2001 that a research institute claiming to measure efficiency in the universities concluded "...a factor such as the proportion of students gaining firsts is, in isolation, judged to increase an institution's inefficiency because it reflects particularly high-quality teaching, which is a costly service."[5]

The proponents of PIs are often those who want to push the new masses of students (particularly blacks and Latinos in the United States, and children of the working class everywhere) into mass "practical," cheap, and electronic education defined by PIs—a form of education they would never choose for their own children.[6]

The first question to be asked of any PIs system is whether the system is about cuts and control, or about the public interest.

One way of answering that general question in particular cases is to describe the kind of university or college that could win the PIs race. Motives and effects then become painfully clear. Would our "winning" university have a fondness for secretive and authoritarian administrative practices? Would it devote its energies to making contracts with private and public sector clients that lead to improved PIs (increased endowments, decreased public expenditure on faculty/student hourly teaching costs, and so on)? Would it want to increase the number of students per square foot, or decrease faculty costs by the same measurement? Would it treat library and computer costs as areas that should be pruned to the bone in order to reduce the unit costs of instruction? Does the winning university define success as reduction in input/output costs? Has the winning university a strong management team, but a weak senate? Is the winning place a highly flexible and responsive entity, willing and able to adapt to each year's "new great thing," but incapable of training students in long-haul fundamentals?

The Hoover Institute at Stanford, the American Enterprise Institute, the Fraser Institute, the C.D. Howe Institute, and their like would view this winning university in roseate hues. Indeed, these organizations have a whole vocabulary to describe efficient, responsive, and nimble universities. In their language, the winning university or college is part of a much larger market in which choice and chance have complete power. In our view, the appropriation of language in discussion of post-secondary education has

---

[5]*THES*, 2001 October 19.
[6]William Durden, President, Dickinson College in the United States, "Liberal Arts for All, Not Just the Rich," *Chronicle of Higher Education*, 2001 October 19.

been as destructive as any single action the neo-conservatives have done. There is no reason whatever to say that efficiency, resilience, effectiveness, choice, quality, and accountability are the property of the New Right, or the property of privatized universities and colleges. Our recommendations are all about taking back that language, and restoring public purpose, public obligation, and true quality.

We emphasize here that normative statistics have an important place in public post-secondary education. Student-teacher ratios do matter, as do the costs and quantities of building up the book collections, data bases and staffing of a great library. Nor would one doubt the use of maintaining detailed records about the participation rates of various social groups, or classes of citizens, in the student, staff, and teaching forces of colleges and universities. It makes good sense to keep detailed track of universities' and colleges' sources of funding, costs of teaching, and budgets for maintenance and administration. Numbers and institutional studies are valuable where they encourage universities and colleges (and the governments and individuals who fund them) to provide education more completely and equitably to people; and they are a fine thing when they show a university's real mandate is, or illustrate its priorities as, for example, the relative salary costs of administrators versus teaching colleagues. These are the elements of a sustained and necessary programme of independent research studies on higher education. Some is done already, but not nearly enough. Governments, administrators, journalists, teachers, students, and members of the public should do much more research work of this kind.

In Canada we have the happy example of a recent and extensive "ranking" of provinces and analysis of colleges and universities which relies on common-sense definitions of terms, and makes good use of statistics in the service of public post-secondary education. This is the *Alternative Guide to Canadian Post-Secondary Education*, produced by the Canadian Centre for Policy Alternatives in 1999, and supplemented in 2001. The descriptive note to the 1999 *Guide* reads:

> Among Canada's provinces, Ontario is the one that shows the least commitment to post-secondary education in Canada, while British Columbia receives the highest ranking.... This report provides a comprehensive analysis of the state of higher education across the country in accordance with the principles of equity, quality, accountability, and accessibility.[7]

The work of the Canadian Centre for Policy Alternatives shows the wisdom of keeping an open mind about the work of accountants and institutional analysts in colleges and universities. Academics all too

---

[7]D. Doherty-Delorme and E. Shaker, eds., *Missing Pieces: An Alternative Guide to Canadian Post-Secondary Education* (Ottawa: Canadian Centre for Policy Alternatives, 1999), 159 pages, and under the same editors, *Missing Pieces II: An Alternative Guide to Canadian Post-Secondary Education* (Ottawa: Canadian Centre for Policy Altenatives, 2001), 268 pp.

frequently affect to despise accountants. Accountancy and accountants are permanent features of post-secondary administration. It makes good sense to consider the activities and roles of accountants, aiming to integrate them more completely into the overall academic task of the university, while ensuring they are subject at all times to academic policy and academic oversight. In short, academics should work with the accountants in their midst to help improve the universities. The alternative to a constructive engagement with accountancy is grim: to allow the New Right to monopolize the profession in the name of an ideology alien to the universities.

The trouble is that numbers and studies move all too easily from the domain of social and educational research into the domain of routinized performance assessment. The moment that happens, the university becomes a machine. That machine, and those who maintain it, must be concerned with power, input-output ratios, costs and benefits, however arbitrarily these terms may be defined.

It is not just college and university students and teachers who are viscerally upset by the movement toward mechanism and centralization. Simon Jenkins, one of the heralds of neo-conservatism in the United Kingdom, noted the dire effect on the universities of "a mechanistic Treasury model of cost-effectiveness." "The research assessment exercise" (see chapter 3), he wrote, "was crass beyond belief [and] the attempt to quantify research 'outputs' was and still is half-witted."[8]

One way of understanding the danger of mechanism is to remember a straightforward truth in post-secondary education: people are, or at all events wish to be/claim to be, committed to a theory of open and accountable governance. For no particularly good economic reason, they think that open debate on academic matters, combined with autonomous and thoroughly public decision-making, will make good scholars, good arts and science, strong professionals, and a vigorous society in the long run. For every good academic reason, those same people think it madness to choose curricula and teaching methods just because the short-term "job market" says they must, or because technological advances in computing software or hardware are said to dictate repeated wholesale and expensive renovation of teaching technique and course content.

It is ironical that in 2001 the trendy move among students in the United States is to take law rather than computer science—not exactly what the protagonists of the market approach thought would or should happen. Supporters of public post-secondary education in Europe, North America, and elsewhere in the university world will say that the above pressures are sure to produce mediocrity and a curious narrowness of vision, once associated with great wealth and power in elitist societies. "Mechanism" means any arrangement whereby universities and colleges

---

[8]Simon Jenkins, "A bewildered tribe," *THES*, 2001 October 19.

are forced automatically to do what markets and ideologies dictate. It is the opposite of innovation, quality, and judgement.

Thus, after a century when universities and colleges have found themselves the victims of one management fad after another, and one more-or-less explicit administrative ideology after another, the temptation is to posit an imagined golden age when academic freedom and autonomy were secure, professors the rulers of their institutions, all significant decisions made in-house without outside interference, and educational decisions motivated exclusively by educational criteria. There never was such a time, of course.

Instead, we must find ways to impel the whole community, and the post-secondary sector especially to notice from the very moment it begins to happen, that performance indicators are about to make education into a mechanism. We must say loudly and clearly that mechanism operates on behalf of privilege, and of mediocrity, and of a dangerously weak sense of accountability. That it must be stopped; and, where it exists, rolled back.

WHAT IS TO BE DONE?

It would be wrong-headed to expect the many fads and ideologies of the last century suddenly and conveniently to end. Twentieth-century management fads are additive, each superposed on the one previous. The new century is unlikely to be very different from the old.

Supporters of public post-secondary education must not limit themselves to detecting the worst excesses of PIs. Nor can we be satisfied to make lists of what good statistics are like, what they are for, and how they differ from bad statistics. We must go much further, revisiting questions about openness, accountability, and quality in a system of public mass higher education. Given the importance of higher education and the tax dollars involved, both the public and governments have the right to ask questions about these key matters.

Below, we recommend steps the academic community should consider in dealing with PIs systems and PIs supporters. To be effective, these proposals must be addressed at the local level—not as provincial or national bureaucratic schemes. It will need the active participation of faculty members, and their faculty associations, to put a stop to PIs. Students will, we believe, support the work, partly because it aims to re-install quality and accountability at the heart of public post-secondary education but also because PIs are, plain and simple, a waste of money— *their* money and their parents' money.

We have in mind a local programme of action guided by practical understandings of our three leading concepts: openness, accountability, and quality in a system of mass higher education.

Driving Concepts for a New Accountability

OPENNESS
- in the way university teachers and students do their daily work
- in the ways professionals in all fields of inquiry govern themselves, including the way institutions and individuals are accredited and licenced
- in academic governance
- in administrative practice
- in financial dealings
- in relations with government (and this implies a radical and novel degree of transparency in government decision-making about public expenditures on education)

PRACTICAL ACCOUNTABILITY
- in reporting the form and content of *teaching* in colleges and universities
- in reporting the form and content of *research* in colleges and universities
- in describing the kind and extent of *service work* in which teachers, staff members, and students engage

QUALITY
- in teaching, but understanding teaching as a work of continuous transformation—the life-long education of critical thinkers, the preparation of able and self-sustaining professionals, and the creation of a community whose practices and institutions embody fairness, respect for persons, and equity
- in admissions, the distribution of financial assistance, and the creation of offices and devices to ensure that social, ethnic, gender, and other differences do not stand in the way of full participation in university or college life
- in research, widespread understanding that good research has close and indissoluble links to teaching, is driven by underlying social and logical demands of the disciplines and the surrounding society, and that these links and ties are in a relation of creative tension, and
- all these standards and practices depend on guarantees of academic freedom, including the guarantee that teachers and students may not be dismissed except for just cause; that faculty, students and administrators respect professional ethics; and that particular forms of government (most especially the primacy of the senior academic decision-making body, the Senate) are crucial in sustaining quality teaching, learning, and administration.

Some Practical Consequences

Each university and college should have a quality assurance policy of its own, according to the mission, size, and budget of the university. We here suggest several components.

The first is to ensure the quality of university departments and programmes, the places where the work is actually done. This is best accomplished though periodic departmental reviews by outsiders. We suggest every eight years, slightly less than the cycle of American accreditors. These reports should be made public (see below for details).

The second is for the university to publicize in a meaningful way its commitments to academic freedom, professional ethics, collegial self-governance, teaching, and research (details below), and show how these are carried out in practice. These are, or should be, the true performance indicators of the university.

In addition, the university needs to display on its web site the statistical data it already collects so as to indicate the quality of its operations, e.g., the use of full-time faculty as compared to part-time, growth in laboratories and libraries, etc. It should also show the level of government support over time (see below for details). Rolling five and ten year trends are a useful way of reporting trends in finance, admission, and so on.

The Vice-President (Academic) should make an annual quality assurance report to the academic senate, including direct and indirect costs of compiling the report. This report should be available both in summary and in full on the university's web site. Key areas should include academic freedom, governance, professional ethics, teaching and learning, and the quality and scope of research. Universities should think how these elements can best be publicized in the community and to governments. One possibility is to group them in the university's own quality assurance web site, to vigorously publicize that web site, and keep it up to date. Universities must, however, resist any temptation to snow the public with oceans of meaningless data.

Most information we call for is already collected by universities. Very little is statistical. We do not shrink, however, from a limited borrowing from the enemy since not all statistical data are evil. But more importantly, we ask that the public have reading access to information about departmental and faculty curricula, about the senate and its works, decisions of the board of governors, and the main purpose of the teaching, learning and research that university teachers and students do every day, every year, all tailored to reveal the work of a particular university, not a statistical construct across a province or a nation. Since some members of the public are not necessarily well acquainted with the Internet, we suggest that public colleges and universities advertise in the local press, several times each year, the availability of documents and information, with clear instructions on how to access them, for example, using a public library terminal.

The general ethos should be that everything is public unless there is a good reason for it not to be, as when a privacy law rightly restricts sensitive information. One would not, for instance, put student and faculty medical records on the Internet, nor a counsel's notes on a university lawsuit. But the university should explicitly justify any restrictions.[9] This information policy should be an integral part of the university's quality assurance web page. Policies on quality encourage long-term thinking about the meaning and practice of good teaching, good research, and effective service in the local, national, and international communities. If universities will not think in the long term, who will?

Universities should energetically stimulate public research and discussion about their key activities of teaching and research. Universities will find they are better served by a web page that indicates not everything is perfect, rather than an electronic document in the hands of relentless public relations employees and spin doctors.

Quality is not a product nor an outcome subject to market determination or definition. Quality has to do with the activity of free inquiry conducted in the public interest. The high standards of quality we recommend and accept are precisely those undermined in practice by PIs, rankings systems, league tables, the activities of interventionist bureaucrats, and the nostrums of think-tank operatives.

But universities and colleges should not impose internal foolishness in order to prevent state-mandated foolishness. Their quality assurance policies should be concerned with demonstrable quality, not budget slashing. They should be sensitive to differences within the university. They should support, not undermine, academic freedom. And they should be cost-effective. Such policies should be negotiated with the faculty association as part of the collective agreement, since they impact on terms and conditions of employment. In non-unionized universities, they should be developed and approved by the academic senate. No quality assurance policy should be adopted without a detailed accompanying statement about how much it will cost in dollars and in faculty and administrative time to implement.

---

[9]See Stanley Fish, Dean of the College of Liberal Arts and Sciences, University of Illinois at Chicago, on why deans should be truthful to their faculties: "After two-and-a-half years as a dean and 17 years as an administrator of one kind or another, I have learned that, as with most activities, there is a golden rule. The golden rule of administration is at once simple and complex, and it comes in three parts. Part one is, always tell the truth. Part two is, always tell more of the truth than you have to. And part three is, always tell the truth before anyone asks you to." *Chronicle of Higher Education*, 2001 October 19.

RECOMMENDATIONS FOR GOVERNMENTS

1 Role of Governments

Governments ought only to ensure that universities and colleges have quality assurance policies along the lines we have suggested, and to require universities and colleges to arrive at those policies openly. Any more direct government involvement would surely mean the creation of a large and invasive bureaucracy of the kind that has begun to collapse in the United Kingdom (where the PI system's annual administrative cost was £250 million, of which not a penny went to buying scientific equipment, increasing the number of teachers, or improving student aid).

Requirements for formal eight-year reviews of all academic departments or faculties, an annual report by the administration on quality assurance, and rolling reports on finance, admissions, and programmes, and other provisions of reporting to the public on the university Web site and to the government, will ensure that indifferent and ineffectual university administrations or faculties are caught out, in the court of international academic opinion, or in the local community, or both, with the inevitable political consequences. This can be done without crippling administrative costs provided its precise definition remains local and not part of standardized provincial or national reporting schemes that grow in complexity and cost with every passing year. Of course, the auditors will continue to make their annual reports on finances and financial controls. Any crooks who are discovered should be dealt with by the courts, not by spinning out more bureaucracy. The role of the government is to ensure that such policies are in place, not to usurp these roles itself.

Our several proposals mean there will necessarily be more transparency and accountability in the university or the college, but in ways that do not undermine the central core, and most especially, that guarantee freedom of thought and action.

2 Funding of Reviews

The cost of departmental and other reviews should be met by a separate budget account funded by provincial governments; these funds should be provided to the universities to carry out their several reviews. Canadian provinces should not set up an expensive, overbearing, and counter-productive bureaucracy to do this work, as in the United Kingdom and elsewhere. Reviews should be done locally if they are to have practical impact, value, and meaning, because universities are so different one from another. If the provinces won't fund such a scheme, then the federal government should provide the funds through the federal research councils, but in such a way that the universities themselves can carry out the work.

3. Dealing with serious problems

We all know that there are some fundamental problems within the university system, insoluble without additional government funding. PIs are designed to obscure this. Governments insist that universities create PIs in these areas without proper funding and then use the same PIs to attack the universities and to justify further cuts. Nothing happens, but there is an appearance of furious activity. We offer two examples.

One is student aid. If we are to maintain ever-increasing student fees, then we need much more in the way of needs-based grants—unless we want to exclude the children of the working class permanently from universities. Grants on a scale that might have an impact can only happen if governments put up more money. We, of course, still need data about the scope of the problem. And we need the political will to do something about it. What we *don't* need is a permanent centralized PIs bureaucracy to deal with this problem.

The same is true of the problems of disabled students and faculty. It costs money to provide proper accommodation for the disabled so that they can function equally with other students—physical changes such as ramps and doors, electronic equipment for the hearing- and sight-impaired, proper counselling and support staff, etc. The universities can do some of this themselves, but to do it properly they need more money from governments. Once again useful data about the numbers involved and the costs of competing learning systems are readily available. Governments only need the will to attack the problem. They shouldn't hide behind PIs.

RECOMMENDATIONS FOR UNIVERSITIES & COLLEGES

1 Reviews

1.1 Departmental reviews
Every department or major academic programme should be formally reviewed every eight years. Any shorter period is uneconomic and would make it extremely difficulty to find reviewers. Reviews should be undertaken by persons from other universities, preferably from outside the province (to avoid charges of conflict of interest) and should include, especially where there is a graduate programme, one person from outside the country. Reviews should concentrate on teaching, research, and service.

The names of the reviewers should be public. The report should also be public, except where it makes remarks about particular faculty members or students. This latter condition is necessary because the university might otherwise be liable for defamatory statements over which it has no control.

Some universities already undertake such reviews, but few make them public. All should do so. Every department should have a web site and the report posted on its web site.

Our proposal is a cross between the British external examiner system and the American system of accreditation. The former was the traditional form of quality control in the United Kingdom. This still exists but operates with great difficulty, given the British government's enthusiasm for massive and costly centralisation of the university system.

Britain is retreating from its centralising enthusiasms and may well end up with a revised version of the external examiner system. The purpose of such a system is to assure and enhance the exit standards of under-graduate and postgraduate degrees, given the fallibility of all humans including academics, as well as the need for public accountability. The British tradition proved too cosy and too secretive. That is why we recommend that all reports be made public. We realize the danger that authors, knowing their reports will be made public, will pull punches, but secret reports are too easily ignored and encourage reviewer eccentricity and malice. The British government is now thinking of properly funding the external examiner system and possibly creating an accreditation process for examiners. Canada should watch these developments with interest but nevertheless remain sceptical about any attempts to revive centralisation by the back door.

The British system placed too much emphasis on examination results and not enough on the academic functioning of the department. It was traditionally an annual exercise, impossible in the present era in terms of costs and availability of examiners in a mass higher education system. Nevertheless it was right in its concentration on departments rather than universities as a whole.

The American system considers the university as a whole. This has the advantage of giving the accrediting team the ability to view the entire structure, including the functioning of the administration, but the dis-advantage of moving from the departmental level, where the work is done, to the central administrative bureaucracy. Individual departmental failures become lost in university averages. Nor is it reasonable to punish a whole university for the sins of a couple of departments. In practice, therefore, the accrediting system focuses on marginal colleges, where it might be reasonable to call the whole institution into question. Our suggestion deals with the possibility that there might be a deficient department or departments in a great university and that rectifying this deficiency is of considerable importance to the students involved.

Examiners should be proposed by the department concerned. Those proposals should be accompanied by a full curriculum vitae and a formal written statement from the departmental chair that the proposed examiners have no conflict of interest, such as prior service in the department or business connections with it or any of its members. These recommendations should be reviewed by the dean, reserving the power to say no and refer the matter back to the department for another choice. We recognize a danger here—departments might choose those known to be "soft touches"—but only the department in question actually knows the field. They are also much more likely to listen seriously to the recommendations if they have a significant role in the choice. It would be much better if scholarly associations created panels of such outside examiners but, while waiting for this to happen, universities should act as we have recommended. Examiners should be appointed by the university, and should report to the president with copies to the dean and the department. This latter is important because presidents do not always want to share the results of such investigations, particularly when they want to axe a department which turns out to be of high quality according to the outside review. The president, dean, and the department should append official responses, all of which should be public.

Examiners should look at the overall academic functioning of the department. They should consider any statements or documents concerning the academic plans of the department, but spare them from supplying idiotic and anodyne mission statements. They should be provided with a complete set of departmental financial accounts for the previous eight years, to judge whether it is credible for such a programme to be run with high quality. They should examine library resources available, including the number of private or restricted data bases subscribed to. This is especially important at the graduate level. Comparisons should be made only with departments in other universities with similar financing. For course work at the undergraduate and graduate level, examiners should see syllabi, course outlines, and reading lists. They should receive information concerning the use of new technology and non-traditional teaching methods. They should borrow from the British external examiner system and look not only at examination questions, but also a sample of the examination answers including failures and first class marks, or course-work if that is used instead of examinations.

They should have the complete *curricula vitarum* of all the academic staff in the period surveyed, including their publication records and teaching dossiers. They should examine the research and community service programmes of the department. They should look at the application of university policies in such areas as academic freedom, equity, and professional ethics. They should invite comments and suggestions not only from the academic staff but also from the dean and other relevant administrators, the students, the support staff, and others who might have an informed opinion, including those who take on students for an applied segment of a course. They should submit additional questions in written form to the department.

Then examiners should visit the department. Everyone interviewed should be invited to put their views in writing (this to mitigate malicious gossip). In the traditional British system, examiners reviewed marks with members of the academic staff and could require that they be changed. We think that impractical in a modern mass system of higher education. The purpose should be to review the academic functioning of the department, not individual marks, particularly since most Canadian universities have appeal systems for individual students.

Most Canadian universities have an external examining system for theses. Our suggested departmental review should not attempt to substitute for the decisions of those examiners, but instead review the aims, plans, and resources of the graduate programme in the department as a whole.

What should the standards be? Some would say that there should be a single, national standard of excellence in each subject. That too is impractical in a mass system of higher education with a great variety of institutions and programmes. Institutions have to be grouped. Hence the American Carnegie classification system, and hence the three general groups proposed by *Maclean's*. Some variation of this approach would have to be adopted for the purpose of comparative standards. Departments and deans could be asked with whom the department should be compared. To say that each university will decide its own standards alone simply invites the unscrupulous to set low targets and announce success with great fanfare.

The report should be public together with the comments of the department, the dean, and the president.

1.2 Professional reviews
In engineering, business, and other parts of the university, outside reviews are undertaken by the profession. These too should be public, together with faculty comments. The university should try to dovetail professional reviews with departmental or programme reviews to minimize bureaucracy, but it should never totally cede any review process to outside professions (which may be more interested in maintaining the status quo than working on the cutting edge).

1.3 Departmental web sites
- Every department should have a web page, linked to the general university Quality Web Site, which should:
  - ► set out briefly in plain English or French what it does, why it does it, and what it plans to do in the future
  - ► provide a brief history of the department
  - ► record independent public policy research that is, research not tied to the interests of a particular funder focussed on Canada.
  - ► indicate any international dimension to its work.
- All faculty members should be named, with their areas of academic interest indicated, and twenty of their most recent and/or significant publications, research awards, and other honours recorded.
- The department web site should give the percentage of full-time and part-time faculty at work in the department, over time (every five years since 1985).
- The site should tell the size of first and second year undergraduate classes, and whether taught by full-time staff (1995, 2000, and current year).

- The site should include lists of departmental reviews (with clear indications on how and where to obtain full texts of those reviews), academic and service awards; the most recent departmental annual report or reports; all current courses with brief user-friendly descriptions; and lists of Internet and electronic course offerings, including the connection between those offerings and the on-campus work of the department, and whatever else the department itself thinks is important.

A departmental or faculty web site will contain extensive data on its faculty, staff, and students; its programmes and activities; but also—and this is of practical importance in a site that deals with quality in higher education —it will show at least some of the ways the department or faculty maintains ties with the surrounding communities.

For instance, a Fine Arts department or faculty web site would include detailed information on the university's contribution to the performing and fine arts in the community. It would at the same time provide details on programmes of study in those arts, and information about funding, or the want of it, and all the kinds of detail mentioned in sections 1–5.

1.4 Individual professorial web sites
If not cared for under item 5, then: each faculty member should have a web site listing areas of academic interest, courses currently given, degrees and other awards, major grants, twenty publications the faculty member considers of academic or social importance, e-mail address, and information potential students may find helpful. The university should provide technical assistance to make this possible.

2 Academic Freedom
Key to any university is how well it protects and defends academic freedom. The university policy statement on academic freedom should be consistent with the model set out by the Canadian Association of University Teachers (CAUT).
- The university should have a clearly visible section of its web site devoted to academic freedom.
- The university policy statement on academic freedom should be included in this section. So, too, should definitions of academic freedom in faculty collective agreements.

2.1 Whistle-blowers
The university should have a policy, preferably enshrined in collective agreements with faculty and staff, to say they are free to criticize the university, its policies, and its administration in public without fear of reprisal. This policy should appear on the academic freedom section of the university's we site.

The best defence against ignorant criticism is not censorship but more information and more debate. Freedom to criticize the university system, and one's own university, is a central feature of academic freedom. In some universities in Australia, the United States, and the United Kingdom, heads of universities fancy themselves CEOs of business enterprises, able to command silence and the acquiescence of academic staff on all matters of educational policy. This is wrong. Universities are not businesses. The law admits that business employees must toe the line; not so in universities and colleges. Universities are committed to independent thought, publicly expressed, and cannot claim the right to academic freedom unless they apply the same standard to themselves.

2.2 UNESCO Policy
The university web site on academic freedom should have a link to the UNESCO policy on academic freedom entitled *Recommendation concerning the Status of Higher-Education Teaching Personnel*:
http://www.unesco.org/education/educprog/am/recom_e.html
Canada supported the adoption of this document by UNESCO, and the representative of the Council of Ministers of Education cast Canada's vote for it at the UNESCO governing body in 1997.

2.3 Network for Education and Academic Rights
The university should be associated with the Network for Education and Academic Rights created by UNESCO in 2001 for the defence of academic freedom and of the human rights of scholars around the world (*www.nearinternational.org*). Network Reports should be regularly distributed to members of the academic senate.

Among the implications of such a policy would be a review of the way the university or college sees its links to the international community. Rather than thinking of extra-national peoples solely as potential markets, the university or college must surely accept its obligation to extend to all people the rights of free inquiry, free teaching, and general accessibility that we see as central features of public post-secondary education in our own country.

3 Governance
If the public is to be assured that academic freedom and accountability are present, arrangements for open governance must be in place. A crucial indicator of freedom of teaching and inquiry is the proper and open working of the academic Senate.

Two committees of Senate should be especially active in a good university or college: the Senate Finance Committee and the Senate Curriculum Committee. These two committees should together have the right of final review, but not final refusal, on all matters of finance and overall university structure. Someone, somewhere has to limit the excesses of administrations that may want to spend arbitrarily on private ventures, to take a flyer on suspect technology, or to make big investments in experiments such as Universitas 21.

Someone, somewhere must be in a position to force managers and administrators, and all members of the academic community, to consider the consequences of such choices on the public interest, and on the academic mission of the university. The Senate, and its standing committees on Finance and Programmes, are the natural place for this work.

To summarize, the first steps in verifying the quality and accountability of an academic institution will be:

- to verify that the Academic Senate is vibrant and active
- to see that the Senate's Finance and Programme committees have powers of final review on money matters and on certain large-scale administrative decisions.
- to ensure the Senate has an active and comprehensive space on the university web site, and that a particular individual is responsible for keeping it up to date.

4 Ethics

4.1 Ethical policies

The public needs to know the university is committed to policies designed to ensure ethical behaviour, and that it actually carries out these policies. This is an indicator of "performance" that has legal and political force, and which would reassure members of the public and of the post-secondary sector that universities and colleges are living up to their full obligations. A section of the university web site should indicate the university's policies in the sub-sections listed below.

4.2 Research ethics

Most universities have policies on research ethics since these are mandated by the federal research councils. The university web site should either contain these policies or should note a link where the full policies can be found, how they are activated, and the name and business e-mail of the person responsible.

We believe such policies should be negotiated with the faculty and staff unions as part of their collective agreements. This gives them legal force and provides a known grievance and arbitration procedure for the accused. If they are not so negotiated, they should be adopted by the university academic senate, be consistent with the models suggested by the Canadian Association of University Teachers, provide a just and fair appeal procedure, and recognize the different research milieus found in the university.

We think the university should be pro-active in this area. For example, in bio-medical research, it should as a minimum require that all outside sources of research funding be revealed to the departmental chair and dean, no funding be accepted either from private sources or government that allows the sponsor to censor or to suppress the research results, faculty be required to note in any scientific or scholarly articles or books or other formal communications the sources of any research funding received for the project, and medical researchers should be required to inform patients of any commercial interest they may have in a proposed therapy. The university should encourage public debate about these matters.

These rules and policies are useful and proper in their own right because they provide rationally defensible solutions to difficult problems but also because they make it more difficult for anti-intellectual populists to attack the teaching and research work of the university. Serious ethical problems are rarely easy to resolve but the university and the scientific community should provide the venue for ongoing discussion of these matters and for the resolution of specific problems.

The contrast between the United States and the United Kingdom in the debate over therapeutic cloning illustrates the point. The British avoided sweeping and ill-considered populist legislation by adopting clear rules and regulations early on, administered through the Human Fertilization and Embryology Authority. The Authority has proved to be independent and committed to due process, and this is the reason Parliament has entrusted it to develop rules on therapeutic cloning to add to those concerning *in vitro* fertilization and human embryo research.[10] Alas, Canada seems poised to go down the same fundamentalist path on this issues as the United States, rather than following the more sensible British model.

4.3 Reporting: publication of all significant contracts
All significant contracts between the university or college, and the private sector, should be published on the university web site. Each university or college should decide, in public hearings of the Senate and its finance committee, at what point a contract becomes "significant." For many universities, this figure may be $50,000 or above.

Universities must also guard against arrangements that make their faculty and graduate students mere underpaid servants of large corporations or that turn them into the personnel departments of those institutions. They should to be able to show their applied research is demonstrably significant and not just low-level testing. Universities have a larger role in the community than this.

4.4 The Teaching of Professional Ethics
The university should provide courses in professional ethics in its professional faculties. It should encourage discussion and debate about issues arising in the area of professional ethics. The university web site should include this information and/or links to pages where it can be found.

---

[10]Nicholas Wade, "Clearer Guidelines Help Britain to Advance Stem Cell Work," *New York Times,* 2001 August 14.

4.5 Non-Discrimination
Many universities have a general non-discrimination policy. This should either be provided on the university web site or provided through a hyperlink where it can be found; further, there should be a clear indication as to how the policy is to be activated and who is responsible. Most universities have non-discrimination articles in their collective agreements with faculty and staff. These should be displayed on the site as well.

4.6 Harassment
Most universities have policies on sexual or racial harassment or harassment of gays and lesbians. These should have bite but should also provide fair and just procedures for the accused and should allow the relevant university tribunal summarily to dismiss trivial and vexatious cases. The policies should either be on the web site or there should be a link to a page where they can be found, how to activate them, and the name and business telephone and e-mail of the person in charge. There ought also to be links to support groups for the victims of harassment.

4.7 Ethical treatment of the disabled
The web site should either list or give a link to the place containing the university's policies to assist the disabled students, faculty, and staff to participate as equal partners in the university enterprise. That site should offer the names and business telephones and e-mails of those responsible for the policy.

4.8 University policies on cheating including plagiarism
Most university academic senates have adopted policies on cheating, including plagiarism. These should be on the web site, or a link provided where they can be found together with the name and business telephone and e-mail of the person responsible for the policies. The university should also encourage debate about these matters and provide resources where needed to combat plagiarism.

4.9 University policies on allegations of unfair marking
Most university academic senates have adopted policies which permit formal appeals of marks. A link should be provided that gives the details. These should include an assessment by a specialist(s) so that administrators are less frequently faced with lobbying by vociferous students or their parents. No marks should be changed by an administrator unless recommended by a professional in a formal appeal. Corrupt practices can be dealt with by other means.

4.10 Reporting the application of ethics policies
The Vice-President (Academic) should make a written annual report to the academic senate and to the board of governors on the ethical policies of the university as part of the general report on quality assurance, any

changes during the current year, any areas of controversy, and statistics over time on the number of formal complaints lodged, settled, or heard by an arbitrator or tribunal. This report should be on the university's web site.

5 Teaching and Learning

5.1 Teaching and Learning Centres
Most universities these days have teaching and learning centres. Those that don't, should. This is a good indicator of the seriousness of the university's commitment to teaching. The Centre should be responsible for an orientation programme for all new faculty and for a web site available to all. Such Centres should not become simply the dumping ground for faculty disasters nor the plaything of ideologues. They should be pro-active and assist individuals and departments who approach them for help in improving teaching standards. The university web site should give relevant information about the Centre, including its budget appropriations over the past five years.

5.2 Mentoring
Departmental chairs should ensure all new faculty who have not taught at the university level before, are assigned a mentor, or similarly helped to take up their teaching work and responsibilities. This should be part of their job description, and they should report on the functioning of the system to the dean.

5.3 Subject Centres
The national learned societies, as for instance the Canadian Association of Physicists, the Canadian Historical Association, and so on, should study the possible creation of subject centres for research on teaching in their particular areas. Almost everything that the British have done in the area of quality assurance in the past decade is a lesson in expensive and counter-productive futility, but this idea, in the form of the Learning and Teaching Support Network,[11] may have promise. Centres might be funded by the CMEC or by the federal granting councils. It is important they be set up for the improvement of teaching, not for the assessment of departments, which latter would be the kiss of death.

6. Research Policies

6.1 Commitment to independent public policy research
The Quality Web Site of each university or college should indicate the university's commitment to independent public policy research, research

---

[11]See the discussion of such support networks in Chapter 3.

not tied to the agenda of a particular funder, and should provide a link to a page listing such research. Research might deal, among other matters, with Canadian history, culture, and identity; the environment; poverty; educational policy; and the like. The new government in New Zealand, for example, has laid emphasis on standards and indicators relative to the Maori and Pacific Island peoples.

6.2 Commitment to public international research
The Quality Web Site should have a link to pages showing the international work of the university and its sponsors.

6.3 Universities and economic development
Universities make a significant and necessary contribution to the economic development of Canada in educating business and technological leaders but also in research. The federal government has recognized that fact through its research policies, as have some provinces. Most universities already celebrate their achievements in this area and should continue to do so.

7 University Data
The university already gathers a great deal of information for provincial governments, the CMEC, Statistics Canada and others, and display much of this on their web sites. We suggest that it distill some of these data to show the quality of what it is doing including some that it might prefer not to publicize such as first year drop-out rates and the ratio of teaching faculty to administrators. It should also indicate where the curious can access more detailed data provided these are already set up for Internet transmission and reading.

The basis for this should be the quality report which we earlier recommended be made on an annual basis by the vice-president academic to the senate. It is important that this report focus on questions of true intellectual quality, not business babble and not the counter-productive indicators sometimes demanded by governments. Data displayed should be relevant to the mandate of the university, and should be designed for enlightenment, not obfuscation.

Universities need to do this to show the public the quality of their institutions, even if in the short-run it will not persuade the ideologues to lessen their drive to micro-manage the universities through the provincial bureaucracies. In the long run it would become, one hopes, the template for future reporting, and the basis for a counter-revolution.

8 Funding
The quality of a public university or college, however one thinks of quality, has much to do with the funding it receives. Adequate public funding is an essential foundation for quality public post-secondary education. The university's quality web site should show at a minimum:

Provincial government support
- Provincial operating grants per FTEs [full-time equivalent] student measured every five years over at least two five-year periods
- Provincial building grants over the past fifteen years, but with emphasis on results by five-year intervals
- Provincial government research funds over the past five years, in total and per full-time faculty member

Federal government support
- Federal government research funds over the past five years, in total and per full-time faculty member

Private research funds
- Private research funds over the past five years, in total and per full-time faculty member
- A list of all private and public research contracts, and all private and public development contracts (sometimes called "R&D" contracts), showing the names of all signatories, the dates of completion, and the purpose of each contract

All items in 8 could be present in brief form, but should include Web "pointers" to detailed sources of additional information, whether at the department, faculty, or university level.

TOWARD A COUNTER-REVOLUTION

Canadian university administrations are not working nearly as hard as they should in dismantling or at least de-fanging centralized governmental PIs systems. They rarely press governments to do anything at all about such systems. Canada's AUCC, for instance, has had little to say about these centralized attacks on autonomy, accountability and the quality of post-secondary education, not to mention the local costs involved. The quiescence and sometimes acquiescence of university leaders is hard to fathom, considering all that is at stake.

Already several governments in the OECD jurisdictions have set up centralized PI systems and, in some cases, are trying to sell them to the world as the ideal structure for the future. Canadian provinces are well on the way to doing the same. The CMEC has been a cheerleader for such developments. Blocking or dismantling them will require considerable political pressure. The precise form of that pressure will depend on local political culture and the will of the local university and college community. Experience in the United Kingdom suggests the counter-revolution is not likely to work without adequate and extensive studies on the costs and follies of centralized PIs—not just direct dollar costs but also the cost in time for administrators and faculty, which usually turns out to be beyond belief. This data must then become part of a larger political fight—otherwise there is no point in gathering the data and engaging the competition.

But the counter-attack should not be based on illusions.

We do not suggest that universities and colleges shake off their public duties and obligations. We do not think universities should even dream of returning to an imaginary past, a past where they could act as they liked. We do not suggest that universities and colleges, once freed of the useless burdens of PIs, should consider themselves "liberated" from public obligation. Instead we have suggested means whereby their professional and public obligations can come to the fore. We have also noted that quality in the university doesn't come without financial support from governments.

We think it is high time for an inquiry into the costs involved in the web of bureaucracy that has been imposed by governments on the universities. Politicians and bureaucrats rarely raise taxes to pay for their *rouages administratifs* (bureaucratic devices—the French phrase is truly best here). Instead they make the universities and the university community pay for the privilege.

Two types of costs are relevant here. The first is the strict cost accounting of any centralized PIs scheme including the cost of the time of all those in the university community who collect and process the material. Existing PIs should be costed in detail without delay. New ones should not come into play without a full cost analysis. The British have done it. There is no reason why it cannot be done in Canada. Nor should the university exempt itself when it decides to set up such schemes on its own. Folly in these matters needs to be challenged, whoever the author may be. Local faculty associations should play a key role if anything is going to happen. They should work with their administrations to produce the local data and to fire up the community for the counter-attack. This can then be co-ordinated at the provincial level by provincial faculty associations, and at the national level by the CAUT.

The second is the overall cost of the bureaucratic superstructure which dreams up these schemes and grows exponentially to administer them. CAUT should co-ordinate a study of the actual costs of the higher education bureaucracy—all the provincial ministries of higher education or the higher education components of undivided ministries, other ministries or segments of ministries claiming a role in higher education, all provincial and regional bodies such as the Council of Ontario Universities, auditing costs where auditing is done in whole or in part by government plus the private auditing costs mandated by governments, the costs of the Council of Ministers of Education, the administrative costs of federal bodies involved in higher education. Might some of this money be more profitably spent on hiring more professors, increasing student aid, buying more scientific equipment, improving the library, and the like? It might be useful to do a few case studies on the direct and indirect costs to the universities of complying with the demands of all these tentacles of bureaucracy.

We also think that CAUT should work with the provincial associations and the Centre for Policy Alternatives to develop methods to judge provincial governments in an informed and comparative way on such matters as accessibility, student aid, support for disabled students, support for independent fact-based research, and policies that improve or undermine academic freedom and institutional autonomy and the like An example is the work that is being done in Alberta by CAFA. We have also noted a similar development in the United States. If CAUT could persuade the university presidents (or at least some of them), the Canadian Association of University Business Officers, and comprehensive auditing authorities to co-operate, so much the better.

All these data have to be translated into political action. No one will fight the universities' political battle for them, although allies are useful. However one thinks of PIs, universities and colleges eventually will have to bite the bullet, as they have finally done in the United Kingdom. It is simply impossible to produce more for less *ad infinitum*. But the British example also strongly suggests it is important the whole university community join together in the struggle. It is possible to win this war, as the Scots have shown. After all, even neo-conservatives profess to be opposed to bureaucracy and its costs. But the battle will not be successful unless *(1)* universities and colleges demonstrate not only the folly but also the great cost of such centralized schemes, *(2)* they propose alternatives—as we have done, and *(3)* they take collective action to make it all happen.

The alternative is the vision of the Fraser Institute, the Corporate Higher Education Forum, and the nay-sayers in the Harris and Klein governments —namely, complete privatization. This would allow universities to act independently of the state as any other private corporation, securing their funds from high student fees, corporate contracts and charity—the last being the route favoured by the Southam newspapers. This would create a two-tiered system of higher education: quality for the rich, cheap and mediocre for the masses based mainly on canned materials on the Internet rather than face-to-face contact with faculty. We reject that vision and think that most Canadians would as well.

The university, as the AAUP said in 1915, should be "an inviolable refuge from tyranny…. It should be an intellectual experience station, where new ideas may germinate and where their fruit, though still distasteful to the community as a whole, may be allowed to ripen until finally, perchance, it may become part of the accepted international food of the nation or of the world."[12] This is most unlikely to be the case in the brave new world of industrial-style PIs.

---

[12]Declaration of the First Committee on Academic Freedom of the American Association of University Professors, 1915.

Bibliography

Institutions and Governments

Alberta, Alberta Education. *Achieving Quality: Final Report of the Educational Quality Indicators Initiative.* Edmonton: Alberta Education, 1993.

Alberta Treasury. *The Right Balance: Learning Business Plan 1999–2000 to 2001–02 restated.* Edmonton AB: Government of Alberta, 1999, and annual reports since, to 2001.

British Columbia Labour Force Development Board. *Training for What?* Victoria: British Columbia Labour Force Development Board, 1995.

Bovey, C. *Ontario Universities: Options and Futures Report of The Commission on the Future Development of the Universities of Ontario.* Toronto: Ministry of Colleges and Universities, 1984.

Broadhurst, W. *University Accountability: A Strengthened Framework. Report of the Task Force on University Accountability.* Toronto: Ministry of Colleges and Universities, 1993.

Confederation of Alberta Faculty Associations. *Brief to Senate Sub-Committee on Post-secondary Education.* Edmonton: Confederation of Alberta Faculty Associations, 1997.

Confederation of Alberta Faculty Associations. "Performance Funding and the University," *CAFA Report*, 14, 1 (September 1998): 1–3.

Québec. *The Estates General on Education, 1995–1996: The State of Education in Quebec.* Québec: Ministère de l'Éducation, 1996.

Council of Ministers of Education, Canada. *A Report on Public Expectations of Post-secondary Education in Canada.* Toronto: Council of Ministers of Education, Canada, 1999.

CMP. Council of Maritime Premiers 1997–1998 Annual Report. *http://www. cmp.ca/anrep98eng.htm*

Commission d'orientation de l'Université Laval. *Rapport final de la Commission d'orientation.* Ste-Foy: Université Laval, 1998.

Conseil Supérieur de l'Éducation (CSE). *Le Financement des Universités: Avis à la ministre de l'Éducation.* Québec: Gouvernement du Québec, 1996.

Côté, G. Des outils nouveaux et originaux pour bonifier le processus budgétaire. Le Fil des Événements [Internet]. 12 mars. Disponible à: *http://www.ulaval.ca/scom/ Au.fil.des.evenements* [1998].

Côté, G. Levée de boucliers contre le projet de politique de financement des universités. Le Fil des Événements [Internet]. Disponible à: *http://www.ulaval.ca/scom/Au.fil.des.evenements.*

Dearing, S. R. *Higher Education in the Learning Society: The National Committee of Inquiry on Higher Education.* Hayes: NICHE Publications, 1997.

Ministère de l'Éducation du Québec (MEQ). *Politique à l'égard des universités: Pour mieux assurer notre avenir collectif.* Québec: Gouvernement du Québec, 2000.

Maritime Provinces Higher Education Commission. Minute 163-D: Quality Assurance. 163rd Meeting, Holland College, 1997 November 3. Available at: *http://www.mphec.ca/htm/information/ 163/163-d.htm.*

MTCU. Ministry of Training, Colleges and Universities 1999–2000 Business Plan. Toronto: Queens Printer for Ontario, 1999.

PAIR. *UBC Performance Indicators*. Department of Planning and Institutional Research, University of British Columbia, 1997.

QUAFA. Queens University Faculty Association Collective Agreement, 1997 1999, Article 26, Performance Indicators.

Robbins, A.R. *Towards an MAETT Accountability Framework*. Victoria: Research, Evaluation and Accountability Branch, Policy Services Division, MAETT, 2000.

Shapiro, B.J. Tradition and Innovation: An International University in a City of Knowledge. A Discussion paper for the Ministère de l'Éducation, 1999 September.

Smith, D.C., D.M. Cameron, F. Gorbet, C. Henderson, B.M. Stephenson. *Excellence, Accessibility, Responsibility—Report of the Advisory Panel on Future Directions for Postsecondary Education*. Toronto: Ministry of Education and Training, 1996.

Tavenas, F. *La gestion universitaire par François Tavenas, candidat au poste de recteur*. Ste-Foy: Université Laval. 20 mars 1997.

Tavenas, F. Débats de la commission de l'éducation [Internet]. 9 mars 2000. Disponible à: *http://www.ulaval.ca/recteur/debats.html*.

University of Alberta. *1999–2000 Strategic Business Plan: Building Knowledge and Innovation*. Edmonton AB: University of Alberta, 1999.

Scholarly and Popular Discussions of Performance Indicators

Albright, Brenda N. From Business as Usual to Funding for Results, background paper, Higher Education Commission, Ohio Board of Regents, 1996 June.

Allen, W.H. *Self-Surveys by Colleges and Universities*. Yonkers-on-Hudson, New York: World Book Company, 1917.

Andres, L. "Rational choice or cultural reproduction? Tracing transitions of young Canadians to higher education," *Nordisk Pedagogik*, 18, 4 (1998): 197–206.

Andres, L. and H. Krahn. "Youth Pathways in Articulated Post-secondary Systems: Enrolment and Completion Patterns of Urban Young Women and Men," *Canadian Journal of Higher Education*, 29, 1 (1999): 47–82.

Annan, Noel. *The Dons: Mentors, Eccentrics, and Geniuses*. Chicago: University of Chicago Press, 1999.

Aper, J.P. "Higher Education and the State: Accountability and the Roots of the Student Outcomes Assessment," *Higher Education Management*, 5, 3 (1993 November): 365–76.

Association of University Teachers. *Higher education: preparing for the 21st century*. London: AUT, 1995.

Association of Universities and Colleges of Canada. *Directory of Canadian Universities*. Ottawa: AUCC, 2001.

_____ *Trends: The Canadian University in Profile*. Ottawa: AUCC, 2000.

Atkinson-Grosjean, J., G. Grosjean, D. Fisher & K. Rubenson. "Consequences of Performance Models in Higher Education: An International Perspective," Study for the Humanities and Social Sciences Federation of Canada. Vancouver, B.C.: Centre for Policy Studies in Higher Education, University of British Columbia, 1999.

Averill, H., and G. Keith, "Daniel Wilson and the University of Toronto," in M. Ash, *et al.*, eds., *Thinking with Both Hands: Sir Daniel Wilson in the Old World and the New* (Toronto: University of Toronto Press, 1999), pp. 139–210.

Avery, Donald H. *The Science of War: Canadian Scientists and Allied Military Technology during the Second World War.* Toronto: University of Toronto Press, 1998.

Axelrod, Paul and John G. Reid, eds., *Youth, University and Canadian Society: Essays in the Social History of Higher Education.* Kingston: McGill-Queen's University Press, 1989.

Axelrod, P. "Challenges to a liberal education in an age of uncertainty." *Historical Studies in Education/Revue d'histoire de l'éducation*, 10, 1/2 (1998), available online at *www.edst.educ.ubc.ca/ 98axelrod.htm.*

Barnetson, Bob and Marc Cutright, "Performance Indicators as Conceptual Technologies," *Higher Education*, 40 (2000): 277–92.

Barzun, Jacques. *From Dawn to Decadence, 1500 to the Present: 500 Years of Western Cultural Life.* New York: HarperCollins, 2000.

Beaton, T. "Performance Indicators and Quality Management in the University," Humanities and Social Sciences Federation of Canada Research Report, Ottawa, 1999.

Bellamy, Lesley, J. Parsons, and E. Say. "The Texas Educational Accountability System: Method in the Madness?" Texas Educational Policy Research Report, Texas Center for University School Partnerships, University of Houston, No. 3, 1994 June.

Benjamin, E.G. "The Decline of Academic Autonomy in Higher Education," *Academe*, 80, 4 (1994 July/August): 34–6.

Benjamin, E. G., G. Bourgeault, and K. McGovern. *Government and Accountability: The Report of the Independent Study Group on University Governance.* Ottawa: Canadian Association of University Teachers, 1993.

Bercuson, D., R. Bothwell, and J.L. Granatstein. *Petrified Campus: The Crisis in Canada's Universities.* Toronto: Random House, 1997.

Bercuson, David J., Robert Bothwell, J.L. Granatstein. *The Great Brain Robbery: Canada's Universities on the Road to Ruin.* Toronto: McClelland and Stewart, 1984.

Bernatchez, Jean. "Contextualisation et analyse comparée du point de vue des enjeux des contrats de performance des universités québécoises," unpublished paper, Canadian Society for the Study of Higher Education, Annual Meeting, 2001 May 25, Université Laval.

Birnbaum, Robert. *Management Fads in Higher Education: Where They Come From, What They Do, Why They Fail.* San Francisco: Jossey-Bass, 2001.

Bissell, Claude T. *Halfway Up Parnassus: A Personal Account of the University of Toronto, 1932–1971.* Toronto: University of Toronto Press, 1974.

Bjarnason, S. 'Buffer' Organizations in Higher Education: Illustrative Examples in the Commonwealth [Study supported by the Commonwealth Fund for Technical Cooperation]. London: Association of Commonwealth Universities, 1998. *<http://wwwacuacuk/chems/onlinepublications>*

Blank, R.K. "Developing a System of Education Indicators Selecting, Implementing, and Reporting Indicators," *Educational Evaluation and Policy Analysis*, 15, 1 (1993): 65–80.

Bloom, Allan. "The Crisis of Liberal Education," in his *Giants and Dwarfs: Essays 1960–1990*. New York: Simon and Schuster, 1990.

Bogue, E.G. and R.L. Saunders. *The Evidence for Quality*. San Francisco: Jossey-Bass, 1992.

Bogue, E. Grady. "Quality Assurance in Higher Education: The Evolution of Systems and Design Ideals," in Gerald M. Gaither, ed., *Quality Assurance in Higher Education*. San Francisco: Jossey-Bass, 1998.

Brennan, J. "Evaluation of Higher Education in Europe," in M. Henkel and B. Little, eds., *Changing Relationships Between Higher Education and the State*. London: Jessica Kingsley, 1999, 219–35.

Broadbent, Edward, ed. *Democratic Equality: What Went Wrong*. Toronto: University of Toronto Press, 2001.

Broadhurst, W., *et al.*, *Task Force on University Accountability: Progress Report and Issues Paper*. Toronto: The Task Force, 1992, pp. ii+62.

Bruneau, William. "British Columbia's Right Wing and Public Education," *Our Schools, Our Selves*, 1, 4 (1989 August): 94–106.

_____. "The Perils of Performance Indicators, Working paper, Committee on performance indicators and accountability," Ottawa: Canadian Association of University Teachers, 1994.

_____. "Privatization in School and University: Renewal or Apostasy?" in M. Charlton and P. Barker, eds., *Crosscurrents*, 3rd ed. Toronto: ITP Nelson, 1998, 472–83.

_____. and D. Savage. "Not a magic bullet: Performance indicators in theory and practice." Paper at the annual meeting, Canadian Association for the Study of Higher Education. Montréal, PQ, 1995 June 02.

Burgan, Mary "The Corporate University and Its New Ways," unpublished manuscript, Spring Council, Canadian Association of University Teachers, Ottawa, 1997.

Burke, Joseph C., Jeff Rosen, Henrik Minassians, and Terri Lessard, *Performance Funding and Budgeting: An Emerging Merger?*, The Fourth Annual Survey, Higher Education Program, The Nelson A. Rockefeller Institute of Government, State University of New York, Albany, New York, 2000.

Burke, Joseph C. and Andrea M. Serban, *Current Status and Future Prospects of Performance Funding and Performance Budgeting for Public Higher Education: The Second Survey*. Public Higher Education Program, The Nelson A. Rockefeller Institute of Government, State University of New York, Albany, New York, 1998.

Burt, Cyril. *Factors of the Mind: An Introduction to Factor-Analysis in Psychology*. London: University of London Press, 1940.

Butterworth, Ruth and Nicholas Tarling. *A Shakeup Anyway: Government and the Universities in New Zealand in a Decade of Reform*. Auckland: Auckland University Press, 1994.

Callahan, Raymond. *Education and the Cult of Efficiency: A Study of the Social Forces that Have Shaped the Administration of the Public Schools*. Chicago: University of Chicago Press, 1962.

Carlin, James F. "Restoring Sanity to an Academic World Gone Mad," *Chronicle of Higher Education*, 1999 November 5.

Carr, Sarah and Andrea L. Foster, "States Struggle to Regulate Online Colleges That Lack Accreditation," *Chronicle*, 2001 March 23.

Carter, N., R. Klein, and P. Day. *How Organisations Measure Success: The Use of Performance Indicators in Government.* London: Routledge, 1992.

Cassin, A. M. and J.G. Morgan. "The Professoriate and the Market-Driven University: Transforming the Control of Work in the Academy," in W. K. Carroll, L. Christiansen-Ruffman, R. Currie, and F. D. Harrison, eds., *Fragile Truths: Twenty-Five Years of Sociology and Anthropology in Canada.* Ottawa: Carleton University Press, 1992, 247–60.

Cave, Martin *et al. The Use of Performance Indicators in Higher Education: The Challenge of the Quality Movement,* 3rd ed. London: Jessica Kingsley Publishers, 1997.

Cave, Martin, S. Hanney, and M. Kogan. *The Use of Performance Indicators in Higher Education: A Critical Analysis of Developing Practice.* London: Jessica Kingsley, 1991.

Clark, B.R. *The Higher Education System: Academic Organization in Cross-National Perspective.* Berkeley, University of California Press, 1983.

Clarke, G. Grant, E. DesRosiers, and Stephen Hawkins. *An Information Framework for Higher Education in the Maritimes.* West Hill, Ontario: Edward DesRosiers and Associates, 1995 October 18.

Clayton, Mark. "Pressuring professors to put in more face time," *Christian Science Monitor,* 2000 November 07.

Climaco, C. "Getting to Know Schools Using Performance Indicators Criteria, Indicators and Processes," *Educational Review,* 44, 3 (1992): 295–308.

Coate, L. Edwin. "Implementing Total Quality Management in a University Setting" in Harry Costin, ed., *Readings in Total Quality Management.* Toronto: Dryden Press/Harcourt Brace, 1994.

Cooke, M.L. *Academic and Industrial Efficiency: A Report to the Carnegie Foundation for the Advancement of Teaching.* New York: Merrymount Press, 1910.

Council of Ministers of Education, Canada [CMEC]. *A Report on Public Expectations of Postsecondary Education in Canada.* Toronto: CMEC, 1999 February.

Craft, Alma, ed. *Quality Assurance in Higher Education: Proceedings of an International Conference Hong Kong.* London: Falmer Press, 1992.

Croft, Maurice. "External Examining: A review of its rationale and mode of operation," paper presented, Conference of the International Network of Quality Assurance Agencies in Higher Education (INQAAHE), Montréal, May 1993.

Crozier, Rob, ed. *Troubled Times: Academic Freedom in New Zealand.* Palmerston North, NZ: Dunmore Press, 2000.

Cullen, Michael J. *The Statistical Movement in Early Victorian Britain: The Foundations of Empirical Social Research.* New York: Harvest Press/ Barnes and Noble, 1975.

Currie, Jan and Janice Newson. *Universities and Globalization: Critical Perspectives.* Thousand Oaks, California: SAGE Publications, 1998.

Curtis, Bruce. *Building the Educational State: Canada West, 1836–1871.* London, Ontario: Althouse Press, 1988.

Cutt, J. and R. Dobell, eds. *Public Purse, Public Purpose: Autonomy and Accountability in the Groves of Academe.* Halifax, NS: Institute for Research on Public Policy, 1992.

Damer, Eric J. *Mechanical Engineering at UBC, 1915–2000.* Vancouver: Ronsdale Press, 2002.

Davie, George. *The Democratic Intellect: Scotland and Her Universities in the Nineteenth Century,* 2nd ed. Edinburgh: Edinburgh University Press, 1997.

Demers, Guy. "Autonomie, imputabilité et évaluation," unpublished paper, Canadian Society for the Study of Higher Education, Annual Meeting, 2001 May 25, Université Laval.

Denise Doherty-Delorme and Erica Shaker, eds. *Missing Pieces II: An Alternative Guide to Canadian Post-Secondary Education.* Ottawa: Canadian Centre for Policy Alternatives, 2000.

Dennison, John. "Accountability: Mission Impossible?" unpublished paper, University of British Columbia, 1994.

Deschenes, Sarah, David Tyack, and Larry Cuban, "Mismatch: Historical Perspectives on Schools and Students Who Don't Fit Them," *Teachers College Record,* 103, 4 (2001): 525–47.

DesRosiers, E. *et al. An Information Framework Linking Educational Outcomes to Economic Renewal.* West Hill, Ontario: Edward DesRosiers and Associates, 1993 October 15.

_____ *An Information Framework for Higher Education in the Maritimes,* 1995 October 18.

Dochy, F.J.R.C., M.S.R. Segers, and W.H.F.W. Wijnen, eds. *Management Information and Performance Indicators in Higher Education: An International Issue.* Assen: VanGorcum, 1990.

Doherty-Delorme, D. and E. Shaker, eds. *Missing Pieces: An Alternative Guide to Canadian Post-Secondary Education.* Ottawa: Canadian Centre for Policy Alternatives, 1999.

_____. *Missing Pieces II: An Alternative Guide to Canadian Post-Secondary Education.* Ottawa: Canadian Centre for Policy Alternatives, 2001.

Dominelli, L. and A. Hoogvelt, "Globalization, Contract Government and Taylorization of Intellectual Labour in Academia," *Studies in Political Economy,* 49 (1996).

Drewes Committee, "Measuring up to Our Standards: Final Report on Performance Indicators for Trent University," Trent University, Peterborough, Ontario, 1994 November. Typescript, 11 pages.

Duff, James and R.O. Berdahl. *University Government in Canada.* Toronto: University of Toronto Press, 1966.

Easton, Stephen. *Education in Canada: An Analysis of Elementary, Secondary, and Vocational Schooling.* Vancouver: Fraser Institute, 1988.

Easton, Brian. *The Commercialization of New Zealand.* Auckland: Auckland University Press, 1997.

_____. *The Whimpering of the State.* Auckland: Auckland University Press, 1999.

Edward DesRosiers and Associates. *An Information Framework Linking Educational Outcomes to Economic Renewal.* West Hill, Ontario: Edward DesRosiers and Associates, 1993 October 15.

Elkin, R. and M. Molitor. *Management Indicators in Non-profit Corporations.* Baltimore: University of Maryland School of Social Work and Community Planning, 1984.

Elliott, Marianne. *The Catholics of Ulster: A History*. New York: Basic Books/ London: Allen Lane, 2001.

Emberley, Peter C. *Zero Tolerance: Hot Button Politics in Canada's Universities*. Toronto: Penguin Books: 1996.

Evers, F.T. and Sid Gilbert, "Outcomes Assessment: How Much Value Does University Education Add?" *Canadian Journal of Higher Education*, 21, 2 (1991): 53–69.

Farnham, David, ed. *Managing Academic Staff in Changing University Systems: International Trends and Comparisons*. London: Society for Research into Higher Education and the Open University Press, 1999.

Fédération québécoise des professeures et professeurs d'université. *Pour l'Etat, malgré lui: Mémoire présenté au Conseil supérieur de l'éducation*. Montreal: FQPPU, 2001.

Ferguson, Niall. *The Cash Nexus: Money and Power in the Modern World, 1700–2000*. New York: Basic Books, 2001.

Fitzgibbon, Carol T. *Performance Indicators*. Clevedon, Avon, Eng.: Multilingual Matters, 1990.

Gaither, G. B.P. Nedwek, J.E. Neal. *Measuring Up: The Promises and Pitfalls of Performance Indicators in Higher Education*, ASHE-ERIC Higher Education Reports, No. 5, Washington, 1994.

Gaither, Gerald H., ed. *Quality Assurance in Higher Education: An International Perspective*. [New Directions for Institutional Research, Number 99] San Francisco: Jossey-Bass, 1998.

Gale, Robert T. "Market Perceived Quality: Key Strategic Concept," *Planning Review*, 1989 March April: 615–48.

Geiger, Roger. *To Advance Knowledge: The Growth of American Research Universities, 1900–1940*. New York: Oxford University Press, 1986.

Gidney, R. and W.P. J. Millar. *Inventing Secondary Education: The Rise of the High Schools in Nineteenth Century Ontario*. Montréal and Kingston: McGill-Queen's University Press, 1990.

_____. *Professional Gentlemen: The Professions in Nineteenth-Century Ontario*. Toronto: University of Toronto Press, 1994.

_____. "Quantity and Quality: The Problem of Admissions in Medicine at the University of Toronto, 1910–51," *Historical Studies in Education/ Revue d'histoire de l'éducation* 9, 2 (Fall/automne 1997): 165–89.

Gidney, R.D. *From Hope to Harris: The Reshaping of Ontario's Schools*. Toronto: University of Toronto Press, 1999.

Gilbert, Sid. "Search for Education Indicators," *Education Quarterly Review* (1994): 44–53.

_____. "Performance indicators for universities: Ogres or opportunities?." OCUFA Forum, Spring 1999, at Web site: *http://www.ocufa.on.ca/*.

Glotzer, Richard. "The Influence of Carnegie Corporation and Teachers College, Columbia, in the Interwar Dominions: The Case for Decentralized Education." *Historical Studies in Education/Revue d'histoire de l'éducation*, 12, 1/ 2 (2000 spring/fall): 93–110.

Goedegebuure, C.J., P.A.M. Maassen, and D.F. Westerheijden. *Peer Review and Performance Indicators: Quality Assessment in British and Dutch Higher Education*. Utrecht: Uitgverij Lemma, 1990.

Goodlad, Sinclair. "Benchmarks and Templates Some Notes and Queries from a Sceptic" in *Benchmarking*, 79.

Graham, Amy and Nicholas Thompson, "Broken Ranks: U.S. News' college rankings measure everything but what matters," *The Washington Monthly*, 2001 September.

Grosjean, G., J. Atkinson-Grosjean, K. Rubenson, and D. Fisher. Measuring the Unmeasurable: Paradoxes of Accountability and the Impacts of Performance Indicators on Liberal Education in Canada, unpublished research report, Humanities and Social Sicence Federation of Canada, 2000 May 3.

Grosjean, J.A., Garnet Grosjean, Donald Fisher, Kjell Robinson, *Consequences of Performance Indicators in Higher Education: An International Perspective*. Vancouver: Centre for Policy Studies in Higher Education and Training, University of British Columbia for the Humanities and Social Sciences Federation of Canada, 1999.

Gupta, D.K., A.J. Longman, and A.P. Schmid. "Creating a Composite Index for Assessing Country Performance in the Field of Human Rights: Proposal for a New Methodology," *Human Rights Quarterly*, 16, 1 (1994): 131–62.

Halsey, A.H. "Oxford and the British Universities," in Brian Harrison, ed., *The History of the University of Oxford, VIII: The Twentieth Century* (Oxford: Clarendon Press, 1994), 577–606.

Hanson, G. "Using Multiple Program Impact Analysis to Document Institutional Effectiveness," unpublished paper, Association of Institutional Research, Atlanta, Georgia, USA, 1992.

Hardy, Cynthia. *The Politics of Collegiality: Retrenchment Strategies in Canadian Universities*. Montréal and Kingston: McGill-Queen's University Press, 1996.

Harris, J. "Performance models." *Public Productivity and Management Review*, 22(2) (1998 December): 135–40.

Helsby, G. and M. Saunders, "Taylorism, Tylerism and Performance Indicators: defending the indefensible?" *Educational Studies*, 19, 1 (1993): 55–77.

Hodder, J. Uunpublished manuscript talk, First National Consultation, Counsel of Ministers of Education, Canada, Edmonton, Alberta, 1994.

Horn, Michiel. "Under the Gaze of George Vancouver: The University of British Columbia and the Provincial Government, 1913–1939," *BC Studies* 83 (1989): 29–67.

Horton, Sylvia. "The United States: Self-Governed Profession or Managed Occupation," in David Farnham, *Managing Academic Staff in Changing University Systems: International Trends and Comparisons* (The Society for Research into Higher Education and Open University Press, UK, 1999).

Hoskin, Keith and Richard Macve, "Writing, examining, disciplining: the genesis of accounting's modern power," in A.G. Hopwood and P. Miller, *Accounting as Social and Institutional Practice* (Cambridge: Cambridge University Press, 1994), 67–97.

Izquierdo S., Miguel A. *Sobrevivir a los estímulos: académicos, estrategia y conflictos*. México, D.F.: Universidad Pedagógica Nacional, 2000.

Jager, G. de, and S. Goedhart. "The Contribution of Cost Measurement to the Development of Performance Indicators," *Higher Education Management*, 5, 1 (1993 March): 7–11.

James, Cathy. "Practical Diversions and Educational Amusements: Evangelia House and the Advent of Canada's Settlement Movement, 1902–09,"

Historical Studies in Education/Revue d'histoire de l'éducation, 10, 1&2 (Spring/printemps & Fall/automne 1998): 48–66.

Johnes, J. and J. Taylor. *Performance Indicators in Higher Education*. Buckingham: Society for Research into Higher Education and Open University Press, 1990.

Johnson, Ann Dowsett. "Measuring Excellence," *Maclean's Guide to Canadian Universities and Colleges*. Toronto: Rogers Media, 2001), 10–15.

Kelly, P.H., ed. *Locke on Money*. Oxford: Clarendon Press, 1990 1 (2 volumes).

Kent, Christopher. *Brains and Numbers: Elitism, Comtism, and Democracy in Mid-Victorian England*. Toronto: University of Toronto Press, 1978.

Kingwell, Mark. *The World We Want: Virtue, Vice and the Good Citizen*. Toronto: Viking, 2000.

Labaree, D.F. "An Unlovely Legacy: The Disabling Impact of the Market on American Teacher Education," *Phi Delta Kappan*, 75, 8 (1994 April): 591–95.

Laroche, Mireille and Marcel Mérette, "Measuring Human Capital in Canada," unpublished paper, Statistics Canada [Economic Conference 2000], 34 pp.

Leacy, F.H., M.C. Urquhart, and K.A.H. Buckley, eds. *Historical Statistics of Canada*, 2nd ed. Ottawa: Statistics Canada, 1983.

Lee, Gloria. "Whatever Happened to the Ivory Tower? Process Change in Higher Education: From TQM to BPR," *Journal of Business and Management*, 2, 2 (1996): 114–31.

Litt, Paul. *The Muses, the Masses, and the Massey Commission*. Toronto: University of Toronto Press, 1992.

Logan, Harry. *Tuum Est: A History of the University of British Columbia*. Vancouver: University of British Columbia, 1958.

Lucier, Pierre. "Performance Indicators in Higher Education: Lowering the Tension of the Debate," *Higher Education Management*, 4, 2 (1992 July): 204–14.

Lyke, Richard Wayne. *Higher Education and the United States Office of Education 1867–1953*. Washington, DC: U.S. Office of Education, 1930.

Macdonald, John. *Chances and Choices: A Memoir*. Vancouver: University of British Columbia and UBC Alumni Association, 2000.

MacKillop, A.B. *Matters of Mind: The University in Ontario, 1791–1951*. Toronto: University of Toronto Press, 1994.

Mackintosh, N.J. *Cyril Burt: Fraud or Framed?* Oxford: Oxford University Press, 1995.

Macmillan, Keith. "National Organizations," in A. Walter, ed., *Aspects of Music in Canada*. Toronto: University of Toronto Press, 1969.

MacMullen, E.N. *In the Cause of True Education: Henry Barnard and Nineteenth-Century School Reform*. New Haven: Yale University Press, 1991.

Magnuson, Warren, ed. *The New Reality: The Politics of Restraint in British Columbia*. Vancouver: New Star Books, 1984.

_____. *After Bennett: A New Politics for British Columbia.* (Vancouver: New Star Books, 1986.

Marchak, Patricia. "The New Economic Reality: Substance and Rhetoric," in W. Magnusson, *et al.*, eds., *The New Reality: The Politics of Restraint in British Columbia* (Vancouver: New Star Books, 1984), 22–40.

Marsh, Leonard C. Report on Social Security for Canada. Toronto: University of Toronto Press, 1975, repr. of 1943 report for the Federal Committee on Post-War Reconstruction.

_____. *Canadians In and out of Work: A Survey of Economic Classes and Their Relation to the Labour Market*. Toronto: Oxford University Press for McGill University, 1940.

_____. *Health and Unemployment: Some Studies of their Relationships*. Toronto: Oxford University Press for McGill University, 1938.

Martin, G.H. "Assessment Issues in Canadian Higher Education: A Review of Recent Literature," Educational outcomes Measurement Strategic Workshop, University of New Brunswick, Freericton, NB, 1992 October 16–17.

Marwick, Arthur. *The Sixties*. Oxford: Oxford University Press, 1998.

McConica, J.K. *English Humanists and Reformation Policies under Henry VIII and Edward VI*. Oxford: Clarendon Press, 1965.

McEwen, N. "Educational Quality Indicators," *Alberta Journal of Educational Research*, 39, 2 (1993): 167–78.

McPherson, C.B. "The Social Bearing of Locke's Political Theory," *Western Political Quarterly*, 7, 1 (1954 March): 1–22

McPherson, E. "Measuring Added Value in Schools," *Briefing* [National Commission on Education, United Kingdom], NCE Briefing No. 1, 1992 February.

Miller, P. "Accounting as a Social and Institutional Practice: An Introduction," in A. G. Hopwood and P. Miller, eds., *Accounting as a Social and Institutional Practice* (Cambridge: Cambridge University Press, 1994), 1–39.

Mintzberg, H. *The Rise and Fall of Strategic Planning: Reconceiving Roles for Planning, Plans, Planners*. New York: Free Press, 1994.

Mitchell, B.R. ed. *International Historical Statistics: Europe, 1750–1993*, 4th ed. London: Macmillan, 1998.

Moffitt, J. "On to the Past: Wrong-Headed School Reform," *Phi Delta Kappan*, 75, 8 (1994 April): 584–90.

Nadeau, Gilles G. "The Use of Quality and Excellence Indicators in Post-Secondary Education," CSSHE Professional File, Report No. 10, 1992 Fall.

Newson, Janice and Howard Buchbinder. *The University Means Business: Universities, Corporations and Academic Work*. Toronto: Garamond Press, 1988.

Noble, David. *Forces of Production: A Social History of Industrial Automation*. New York: Oxford University Press, 1984.

Northern Telecom [Nortel]. *The Supply of High-Technology Professionals: An Issue for Ontario's and Canada's Future*. Ottawa: Nortel, 1998.

Novak, R., and D. Leslie, "A Not So Distant Mirror: Great Depression Writings on the Governance and Finance of Public Higher Education," *History of Higher Education Annual*, 20 (2000): 59–78.

Nussbaum, Martha. *Cultivating Humanity: A Classical Defense of Reform in Liberal Education*. (Cambridge: Harvard University Press, 1997.

NZVCC. *Committee on University Academic Programmes: Functions and Procedures 1998*. Wellington: NZVCC, 1998.

Oakes, Jeannie. "What Educational Indicators? The Case for Assessing the School Context," *Educational Evaluation and Policy Analysis*, 11, 2 (1989 Summer): 181–99.

_____ *Educational Indicators: A Guide for Policymakers*. Madison, WI: Center for Policy Research in Education [Rand], 1986.

Organisation for Economic Co-operation and Development. *Education at a Glance: OECD Indicators, Education Skills*. Paris: OECD, 2001.

Owram, Doug. *Born at the Right Time: A History of the Baby Boom Generation*. Toronto: University of Toronto Press, 1996.

Parry, J.H. *The Establishment of the European Hegemony, 1415–1715: Trade and Exploration in the Age of the Renaissance*, 3rd ed. New York: Harper Row, 1966.

Paterson, L. "A Comparison of Methods Currently Being Used to Evaluate Schools in Scotland," unpublished paper, at Conference on the Practice of Evaluating Schools in Scotland, Edinburgh University, 1992 August 25.

Peters, H.P.F. and A.F.J. Vanraan. "A Bibliometric Profile of Top Scientists A Case-Study in Chemical-Engineering," *Scientometrics*, 29, 1 (1994): 115–36.

Peters, Michael. "Performance and Accountability in 'Post-Industrial Society': The Crisis of British Universities," *Studies in Higher Education*, 17, 2 (1992): 123–39.

Peters, Michael. "Performance Indicators in New Zealand Higher Education," *Journal of Education Policy*, 7, 3 (1992): 270–98.

Peters, Michael C., John Freeman Moir, Education Department, University of Canterbury, and Michael A. Peters, Education Department, University of Auckland. *Accountability and Performance in Tertiary Education*, AUSNZ, 1993 July.

Peters, Michael C., J. Freeman-Moir, and Michael A. Peters. "Performance and Accountability in Tertiary Education," *Bulletin* [of the Association of University Staff of New Zealand], no. 14 (1993 July August): 3–4.

Peters, Roger. "Some Snarks Are Boojums: Accountability and the Ethos of Higher Education," *Change*, 1994, 26, (6), 16–23.

Plomp, R. "The Highly Cited Papers of Professors as an Indicator of a Research Groups Scientific Performance," *Scientometrics*, 29, 3 (1994): 377–93.

Pocklington, Tom. "The Marketing of the University," in T.W. Harrison and J.L. Kachur, eds., *Contested Classrooms: Education, Globalization, and Democracy in Alberta*. Edmonton: University of Alberta Press and Parkland Institute, 1999, 45–55.

Polster, C. and J. Newson. "Don't count your blessings: The social accomplishments of performance indicators," in J. Currie & J. Newson, eds., *Universities and Globalization: Critical Perspectives* (Thousand Oaks: Sage, 1998), 173–91.

Porter, Theodore M. *Trust in Numbers: The Pursuit of Objectivity in Science and Public Life*. Princeton: Princeton University Press, 1995.

Power, M. *The Audit Society: Rituals of Verification*. Oxford: Oxford University Press, 1995.

Prentice, Alison. *The School Promoters: Education and Social Class in Mid-19th Century Upper Canada*. Toronto: McClelland Stewart, 1975, 1999.

Putman, J.H. and G.M. Weir. *Survey of the School System*. Victoria: King's Printer, 1925.

Readings, B. *The University in Ruins*. Harvard: Harvard University Press, 1996.

Reuben, Julie. *The Making of the Modern University: Intellectual Transformation and the Marginalization of Morality*. Chicago: University of Chicago Press, 1996.

Ringer, Fritz. *Education and Society in Modern Europe*. Bloomington, Indiana: Indiana University Press, 1979.

Roberts, J.M. *Twentieth Century: The History of the World, 1901 to 2000*. London: Penguin/Viking, 1999.

Rothblatt, Sheldon. *The Modern University and Its Discontents: The Fate of Newman's Legacies in Britain and America*. Cambridge: University Press, 1997.

Royal Society of Canada. *Realizing the Potential: A Strategy for University Research in Canada: Report*. Ottawa: Royal Society of Canada, 1991.

Russell, Conrad. *Academic Freedom*. London: Routledge, 1993.

_____. "Leave it to the Teachers," *London Review of Books*, 19, 6 (1997 March 20).

Ryan, Alan "The Twisted Path to the Top," *New York Review of Books*, 19 November 1999 [*http://www.nybooks.com/*] (review of Nicholas Lemann, *The Big Test: The Secret History of the American Meritocracy*).

Savage, Donald C. "Academic Freedom and Institutional Autonomy in New Zealand Universities," in Rob Crozier, ed., *Troubled Times: Academic Freedom in New Zealand* (Palmerston North, NZ: Dunmore Press, 2000), pp. 7–225.

Schmitz, C.C. "Assessing the Validity of Higher-Education Indicators," *Journal of Higher Education*, 64, 5 (1993): 503–21.

Scott, G. "What's Wrong with Managerialism," *Public Sector* 16, 1, 1993.

Scott, P. *The Meanings of Mass Higher Education*. Buckingham: Open University, 1995.

Scott, Guy and Helen Scott, *New Zealand University Funding Over The Last Two Decades*. NZVCC and AUSNZ: Wellington: n.p., 2000.

Shrimpton, G. "A Decade of Restraint: The Economics of B.C. Universities," in W. Magnusson, *et al.*, eds., *The New Reality: The Politics of Restraint in British Columbia*. Vancouver: New Star Books, 1984, pp. 258–68.

Simon, Brian. *Intelligence Testing and the Comprehensive School*. London: Lawrence & Wishart, 1953.

Simon, Herbert A. *Administrative Behavior: A Study of Decision-Making Processes in Administrative Organization*. New York: Macmillan, 1947.

Sirluck, Ernest. *First Generation: An Autobiography*. Toronto: University of Toronto Press, 1996.

Sizer, J. "Assessing Institutional Performance: An Overview," *European Journal of Institutional Management in Higher Education*, 3 (1979): 49–75.

Slaughter, Sheila. "From Serving Students to Serving the Economy: Changing Expectations of Faculty Role Performance," *Higher Education*, 14 (1985): 41–56.

Smith, D. C. *And How Will I Know If There is Quality? Report on quality indicators and quality enhancement in universities: issues and experiences*. Toronto: Council of Ontario Universities, 2000.

Snowden, Ken. "The Development of Performance Indicators at Queen's University." Unpublished paper, Annual Meeting, Canadian Association of Institutional Researchers, Vancouver, 1993.

Sobel, Dava. *Longitude: The True Story of a Lone Genius Who Solved the Greatest Scientific Problem of His Time*. New York: Penguin, 1996.

Steele, Joe M. "Evaluating College Programs Using Measures of Student Achievement and Growth," *Educational Evaluation and Policy Analysis*, 11, 4 (1989 Winter): 357–75.

Stein, Janice Gross. *The Cult of Efficiency*. Toronto: Anansi, 2001.

Steinberg, J. and D.B. Henriques, "None of the Above: When a Test Fails the Schools, Careers and Reputations Suffer," *Our Schools*, 11, 1 (2001 October): 71–87 [orig. *New York Times*, 2001 May 21].

Stephen Court, "Memories of Jobs for Life," *CAUT Bulletin*, 1998 March.

Storm, Christine, ed., *Liberal Education and the Small University in Canada*. Montreal and Kingston: McGill-Queen's University Press, 1996.

Strangway, David. "The Scope of University Accountability," in J. Cutt and R. Dobell, eds., *Public Purse, Public Purpose: Autonomy and Accountability in the Groves of Academe*. Halifax: Institute for Research on Public Policy/ Canadian Comprehensive Auditing Foundation, 1992, 251–2.

Taft, K. *Shredding the public interest: Ralph Klein and 25 years of one-party government*. Edmonton AB: The University of Alberta Press and the Parkland Institute, 1997.

Tavenas, François. "The Use and Pitfalls of Performance Indicators for Universities." Unpublished paper, AUCC Symposium on Performance Indicators, Winnipeg, MB, 1993 November 11–13.

Taylor, F.W. *The Principles of Scientific Management*. New York: Harper and Row, 1911.

Terezini, Patrick T. "Assessment with Open Eyes: Pitfalls in Studying Student Outcomes," *Journal of Higher Education*, 60, 6 (1989 Nov. Dec.): 644–64.

Thompson, Jon, Patricia Baird, Jocelyn Downie. *The Olivieri Report: The complete text of the report of the independent inquiry commissioned by the Canadian Association of University Teachers*. A CAUT Series Title. Toronto: James Lorimer & Company Ltd., 2001.

Thomson, Gerald E. "Remove From Our Midst These Unfortunates," Ph.D. thesis, University of British Columbia, 1999.

Tippett, Maria. *Making Culture: English-Canadian Institutions and the Arts before the Massey Commission*. Toronto: University of Toronto Press, 1990.

Tomkins, George. *A Common Countenance: Stability and Change in the Canadian Curriculum*. Scarborough: Prentice-Hall, 1986.

Towers, J.M. "The Perils of Outcome-Based Teacher Education," *Phi Delta Kappan*, 75, 8 (1994 April): 624–27.

Turk, James, ed. *The Corporate Campus*. Toronto: James Lorimer, 2000.

Tyler, Ralph Winfred. *Basic Principles of Curriculum and Instruction*. Chicago: University of Chicago Press, 1949.

Wagner, Robert B. *Accountability in Education: A Philosophical Inquiry*. New York: Routledge, 1989.

Waite, P.B. *Lord of Point Grey: Larry Mackenzie of UBC*. Vancouver: UBC Press, 1987.

Watson, David and Rachel Bowden, "Why did they do it? The Conservatives and access to higher education," *Journal of Education Policy* 14, 4 (1999): 243–56.

West, Edwin G. *Higher Education in Canada: An Analysis.* Vancouver: Fraser Institute, 1988.

_____. *Higher Education and Competitiveness.* Kingston, Ont.: Government and Competitiveness, School of Policy Studies, Queen's University, 1993.

Willinsky, John. "The Construction of a Crisis: Literacy in Canada," *Canadian Journal of Education/Revue canadienne de l'éducation,* 15, 1 (1990 hiver/ Winter): 1–15.

Willms, J. Douglas. *Monitoring School Performance: A Guide for Educators.* Washington, DC: Falmer Press, 1992.

Wilson, J.D. "The Ryerson Years in Canada West," in Titley, E. Brian and Peter J. Miller, eds., *Education in Canada: An Interpretation.* Calgary: Detselig, 1982.

Wilson, J.D., R. Stamp, and L.-P. Audet, eds. *Canadian Education: A History.* Scarborough, Ontario: Prentice-Hall, 1970.

Wolfe, D.A. "Quality and Accountability in PSE Research: The Measurement Challenge," background paper prepared for the Council of Ministers of Education, Canada, 1998 November Toronto: CMEC, 1998, 20 pp.

Zappia, Charles. "The Private Sector and Public Higher Education," *Perspectives* (2000 May): 34–44.

_____. "Politics and Standards," *Perspectives* (2000 May): 51–9.

Zeeveld, W. Gordon. *Foundations of Tudor Policy.* Cambridge: Harvard University Press, 1948.

Index nominorum

MEMBER OF SCABRINI MEDIA

Quebec, Canada
2002